WINCKELMANN

WINCKELMANN

by

WOLFGANG LEPPMANN

London
Victor Gollancz Ltd
1971

Printed in Great Britain by
Lowe and Brydone (Printers) Ltd., London

"Winckelmann must be regarded as one of those
who developed a new organ and opened up
frooh perspectives in the world of art."

Hegel

"While the characters of many men,
and especially of scholars, tend to
disappear from view as we look at their achievements,
the opposite is true of Winckelmann:
everything that he produces is great
and remarkable because it reveals his character."

Goethe

FOREWORD

Great scholars, especially classical scholars, are rarely made subjects of biographies. Their lives are considered to be uneventful, and their personalities colorless compared with those of, say, famous explorers, artists, soldiers, scientists, or lovers. Such men conjure up pictures: Columbus's caravel standing out against the horizon, Michelangelo atop his scaffold in the Sistine Chapel, Napoleon glowering across the Beresina, Galileo before the Inquisition, Casanova in some lady's boudoir. Scholars, on the other hand, remain nameless and faceless. Even the most enterprising among those that deal with classical antiquity, the archaeologists, tend to be forgotten nowadays unless they also excelled at something else, as Schliemann did at making money. But it was not always thus. Columbus, Michelangelo, Napoleon, Galileo, and, yes, Casanova too, knew and admired the classical scholars of their day. In the eighteenth century, especially, educated men everywhere followed each other's work with interest and understanding. In a few instances, pictures of scholars from that period can still be dimly perceived through the mists of time: Gibbon in the Colosseum, or the discoverer of the Rosetta Stone sailing to Egypt with General Bonaparte. One picture of this kind that deserves to be redrawn is that of Johann Joachim Winckelmann.

But do we have any right—it may be asked—to take time out from the problems of our own age in order to follow the career of a long-dead personage who to most of us is little more than a name? Are there not too many books in print already about men whose work appears to bear so little relevance for the modern world that they might as well have been contemplating their navels? These are legitimate questions. Yet Winckelmann stands above them, not so much because he was among the initiators of what came to be called the Greek Revival (a fashion, when all is said and done, that is more foreign to us in spirit than ancient Greece itself), but because he is the father of archaeology as we know it. Introducing methodical procedures into a field that had previously been the preserve of treasure hunters, he transformed a fad into a science, and incidentally made Pompeii and Herculaneum the proving ground of techniques that were later used in excavations all over the globe. The specific appeal that he holds for the twentieth-century reader, however, extends beyond his achievements as an archaeologist and art historian. This idealist who mastered the harshest facts of everyday life, this non-believer in the Vatican, this self-made man in an unegalitarian age, this homosexual in a century dominated by women, this republican in the *ancien régime*, and this educator who hated schools also has more in common with us, and is therefore in essence more modern, than many a more recent writer. Not that we live suspended between the same paradoxes that tormented him; nor are we necessarily homosexuals, or educators, or whatever. But to the extent that ours, too, is a reproductive and antiquarian rather than a creative age, an age that will be remembered for its museums and symphony orchestras rather than for its sculptors and composers, to that extent our own mental habitat is closer to his than to that of the Romantics or the Victorians. In short, his life and his personality are as intriguing as the fact that he coined the terms of Noble Simplicity and Quiet Grandeur as hallmarks of classical Greek sculpture, and launched a number of other concepts as well that are still common currency—smooth-edged with much usage, but of high silver content even now—wherever art is discussed. In the words of one expert, "his critical estimates have become part of our folklore; the man in the street who has never heard of Winckelmann will nevertheless quote him if asked to express an opinion about art. No other art historian has had a comparable influence . . ." (John Ives Sewall in 1953).

While it would be a shame to dismiss such a man from consideration simply because he happens to have lived in eighteenth-century Europe, it would surely be naïve to assume that the men and events of that time are as familiar to us as are those of our own. The best of his biographers, Carl Justi, knew this when he entitled his work *Winckelmann and his Contemporaries* (1866–72). We, too, will have to approach him obliquely on occasion, on detours that touch on the men and movements that affected him and that he affected in turn; for his life and work make no sense unless they are viewed against the background of his period. Since it was a period in which scant attention was paid to the common people, many details about his early days are lost: a state of affairs which has led another expert to conclude that "we cannot psychoanalyze Winckelmann" (Richard Biedrzynski in 1968). Given the similarities that exist between psychoanalytical and archaeological procedures, it is a pity that we cannot adequately trace the childhood of this first and perhaps greatest of all archaeologists. What we can do is to remove the accretions and incrustations of dead scholarship that have all

but obscured him from view, and to let him and his friends—
an articulate generation if ever there was one—speak for themselves. Even in translation their voices ring out clear, clearer
than many that are raised in our days.

Wolfgang Leppmann

Rome, summer 1969

Acknowledgments

It is a pleasure to thank the following individuals and institutions for their advice, help, and encouragement in the writing of this book: Horst Rüdiger of Bonn; Silvio Rutteri of Trieste; Chandler Beall, Peter Gontrum, and Frederick Combellack of Eugene; Barker Fairley of Toronto; Ulrich Rüdiger, Hellmut Sichtermann, and Prince Alessandro Torlonia of Rome; Ruth Kromer of Anacapri; Klaus Polte of Stendal; Johannes Winckelmann of Munich; and my wife. Also the University of Toronto, Vassar College, and the University of Oregon; the *Winckelmann-Gesellschaft* in Stendal; the *Deutsches Archäologisches Institut* in Rome; the British Museum in London; the American Council of Learned Societies in New York; and the *Staatsbibliothek Preussischer Kulturbesitz* in Berlin. I am also grateful to Elek Books of London for permission to use, in amended form, a few passages from a previous book of mine. Translations are mine unless otherwise indicated.

CONTENTS

ILLUSTRATIONS

xvii

Chronologies

Johann Joachim Winckelmann, 1717–68

KINGS OF PRUSSIA

Frederick William I, 1713–40

Frederick II (the Great), 1740–86

ELECTORS OF SAXONY

Frederick Augustus I, 1694–1733
(*after 1697, also King of Poland as Augustus II*)

Frederick Augustus II, 1733–63
(*also King of Poland as Augustus III*)

Frederick Christian, 1763
(*Poland no longer part of Saxony*)

Frederick Augustus III, 1763–1806

POPES

Clement XI, 1700–21

Innocent XIII, 1721–4

Benedict XIII, 1724–30

Clement XII, 1730–40

Benedict XIV, 1740–58

Clement XIII, 1758–69

KINGS OF THE TWO SICILIES

Under Austrian rule, 1713–38

Charles III, 1738–59

Ferdinand IV (I), 1759–1825

EPILOGUE AND PROLOGUE: TRIESTE

Only one passenger, a middle-aged man, alighted from the diligence which arrived in Trieste from Laibach just before noon on Wednesday, June 1, 1768. Declaring that he intended to continue his journey in a day or two, the traveler found accommodation in the Locanda Grande, on what is now Piazza dell'Unità d'Italia in the center of town. The three-story building had just been renovated. With forty rooms as well as stables and an all-night café, it was Trieste's largest inn, a fit abode for such demanding visitors as Giacomo Casanova and the Emperor Joseph II of Austria.

The new guest, who said that he was traveling incognito and preferred to be called simply Signor Giovanni, was shown to room No. 10 on the first floor. He was pleased. Six lire including meals seemed a reasonable price, and the location was perfect: for it was by ship that he intended to go on, to Venice or Ancona and thence overland to Rome, and the room was not only large but had two windows from which he could look out over the Mandracchio, or inner harbor. When he had washed up and taken his seat in the dining room, with twelve or fifteen other guests at lunch, he asked the innkeeper whether there might be a ship in port that could take him to Venice. "There is indeed," someone replied, "sailing tonight, with Stefano Tagusini as master." Turning to the person who had provided this news, Signor Giovanni saw a youngish man of medium height, with a pockmarked face and his own dark hair instead of the customary pigtail, who introduced himself as "Francesco Angelis, at your service." When the traveler asked, "Would you be good enough to point it out to me?" the other led him to the window and showed him the masts of Tagusini's vessel. After lunch the two men walked down to the harbor, only to find that the master could not sail after all because he still lacked a full cargo. Disappointed, they returned to the Locanda Grande, where they discovered that they were neighbors; Angelis, who had arrived a few days before, had been given room No. 9 on the same floor. After siesta they tried again, and this time they had better luck. The captain of a ship bound for Ancona accepted Signor Giovanni's deposit, promising to notify him in good time when he was ready to set sail. It would be a matter of a few days at most.

Although Signor Giovanni refused the coffee which Angelis had sent to his room that evening, the two men spent much time together in the days that followed. They were seen strolling along the harbor and along the road that led to the old hospital, taking their coffee and scanning the papers several times a day in Gasparo Griotti's café behind the piazza. They repeatedly took their dinner in Angelis's room, where Signor Giovanni, who rarely ate at night, at least kept his friend company. On June 3 the innkeeper, who knew Angelis from a previous stay in the Locanda Grande, asked him whether he knew who the new arrival was. He had no idea, the other replied, adding that he had been taken aback to see a large book on the desk in No. 10, a volume written "not in Italian or French or German,

4

but in a strange language." When Angelis reported the innkeeper's question to Signor Giovanni, the latter said that he was
a perfectly respectable man and that in order to prove it, he
would let Angelis see some medals that he had just been given
by the Empress Maria Theresa in Vienna. And he was as good
as his word: in his room that evening, he took a wooden box
out of his trunk and showed his neighbor two gold and two
silver medals. Without divulging the subject of his conversation
with the Empress, he claimed that he had been taken through
the servants' quarters of the palace in Vienna to see Her Majesty
and the Chancellor, Prince Kaunitz, and that he had been dressed
on that occasion in the clothes he was wearing now: black silk
stockings, black leather trousers with silver buckles, a white
linen shirt with wide cuffs and gold buttons inlaid with carnelian.
Angelis, who had listened in open-mouthed astonishment, later
gave an account of this conversation to the café owner Gasparo.

If Signor Giovanni, who not only knew Greek (for the book
on his desk was the *Odyssey*) but much else besides, nonetheless took pleasure in the company of his uneducated neighbor,
it may have been because he was himself a son of the people,
who a few short years before would not have dreamt of being
received in private audience by the Empress. He may have
liked to relax with the uncomplicated Angelis; and besides, the
man was decidedly useful: he knew the city and spoke the local
dialect. It is, therefore, not surprising that they should have gone
together to Pfneisel's fancy-goods shop on June 7, when Signor
Giovanni, who had much correspondence to look after during
his enforced stay in Trieste, bought a penknife and a pencil.
And it was equally natural that Angelis should have left him
alone at other times; after all, a gentleman who said that he
had just spoken with Maria Theresa in Vienna, and who was
bound for Rome where he claimed to know Cardinal Albani,
could not be expected to spend every hour of the day with an

unemployed cook whom he had chanced to meet in a minor port of the Empire. On one such occasion Angelis visited Father Bosizio, a Jesuit priest whom he had known for some time, and returned to Pfneisel's—on June 7—in order to purchase a knife of his own, of Venetian manufacture and with an octagonal handle. He is also known to have bought, in another store, a five-foot length of rope, which he now fashioned into a noose.

The events which took place in Trieste at about ten o'clock in the morning of June 8, 1768, have been described many times. Angelis's own account, the last of several versions he gave when arraigned in court, is likely to be more accurate than any reconstruction attempted across the gulf of two centuries:

> Asked why he, the defendant, had twisted and knotted said rope, he replied: "I truthfully state that I did not know who that man was, because it was not I who sought his acquaintance but he who wanted my friendship, just as it was he who told me the details that I have already testified to, namely, that the Empress had received him in that wretched costume with the leather trousers. To tell the truth, it was then that I thought that he must be some kind of a Jew or Lutheran. This suspicion gained on me after I had seen on his desk the book that I could not read, and even more when I noticed that he never attended Mass or wished to enter a church when I invited him to partake of the benediction; also, I could not help observing that he never bared his head, as I did, when we passed a church where the Host was being shown. That happened before St. Peter's here in town, and before the Capuchin Fathers' chapel on the way to the old hospital. Furthermore, it seemed to me that he could not be very bright, because I saw that he could not even figure out the change when paying for his tobacco. My belief that he might be a Lutheran or a Jew was strengthened when Gasparo, the café owner, asked me about him, and I answered that I did not know who he was, but that he had been received by the Empress and given two gold and two silver medals; whereupon

6

Gasparo remarked that he might have bought them in a store. Thus the idea of robbing him of these medals came to me, the more so as I never managed to discover whether he had any other valuables or money, since he had shown me only the medals. So I decided to kill him.

"With this in view I equipped myself with rope and a knife, thinking that I would throw and tighten the rope around his neck to keep him from crying out, and stab him.—As a matter of fact, I had determined to do this in the evening, after dinner. But when we were sitting in my room I could not work up the courage to do as I had planned. So I left it until morning, when we had taken a stroll and had our coffee in the café, where each paid for himself. We had returned to the inn, and he said that he would write from Rome and that if I went there, he would show me Cardinal Albani's palace and let me see who he was, a respected and famous man. He added that he had revealed something to Her Majesty which it would be very useful for her to know, and that she had urged him to stay in Vienna, I know not in what capacity, and that he was thinking of returning there eventually. All of this confirmed me in thinking that he must be some kind of a Lutheran or Jew or informer, a man of no account.

"Determined to carry out my plan, I went to my room, unsheathed the knife and stuck it in my vest pocket, along with the rope that I had made into a noose, and returned to his room. There we walked up and down a little. 'Signor Giovanni,' I asked jokingly when we had stopped by the window, 'are you going to show the medals at the dinner table?'—'I could let them see the large ones, I suppose,' he replied; but on reconsidering, he added with a smile: 'However, if the innkeeper discovers that I am rich, he will add a guilder to the bill.'—I told him that he should do as he thought best.

"After we had taken a few turns around the room, he sat down at the desk . . . and I, trembling and misled by the devil, took the rope from my pocket and, stepping behind him, threw it around his neck and drew it tight. But he jumped up

7

and gave me a shove, and being a strong man, pushed me away altogether. I do not recall whether I let go of the rope or he tore it out of my hand. All I saw was that he pulled it away from his throat, and that is how I knew that the noose had come open. Shaking and panicky, I took the knife and threw myself on him. He seized it by the blade with all his strength while grabbing me across the chest by my vest and shirt. As we wrestled in this manner we both lost our footing, but while I landed on one knee, he fell on his back with legs apart, and now that I had pried loose the knife from his grip, I stabbed him with it three or four times. I do not know whether it was in the chest or farther down because I wielded the knife so furiously that I did not watch where it struck. Then I jumped up and fled from the room. I do not remember where I left the knife. Such is the crime that I committed and which I truthfully confess. This is all I have to say."

When he was asked why he had fled after repeatedly stabbing Signor Giovanni, he replied: "Because I had seen the waiter Andreas stand in the door while we were still fighting [the sounds of the struggle had been heard all over the building, leading at least one guest to believe that furniture was being moved]. Seeing my crime discovered, I feared to be arrested. That is why I lost my head and ran. Had I kept my wits about me, I could have snatched up the medals because I knew where they, or rather the little box that held them, had been kept in the trunk. After all, I had watched Signor Giovanni take them out in order to show them to me, and replace them in the trunk, which he left unlocked. But fear and rage made me flee without taking anything at all, not even my own things. I ran away without so much as a hat, coat, or handkerchief."[1]

The murderer signed the confession with his real name, which he had not dared to use in Trieste because he had a criminal record as a thief: Francesco Arcangeli.

Bleeding profusely and close to fainting, Signor Giovanni staggered to his feet. He made his way down the stairs, mur-

muring "Look what he did to me!" to the slow-witted waiter who had failed to block the assassin's escape. People came running now, some supporting the wounded man as he stood grasping the railing, others hurrying to fetch a doctor and the priest, still others staring in disbelief at what they saw. Thinking that the victim had attempted to commit suicide, one of the maids mistook the blood-soaked cord which still hung from his neck for his intestines, and imagined that he had disemboweled himself. They led him back to his room and made him lie on a settee. He tried to speak and seemed to wish to write, but the hastily applied bandages could not still the bleeding. When he asked how serious his injuries might be, he was told that they were fatal. The police, trained to take down everything in proper sequence, asked the dying man who he was. Whispering that he was too weak to speak, he pointed to a corner of the room. Someone walked over and unfolded the piece of paper that lay on the trunk. It had been issued in Vienna on May 28 and bore the legend *Joanni Winckelmann Praefecto Antiquitatum Romae, in almam urbem redit* (J. W., Prefect of Antiquities in Rome, on his way back to the City). Having made his will and forgiven his enemy, Winckelmann died at four in the afternoon, in the bosom of the Church to which he had been converted many years before.

The body was found to have a cut in each hand, a superficial lesion in the costal cartilage near the left nipple, two stab wounds—of which one had perforated the right lung—and two others that had punctured the diaphragm and the stomach wall. Five pounds of blood had collected in the chest and a like amount in the abdominal cavity. "On account of the great and irremediable loss of blood," the autopsy report concluded over the signature of three doctors, "and of the tear in the stomach wall which caused the intestines to enter the chest cavity . . . we consider the two last-mentioned wounds as absolutely lethal and as the direct cause of death, which took place a few hours after the injuries had been inflicted."

Once the victim's identity had become known, the authorities received orders from Vienna to set aside all other business until the case had been solved. Arcangeli, who had been captured soon afterward in the countryside, was brought to trial and freely confessed. Convicted of murder and having publicly repented of his deed, he was condemned to death and broken on the wheel before a large crowd, on July 21 in the piazza before the Locanda Grande.

Justice was done, but the case remains essentially unsolved. It is not likely that we shall ever know what message, if any, Winckelmann had given Maria Theresa, and what verbal reply if any she had given him to carry back to Rome: when an inventory of his effects was made, nothing relevant was found in writing. It has been surmised that the Jesuits, embattled even then, and soon to be suppressed by Clement XIV, were either the subject of this hypothetical message or else were somehow involved in the case itself; and it does seem odd that Father Bosizio, the Rector of the Society of Jesus in Trieste, who had been a prison chaplain in Vienna when Arcangeli was serving time there for theft, should have been permitted to report on his contacts with the defendant in writing rather than being called to testify in person. Yet there is no reason to suppose that the order wanted to have Winckelmann, already in his lifetime one of the most prestigious converts ever made by the Roman Church, silenced in any manner whatever—least of all by means of a brutal assassination carried out in the semipublic setting of an inn, by a man whom he would in all likelihood have been able to disarm had he not happened to slip on the floor. Although Winckelmann—discreet, respected, and experienced in affairs of state—would have made an ideal diplomatic courier, politics seem to furnish no clue to Arcangeli's motive.

Did Arcangeli act on his own? And if so, what made him commit the crime? He was a confirmed felon, and, if robbery had been his aim, would surely not only have taken the medals but searched the trunk, earlier and while sending its owner out of the room under some pretext or other. Had he done so he would have discovered, as the police later did, that it contained six times as much cash as the medals were worth. Was he a religious maniac eager to rid society of a heretic? There is nothing to indicate that he used the words "Jew" and "Lutheran" as more than terms of opprobrium, and Winckelmann's mention of Cardinal Albani must have at least suggested the truth to him—namely, that he was about to kill a fellow-Catholic. Was Arcangeli a homosexual, like Winckelmann? We know from Boswell and others that such people were sometimes called "men of Italian taste"; yet Trieste is a harbor city, and Winckelmann, had he wanted, could no doubt have followed any such inclinations without benefit of a go-between or procurer. Arcangeli himself was not only a pockmarked and by all accounts ill-favored man of thirty-one, but in view of his past is also likely to have known that in a decree issued by the Emperor Ferdinand III in 1656, "unnatural" sex acts were punished by burning alive the guilty party and scattering the ashes to the wind. He needed only to have pleaded self-defense in order to escape the death penalty. But although the man was in some respects a confirmed liar, he never denied the main sequence of events or his sole responsibility for them. Was Winckelmann, recuperating just then from a nervous breakdown, perhaps himself to blame in some fashion or other? Was the extraordinary career that had led him from a country town in remotest Prussia to a Roman cardinal's palace somehow *bound* to end in an extraordinary manner? Did he die a death of his own, as he had lived a life that was very much his own?

PRUSSIA

I

Johann Joachim Winckelmann was born as one of the humblest
among the three million subjects of Frederick William I, by the
Grace of God King in Prussia, Margrave of Brandenburg, the
Holy Roman Empire's Arch-Chamberlain and Elector, Sovereign
Prince of Orange, Neufchâtel, and Vallangin, Duke in Geldern
and of Magdeburg, Cleves, Julich, etc., Burgrave of Nuremberg
and Seigneur of Halberstadt, Minden, Camin, etc., Duke of
Hohenzollern, Ruppin, the Mark, Ravensberg, etc., etc. Since
the sovereign's will affected every aspect of national life in the
Age of Absolutism, it is well to spend a few minutes with this
man who left the imprint of his formidable personality on
Winckelmann as on all his subjects. As his titles indicate, Frederick William ruled over a conglomeration of lands scattered
over northern Germany, from Geldern on the French to Memel
on the Russian border. Varying in size from mere specks on
the map to substantial provinces, and held together only by a
common crown, army, and bureaucracy, these lands were separated from one another, and from the Electorate of Brandenburg, which formed the heartland of the Hohenzollern dynasty,

by Hanover, Saxony, and sundry other of the three hundred states which then made up the Holy Roman Empire. His father, the former Margrave-Elector of Brandenburg, a vain and luxury-loving man who had patterned his court after that of the Sun King himself, had only recently prevailed upon the Emperor to grant him the rank of "King in Prussia"—*in* and not *of* Prussia because much of that territory lay, and was intended by the Emperor to remain, outside of the ex-Margrave's jurisdiction.

Important as this gain in prestige was, it remained for Frederick William, the second Prussian king, to make the state strong enough to be a kingdom in fact as well as name. His father had no sooner died, in 1713, than he assumed personal control over two weapons by the use or threatened use of which Prussia could alone hope to preserve her independence of the giants by whom she was surrounded: the France of Louis XIV and XV; the England of the Hanoverian kings; the Emperor Charles VI in Vienna, who was Frederick William's nominal overlord; and the Russia of Peter the Great and his successors. If Prussia, a patchwork state poor in resources and lacking the protection afforded by natural borders, was to survive at all, it would be because (1) her coffers were full and (2) her army was ready to strike at any time and in any direction. In later years, Frederick William liked to boast that he was the only solvent monarch in Europe. It was a distinction that had had to be achieved by a radical change of course: if his father had steered the Prussian ship of state by the lights of Versailles, the son chose ancient Sparta for his lodestar. He did not have himself crowned and anointed, declaring that the coronation of the first King of Prussia, in Königsberg back in 1701, had cost so much that it would have to suffice for two reigns.

Instead, he sold his father's Gobelins and jewels, dismissed all but a handful of courtiers, ordered that the buttons from his discarded uniforms be kept and reused, and moved his family into a five-room apartment while using the rest of the palace as offices for his civil servants—whose efficiency knew no bounds now that the royal gaze was forever fixed upon them. He even arranged a barter with Augustus the Strong of Saxony, by the terms of which that sovereign provided the Prussian army with two regiments of infantry in exchange for the porcelain service from which the Electors of Brandenburg had hitherto eaten. He was thus able to indulge two passions which, though far from kingly in nature, proved to be useful under the circumstances: saving money, and squeezing the last drop of work out of his subjects. He soon came to be called *Der Plusmacher:* the man who could show a plus or make a little profit. But there is nothing to show that he resented the nickname, as he is known to have resented that of *Der Dicke,* or "Fatty." When he died at fifty-one of gout and dropsy, he weighed well over 250 lbs. Unlike many other fat men, however, he was irascible and not at all jolly.

Radiating outward from the palace, the spirit of economy soon permeated every corner of the realm. It extended to the marketplace, where the women sitting in stalls behind their wares were made to knit when not actually waiting on customers (an idea perhaps borrowed from Venice, whose famous courtesans had to do needlepoint between assignments), and reached into the churches, where the clergy were enjoined to shorten the Sunday sermons, during which the congregation had to sit idle. Reasons of state, a peculiarly Prussian blend of the Protestant ethic of thrift and hard work, and his own highstrung and meddlesome personality thus urged him on in the never-ending struggle against waste and sloth. Although many of his edicts were merely ludicrous, it may be said that his principles were sound, and their wider application based on procedures which were rational enough within the context of a mercantilist society. High tariffs protected Prussian manufacturers from foreign competition; tax exemptions and state loans were made available to businessmen, canals dug to reduce transportation costs, and the underpopulated stretches of East Prussia opened to French Huguenots, Protestant refugees from Salzburg, and anyone else who cared to settle there. The legal and educational systems were centralized, and if such social progress could be combined with financial gain, the King was that much happier. He saw nothing wrong with appointing retired colonels as judges or with re-employing, at no expense to the exchequer, disabled veterans as rural schoolmasters.

In Frederick William's Prussia, economic self-sufficiency, industrial growth, and fiscal stability represented not ends in themselves, as they did in other physiocratically oriented states, but prerequisites for strengthening the army. Reluctantly, the King excused from military service the commercial middle class, which paid the bulk of the taxes. But conscription of the peasantry was ruthlessly enforced, and supplemented by an ingenious recruiting program. A whole network of agents and press gangs supplied the King with soldiers, especially recruits for his *Riesengarde,* or Giant Guard, an elite formation composed of men of exceptional height. Inspecting these puppets and marching them up and down the barracks square was the only luxury that Frederick William, who for all his martial airs was not really a fighter at heart, ever permitted himself. Peter the Great was thus well advised when he presented his host, as a parting gift after a visit to Berlin, with 150 very tall Russians who had been hurriedly rounded up among his own serfs. To cement the friendship between the two autocrats, an additional 100 giants were shipped from St. Petersburg every year until Frederick William's death in 1740.

If one of the King's own subjects had the misfortune of being of military age and over six feet tall, he was not safe anywhere in Prussia. There are even instances on record of foreign diplomats and citizens of neighboring German states being shanghaied: drugged, made drunk or knocked over the head, if necessary smuggled across the border into Prussia, and waking up to find themselves enrolled in the Giant Guard. Since they had been made to take the oath before they had had a chance to collect themselves, they were then faced with the choice of serving their term as soldiers or risking execution as deserters. Even Winckelmann, who was of no more than average height, once had to cut short a trip in order to escape being forcibly enlisted. But the most celebrated episode of the sort was that of Johann Christoph Gottsched, an immensely tall man who while a student in Königsberg had to flee all the way to Saxony. This turned out to be a blessing in disguise because Leipzig was a much better place in which to launch the career of writer, critic, and translator which eventually gained him a niche in the annals of German literature. That the King had lost a prize recruit is borne out by Goethe, who tells of visiting Gottsched more than forty years later and being led into his living room before the latter had had an opportunity to cover his bald pate. When the valet finally brought him his *perruque*, the angry giant put the hairpiece on his head with one ham-sized fist and with the other sent his man reeling across the room.

By such means, Frederick William not only maintained his *Riesengarde* but increased the army's total strength from 13,000 to 80,000. Excepting only that of France, it was the biggest army in Europe. More telling than numbers is the fact that he was able to preserve his territories, and enlarge them at the expense of the Swedes, whom he relieved of Stettin and a portion of the Pomeranian coast, without ever having to take the field.

Frederick William was as puzzling a phenomenon in the domestic as in the political sphere. Here again, preposterous methods led to achievements that were in part very creditable.

Although he was fond of children (he had little choice, having fathered fourteen) and remained a spectacularly faithful husband in a period when the royal *maîtresse* had become almost an institution, he so tyrannized his family that at least two of the children—the Crown Prince Frederick and his sister Wilhelmina—often and literally yearned for death as an escape from parental discipline. It was Frederick's particular misfortune to have been the frail and nervous oldest son of a father who had so loved the military life, as a youth in the War of the Spanish Succession, that the anniversary of the Battle of Malplaquet remained for him a nostalgic occasion forever after. Frederick William was gruff and crude, bellowed rather than spoke, and reveled in the title *Der Soldatenkönig.* As such, he despised not only the arts but all communication beyond military orders. Young Frederick, who recoiled from violence and was given to jumping at unexpected noises, must have shuddered when he was first introduced to the members of the *Tabakskollegium,* the rough old generals and other cronies among whom the King relaxed in the evening over a pipe and a mug of beer. For this weakling son of his who showed no desire to become like himself, Frederick William devised a rigid schedule of daily activities which included instructions about the use of cold water only (before breakfast) and water and soap (before lunch) for the Prince's ablutions. The boy was made to wear a uniform from the age of seven; dynastic history and military science formed his chief subjects during a decade's schooling; Latin, music, and all other intellectual and aesthetic pursuits were not only neglected but expressly forbidden, while instruction in the tenets of the Calvinist faith was tested during the family prayer session which was held every afternoon and followed by a sermon read by the King himself. Since the latter believed in public humiliation as the most effective form of punishment, young Frederick, whenever disobedient, was struck and pulled by the hair before the cowering courtiers and sometimes in front of the assembled troops. On one occasion, the irate King had drawn his sword and would have run his son through had an aged general not opened his tunic and cried "If Your Majesty must have blood, take mine: but that other blood you shall not have so long as I have voice to speak."[1] The Prince was then eighteen and had just been caught trying to escape to England, where his maternal grandfather, George I, had recently died. Having barely escaped the death penalty himself, he was locked up in a fortress and forced to watch the beheading of his best friend, a young Prussian officer who had helped him in his abortive flight from the realm. Somewhat later, when he had promised to do his father's bidding in all things and had been released from prison, Frederick obediently married the princess who had been chosen for him, an unattractive and unloved niece of the Empress of Austria.

In all respects but one, the results of this upbringing were predictable: the older children hated their father, and he ended by despising them. "The King could not stand the sight of my brother," Wilhelmina was to write when she had married and become the Margravine of Bayreuth, "and maltreated him whenever he could." Rejecting not only the Protestant but all religions, the Prince became a freethinker. Although he continued to wear a uniform to the end of his life, he wore it with a pronounced disdain for regulations and was rumored to have forsworn the use not only of soap, but of water. Thanks to a French tutor who had surreptitiously provided him with books and musical instruments, he became a fair scholar and an expert on the flute. While he seems to have consummated the marriage arranged for him by his father, he did so without enthusiasm and in later years lamented that, whereas Solomon had had a thousand wives and yearned for more, he had only one and found her *de trop*. Although he treated his consort, on their

B*

Infrequent meetings, with that exquisite ceremoniousness which is but a subtle form of contempt, he rarely addressed her in person: "Madame has put on a little weight" was his only comment on returning from the Seven Years' War, in which he had so often faced death. The only unexpected result of it all was that he also turned out to be an extraordinary monarch. He became Frederick the Great, who was to finish what his grandfather and father had begun: the transformation of Prussia—the real, pre-Hitler and pre-Hollywood Prussia, which for all its bluster also exemplified a frugal tenor of life and self-effacing devotion to duty—from a minor province into the cornerstone of Germany.

It is clear that the arts could not thrive under a man like Frederick William. He had no love of music or painting and was glad to see the last of Andreas Schlüter, the gifted architect of the Berlin Zeughaus, or armory, who had returned to the relative freedom of Russia. The King's particular scorn, however, was directed at writers and professors, whom he dismissed as so many *Schwarzscheisser*, men who "shit black," because they made their living by excreting black ink. He used the royal library's acquisition funds to supplement the pension of a retired general, and on a visit to the University of Frankfort-on-Oder forced the professors to hold a public debate with his court reader, who had been put in clown's costume for the occasion. Even this might have been passed over as an embarrassing instance of the royal sense of humor if worse had not followed:

Christian Wolff, a protégé of Leibnitz and Winckelmann's teacher in later years, declared in a lecture at the University of Halle that he had come to think of Confucian ethics as in no way inferior to those of Christianity. This was an unremarkable if not trite thing to say, in the cosmopolitan and tolerant era of the Enlightenment, but it had been said publicly and thus gave Wolff's enemies among the orthodox Lutheran clergy the opportunity for which they had been waiting. Too long, they felt, had this outsider, this Silesian who had such a following among the students, been allowed to spread the poison of his determinist views and to lecture on ethics and other matters that he—a mere mathematician by background and training— knew nothing about. They sent a report to two generals at court whom they knew to be sympathetic to their views, and these stalwarts in turn had no trouble persuading the King that Wolff's philosophy threatened the very foundations of the state. Had His Majesty ever considered what would happen to the *Riesengarde* if a recruit should take it into his head to believe himself predestined to be a civilian? Stung to the quick, Frederick William ordered Wolff to leave Prussia within 48 hours, on pain of hanging. Like Gottsched, Wolff was no worse off for having to flee like a criminal. He went to Marburg, where the Landgrave of Hesse-Kassel promptly offered him a chair in the university. It little mattered that the King eventually relented and urged him to return (an invitation which Wolff did not accept until young Frederick had succeeded his father in 1740, at which time the exiled hero was welcomed back to Halle riding in a four-in-hand preceded by six postilions and fifty students on horseback). The harm had been done: a renowned savant, one of the century's major philosophers, member of several academies including the Royal Society in London and recipient of a lifetime stipend from Catherine the Great, had been threatened with the gallows. Voltaire spoke for many when he declared that, "compared with Frederick William's Prussia, Turkey looks like a republic."

II

The eighteenth century was not, by and large, a period which allowed much scope to the self-made man. The few who did rise above their origins usually kept quiet about the details as much as about the fact itself, and Winckelmann was no exception. In later years, he occasionally referred to his youth, more often than not in maudlin and bitter fashion; but his childhood remains hidden from view on account of his own reticence and because it was spent in a country town which had been touched by history only once, and lightly. Indeed, Stendal had seen its best days long before Winckelmann was born on December 9, 1717, the only child of the cobbler Martin Winckelmann and his wife, Anna Maria.

Stendal lies due west of Berlin, on an undulating plain bisected by the road leading from Magdeburg to Hamburg. The town had at one time been the capital of the Altmark, the westernmost portion of the Mark Brandenburg. In the late Middle Ages, its citizens had traded their wheat for the manufactures of Hamburg, Lübeck, and the cities of Flanders. They had been wealthy enough to build a cathedral and to publish, in 1488, the first book printed in the Altmark. Unlike nearby Magdeburg, which survived after having been besieged and pillaged by the Imperial forces, Stendal never recovered from the devastations it suffered in the Thirty Years' War. In 1717, it had at best 3,000 inhabitants. Grass grew in the deserted streets, and most of the houses were as primitive as that at Lehmstrasse No. 263 (now Winckelmannstrasse), with its thatched roof and two windows whose leaded panes barely admitted enough light for the one room that served as shop, bedroom, kitchen, and dining room. It is tempting to speculate about Winckelmann's heredity, as those of his biographers have done who profess to see in him traces of his father's "Silesian mysticism" and of the "Prussian common sense" that he supposedly inherited from his mother; or about his earliest childhood and the emotional shocks that "must have" made him a homosexual. But this would be guesswork at best, aside from the fact that he was singularly disinclined to be mystical. Suffice it to say that almost nothing is known of his mother, a local weaver's daughter, or of his father, who had immigrated from Brieg in Silesia. They both died when their son was still a young man; there being no other close relatives, he had supported them in their indigent last years. His parents must, however, have had great hopes for him, for they allowed him to study, rather than insisting that he follow the family trades of cobbler or weaver. No doubt they trusted that he would eventually become a teacher, or perhaps even a Lutheran minister.

The first person to emerge from this gloom as a faintly discernible individual is the principal of the Stendal school, Esaias Wilhelm Tappert, who on becoming blind in 1733 took Winckelmann into his house as a reader in exchange for room and board. Winckelmann earned his pocket money by joining an itinerant boys' choir which sang in Latin in order to set itself apart from other such mendicant groups. No less than eighty afternoons a year were given over to this work, from which Winckelmann took away an abiding distaste for the kind of musical event in which the audience is expected to participate. (He came to like the opera during his Italian years, and at one time adored a certain ballerina if not the ballet itself; but he refused to sing, even when asked to do so by the Pope.) Every few months, Tappert distributed among the choristers the take from gifts and collections, with which they in turn bought their clothes and school supplies. Winckelmann, who eventually became choirmaster because he could play the organ as well, received a full fourth, and supplemented this income by giving private lessons and supervising the younger boys when they went skating on the frozen river Üchte.

To judge by his prize pupil, Tappert must have been a capable teacher. Yet the school was poor enough, housed as it was in two rooms in a former Franciscan monastery near the city wall. It had no floor boards, and only one stove so that the wooden partition had to be dismantled in winter if both classes were to keep warm. As a *Lateinschule* of the kind that had been established two centuries before by Melanchthon, it made no distinction between students preparing themselves for university and those who were going to be tradesmen and artisans. Its curriculum was in essence restricted to religion, history, Latin, and some Greek in the higher grades. What little German it offered had had to be surreptitiously introduced by Tappert, for the Pomeranian School Regulations of 1690 were quite specific on this point: teachers were to address students in Latin at all times instead of using their native German, a language that was deemed "frivolous in itself, and actually irritating and harmful when spoken with the young." (With few exceptions, secondary schools did not teach the German language as a separate subject until the end of the eighteenth, nor German literature until the beginning of the nineteenth century.) The stress on spoken Latin, on the other hand, sprang from professional and social rather than literary considerations. Latin was studied not in order to read the ancients and still less to acquire a knowledge of classical antiquity, but to enable the students to shine, from the pulpit or wherever else life might place them, with oratorical *tours de force* and a few Latin proverbs, the recitation of which would identify them as educated men much as the judiciously dropped French phrase will in our day. Religious instruction was therefore bound up with Latin rhetoric, and the mixture tested by means of public disputations between students and faculty, the latter being on occasion reinforced by clergymen from neighboring parishes. Despite such concentrated exposure to the language and although he inevitably used it in his early correspondence, Winckelmann for some reason never was more than a fair Latinist. His real love even then was Greek, which he wrote with a fine hand and eventually came to know very well. For the Protestant clergy, being able to read the New Testament in the original was a matter of doctrinal privilege, so much so that doubting the excellence of *Koiné* Greek—for example, by comparing it on a philological basis with the language of the great dramatists and historiographers—would have been tantamount to questioning Holy Writ itself. Limited to the translation of this one document, the teaching of Greek had become so mechanical that it remained unchanged, in some Prussian communities, from 1600 to 1760: an incredibly long stretch of pedagogical aridity, even for generations as yet unaware of the existence of "underachieving" students and classroom "situations." Winckelmann later observed that, in his youth, Greek studies in the Altmark had been "bogged down in sluggish darkness"—"*ignava caligene mersae.*" Indeed, it was in order to perfect his Greek that he decided to go to Berlin in 1735.

Tappert, who remained fond of Winckelmann even though he had lately detected a certain laxity in the manner in which the latter performed his devotions, had provided him with an introduction to the principal of a grammar school, the Cöllnisches Gymnasium. There he received board and room while being farmed out, as it were, to various Berlin families whose dim-witted or recalcitrant offspring required the services of a private tutor. Although the capital itself, a modest city of some 80,000 souls, does not seem to have greatly impressed the eighteen-year-old country boy, he met two men that winter whom he remembered to the end of his days. Like most of his early friends and acquaintances, they were schoolteachers, members of a profession about which he had begun to harbor certain reservations. But these men were schoolteachers with a difference: one had been an adventurer in life and the other was to become one in spirit.

Johann Leonhard Frisch had been a farm manager on a landed estate, a Protestant preacher in Hungary, and an interpreter in the Empire's interminable wars against the Infidel Turk. On his return to Germany, he took up one of the century's favorite hobbies and became a collector: he classified the birds and insects of northern Europe and published ornithological and entomological reference works with illustrations by one of his sons. An excellent linguist, he also compiled a Latin dictionary and taught Russian, among others to Leibnitz, who saw to it that he was made a member of the Royal Prussian Academy of Sciences. Frisch was enough of a chemist to be credited with the invention of potassium berlinate, or soluble Prussian blue, the $KFe_2(CN)_6$ used in dyeing wool and cotton, and enough of an agricultural pioneer to have taken a hand in the introduction of sericulture to Prussia. Having long reared silkworms on his own, he prevailed upon Frederick William to decree that mulberry bushes be planted on municipal cemeteries. One can imagine the King's delight on discovering that his subjects could be made to contribute to the economy even as they lay rotting in their graves. In short, Frisch was a man of varied gifts and interests who had seen the world. Had he been born in France or England, he might well have achieved national prominence. As it was, he remained one of the many victims of the fragmentation of German cultural and economic life, and as such had to consider himself lucky to spend his declining years as principal of the Gymnasium zum Grauen Kloster. It was a good school, but it can hardly have offered much scope to a man of Frisch's caliber.

If Frisch was already old at the time, Christian Tobias Damm's scholarly achievements still lay before him when he taught Winckelmann Greek in Berlin. As the author of an anthology of Greek fables which saw many printings and was used for over a century, Damm had been among the first to stress the superiority, by any token of literary criticism, of the Greek over the Roman authors. His own favorites were Pindar, and above all Homer, whose vocabulary he reduced—in a voluminous etymological dictionary—to three hundred key, or root, words and their derivatives. Only slightly less ludicrous, for all the knowledge and enthusiasm expended on it, was his endeavor to claim the poet for the cause of monotheism by insisting that the deities so picturesquely drawn in the *Iliad* and *Odyssey* were mere symbolizations of specific aspects (personalized decrees, institutions, and the like) of the one God. This original if erroneous view of Olympus led him to consider the poet Homer as the outer shell, to be discarded at will, of Homer the thinker. After decades spent as a teacher of classics, among whose students were Moses Mendelssohn and Friedrich Nicolai, Damm published in 1764 a translation of the New Testament, with a commentary in which he explained the miracles as no more than reflections of the allegorical propensities of Hebrew thought, and the essence of Christianity as the most rational expression of man's self-knowledge and perfectibility. This was too strong even for the freethinking Berlin of Frederick the Great; shunned by colleagues and forbidden to discuss religious matters in the classroom, he was condemned to a lonely old age. Many years later, in Rome, his former student offered to collect subscriptions for Damm's etymological dictionary and to look after his other teacher's grandson, the painter Johann Christoph Frisch, who reported having met "that nice Mr. Winckelmann, who shows me much kindness . . . and esteem, on account of my late grandfather."[2]

After the sojourn in Berlin and a few months during which he worked as assistant to a teacher in the small town of Salzwedel near Stendal, Winckelmann was ready for the university. Given a free choice he would have preferred to study medicine, but parental pressure and that of his teachers made him register as a student of theology in the University of Halle. It was a sensible decision because that discipline, heavily subsidized by state and church, provided him with the means of continuing his education; in that century and the following, Halle was to do as much for many other bright but poor young scholars and writers, some of whom, like Klopstock and Lessing, later went into more mundane professions. The choice of Halle was altogether preordained for Winckelmann because a law of 1729 had made two years' residence in that university mandatory for candidates for a degree and for all others who aspired to enter the Prussian civil service.

The *Abiturientenexamen* by which a student qualifies for admission to university was introduced in Prussia in 1788. Until then, no clear distinction existed between *Gymnasium* and *Universität*, with the result that the latter had very loose admission standards. In Winckelmann's day, an incoming student would have shaken his head in disbelief at the very notion of having to take tests and being handed over, like the freshman in Goethe's *Faust* and countless others since, to the dubious ministrations of an academic counselor. Yet the young man from Stendal who registered on April 4, 1737, would probably have acquitted himself quite well in these procedures. To be sure, he was by no means a formed personality at the age of nineteen, and there were even some black marks against him, such as his spotty preparation and the notation "An unsettled and capricious man"—"*homo vagus et inconstans*"—behind his name in the records of the Cöllnisches Gymnasium. He was, however, an experienced private tutor by then, having given evidence not only of general pedagogical interests but of possessing, even at his own relatively tender age, a particular aptitude for dealing with the young. It was also true that he was penniless, and would have to eat at one of the tables at which free meals were served to indigent theology students. In the 1730's, Halle boasted several such *Freitische* for a dozen students each, supported through a collection held once a year in the churches of Prussia.

If Winckelmann had this much against him, he had nonetheless shown that he was aware of his own shortcomings and the disadvantages under which he had started out in life, and that he knew how to remedy them quietly and effectively. Being poor and coming from a home in which the Bible is likely to have been the only book, he had acquired early the habit of making excerpts from any and all volumes that passed through his hands. When he arrived in Halle, he had already read and copied his way through a shelf of works ranging from the German edition of a gentleman's guide called *L'art de l'homme de l'épée, ou dictionnaire du gentilhomme* to a self-made anthology of Greek authors, his very own *Breve compendium antiquitatum graecarum.* In the eyes of our hypothetical counselor, then, his character might have overshadowed altogether his knowledge. The fact that he was something of a "loner" would not have been counted against him in that century of the uncommon man. It was no more than might be expected of someone who had supported himself from the beginning, been a dutiful son to his parents, mastered the arduous role of companion to a blind benefactor, and gained the respect of such men as Frisch and Damm. In Berlin, he had been enterprising enough to secure admission to the Royal Library, whose 50,000 volumes helped to flesh out the Gymnasium's meager holdings. During his first year at Halle, he was to give a further demonstration of initiative by walking all the way to Hamburg, where a former professor's library, that of the father-in-law of Lessing's friend Samuel Reimarus, was being auctioned off, and returning on foot with his purchases on his back.

We do not know how Winckelmann looked at nineteen (his few portraits being of later date), or whether he was a virgin (which is likely, in view of the cast of his personality and the environment in which he had been raised), or what his favorite beverage was (beer, or the chocolate of which he grew so fond?). More important, in any event, than peripheral details of this nature is the fact that he must have been troubled even then by two conflicts that he never quite resolved. They sprang from the professions for which he was about to prepare himself: the ministry and teaching. His misgivings about the Lutheran faith in which he had been baptized were too deeply rooted to let him face with equanimity, let alone anticipation, the prospect of becoming a clergyman, and he knew that in accepting so much help from the Church he was laying himself open to the charge of being a hypocrite. But if the prospect of becoming a minister caused him to search his heart, the alternative of be-

coming a teacher caused him to turn up his nose, not so much at
the profession itself as at its run-of-the-mill practitioners.
Winckelmann's compulsive fear of being taken for a schoolteacher, even while he was one himself, dates from this period in
which he faced, with masochistic fatalism, his impending transformation into one of these

men of unsociable cast whose bookishness and misanthropic
conceit leads them to bury themselves in their libraries. With-
drawing from ordinary human beings in the strained endeavor
to appear dignified, they assume a severe and forbidding mien
that would do credit to a stage comedian. They are unkempt and
spitefully obstinate, like children raised in solitude; whenever
they come in contact with good society, they blink and lower
their glance as if blinded by the sun; their awkwardness makes
them tremble, and they are rightly laughed at whenever the
conversation turns to anything beyond their own scholarship.
Although dealing with subjects that seem expressly designed to
make men appreciate form and beauty and to foster a spirit of
humanistic fellowship, they lack any such sensitivities, and
indeed lose what little sense they have. They are not men but
bogeymen.

This appraisal of the typical eighteenth-century philologist is
from the inaugural lecture *De doctore umbratico* ("On the
Gentleman Scholar") which the classicist David Ruhnken de-
livered in 1761 on being appointed Professor of History and
Eloquence in the University of Leiden in Holland. At this time
Ruhnken, who, like a humanist of old, Latinized his name to
Ruhnkenius (just as Winckelmann sometimes called himself
"Goniander," from the Greek *gōnio* [angle], in German
Winkel), had himself "arrived" as a gentleman and a scholar:
with the haughtiness of a country squire who rode to hounds
when he was not in demand as a dancer and flautist, he now

etched in acid his nameless colleagues in country schools. It is ironic that Winckelmann, from whose pen we have similar observations made when he, too, had turned his back on the classroom, should later have called Ruhnken to task over some minute point of textual exegesis. Had he read *these* lines, he would have approved wholeheartedly.

III

One major aspect of the student life that Winckelmann encountered at Halle and Jena is parodied in *Der Renommist* ("The Braggart"), a mock-heroic poem by his contemporary Friedrich Wilhelm Zachariae. Its hero, Raufbold, or "Brawler," is an undergraduate who has just been expelled for some misdeed or other from the University of Jena, where he bullied the *Füchse,* or freshmen, ran up debts, drank as much as he could possibly hold, cursed whenever he opened his mouth, and at night kept awake the *Philister,* or townspeople, by shouting and looking for fights. About to leave town, he casts a nostalgic last glance at his old haunts:

"O Jena!," he exclaim'd, "now must I leave your gate,
Now will the slipp'ry Fuchs my downfall celebrate.
Now will your market-place no more my roaring hear,
And you no sword-play after dark in alleys fear,
O Philistines!—A bitter blow! So must some freedom die,
A certain fame, o Jena, fall as I your city fly."
He spoke and to his steed did spring, and as he sped away,
Him twenty creditors did spy, and call'd for him to stay.

Raufbold no sooner arrives in Leipzig and takes a room than he invites three cronies, *ex-Jenenser* like himself, to join him in a drinking bout of herculean proportions. Having at last disposed of the beer, they buckle on their swords and reel out into the nocturnal streets, singing raucously and smashing the lamp outside a professor's house. They end the evening by crashing a dance of Leipzig dandies and their ladies, held under the patronage of the allegorical goddess of *Galanterie,* or Courtesy, and her servant Sylvan, himself a former rowdy from Jena who has since turned into a fashion plate. After briefly considering, during the next morning's hangover, whether he should not move on to Halle, "where freedom still reigns and the brawler is on top," Raufbold decides to remain in Leipzig and if possible conform to the local fashion. Under Courtesy's guidance, he is transformed into a *Stutzer,* or dandy:

> *"With heavy boots oppress'd," she counsels him,*
> *"leave riders in their plight;*
> *'Tis socks of silk that make a girl's delight.*
> *A smaller sword, with lace, is what a man should wear,*
> *A sign that you me serve and banners for me bear.*
> *Avoid from this point on all quarrels and dispute,*
> *Attract with words polite, to perfume give repute."*

In the end, however, all of Dame Courtesy's efforts are in vain: Raufbold reverts to his savage ways, and after fighting a mock-heroic duel with Sylvan rides off once more—to Halle, where he expects to feel more at home.

Zachariae is forgotten nowadays except for this poem, which for all its indebtedness to Boileau and Pope does not lack a certain stature of its own. More allegorical than *The Rape of the Lock,* it shares with this model the entertaining discrepancy between a pompously dignified form—here, the stately alexandrine

—and a slight subject matter, as well as the short-circuiting through ridicule of Homeric and other similes, the presence of sylphs that hover protectively over body and clothing, and, of course, much down-to-earth satire. For it is true that in Zachariae's and Winckelmann's time, Jena and Halle attracted more than their share of rowdies, while Leipzig, the port of entry of the latest French fashions and manners, was well on the way to becoming a showcase of rococo sophistication. Its very size (a city in contrast to such university towns as Jena, Halle, Erfurt, Wittenberg, and Göttingen) contributed to this distinction, as did its economic eminence and a cultural ascendancy based on the manifold activities of Gottsched, Germany's arbiter of literary taste. All this, in turn, made many parents look on Leipzig as a good place in which their sons could sow their wild oats while attending university and acquiring such skills as dancing, fencing, and gambling. It was here that Lessing had to be upbraided by his mother for having shared, with a group of freethinkers and stage people, the Christmas cake that she had sent him; and it would not be long before Goethe, who immortalized the city's role as a miniature Paris in *Faust*, in his turn almost came to grief on the occasion of his first exposure to the worldlier aspects of life and love. There is little doubt that Winckelmann, too, would have gained poise earlier in life if he had had the means to attend the University of Leipzig.

Although situated only a few miles across the border, his own alma mater projected a very different image. The University of Halle, as dowdy at this time as that of Leipzig was glamorous, was attended by rowdies, paupers, and other students who had fallen afoul of bourgeois standards. Oddly enough, they were taught by a staff made up both of incompetents and of men of high caliber. The institution owed its establishment in 1694 to a coincidence of dynastic, religious, and educational needs: the desire of the Electors of Brandenburg for another Protestant university besides far-off Königsberg; the rivalry between Brandenburg and Saxony; and the intolerance of the academic and ecclesiastical establishment in the latter country. The atmosphere there had become so repressive that several prominent scholars decided to leave Saxony altogether and accept jobs at Halle. Foremost among them was the jurist and philosopher Christian Thomasius, who while teaching at Leipzig had been the first professor to lecture in German rather than Latin. The other faculty members' resentment at this had barely begun to subside when he published, the very next year and again in German instead of Latin or French, a literary review in which he allowed several of his colleagues to be satirized. Since he had also taken issue with their theocratic convictions by arguing, years before Frederick the Great and Joseph II were even born, that a sovereign's duties included not only the supervision over the country's churches but also the safeguarding of the rights of religious minorities, Thomasius soon found it expedient to remove himself to Halle. His Pietist friend Philip Jakob Spener had likewise been persuaded to exchange Saxony for Brandenburg, while August Hermann Francke, founder of the Hallische Stiftungen (a self-contained complex of pietistically oriented schools and orphanages with their own dispensary, printing press, and book store), had just been eased out of Erfurt. What had thus begun, in Halle, as a measure of self-assertion on the part of Brandenburg against Saxony, of the advocates of natural against the defenders of canon law, and of the Pietists against the conservative Lutheran clergy, in due course became an orthodoxy in its own right, until it was in turn supplanted by such new heresies as the aesthetics of Winckelmann's teacher Baumgarten, and Wolff's popularization of Leibnitz's thought.

. . .

Then as now, students spent only a small portion of their time in lecture halls and libraries. According to his friends Gottlob Burchard Genzmer and Konrad Friedrich Uden, Winckelmann, too, liked to frequent the Halle Ratskeller in the evening, exchanging gossip with the regular customers and supposedly "sketching out, from their accounts of their own youthful travels, more than one route to Paris. From Erfurt on he would try to reach a monastery every night, where he hoped to find free lodging by claiming that he wanted to change religion, and make his conversion in Rome." It is unlikely that he should have been so calculating at this time, or naïve enough to believe that Paris lay either on the topographical or the spiritual road to Rome. But he enjoyed talking over a glass of beer, and no doubt participated as much as his modest purse would allow in the social side of university life. Merry as that life was if Zachariae is to be believed, it entailed, even in those halcyon days of political innocence, some risk of a confrontation with the establishment. The latter was represented by so stern a father figure that any potential activist would have trembled in his sandals. In 1750, just after Winckelmann's graduation, Frederick the Great found it necessary to issue the following proclamation, for the guidance of students and their faculty sympathizers in Prussian universities:

WHEREAS HIS MAJESTY THE KING OF PRUSSIA has found, to HIS great displeasure, that discipline and good conduct have lately broken down in HIS universities, the students having been granted an entirely unwarranted licence through the pernicious connivance of their superiors and in particular through the self-interest of certain professors . . . , HIS MAJESTY has been pleased to restrict such licence through the re-establishment of supervision and rules of conduct for said students, in order that they may henceforth continue their studies with the requisite application, and conduct themselves in such fashion that their parents

39

and guardians will be assured that the sums expended on the university education of their sons and charges are not wasted, but that these will return with good manners and fit to render service to the country and for the future benefit of all. This being HIS MAJESTY'S sole intention in regard to the following, and because HE would rather see industrious and well-behaved students than witness the corruption of all through the presence of many impudent and ill-mannered youths, HIS MAJESTY herewith commands once and for all that:

1) Excepting only those of noble birth, all students, be they in Law, Theology, or whatever discipline, shall be forbidden to wear swords.

2) Every student must lead an honorable and law-abiding life, comport himself modestly and peaceably at all times, and avoid all disorderly affairs and excesses. Candidates for a degree in theology in particular must live quietly and respectably, avoiding all scandal, so that it may not be said of them that they cannot be entrusted with teaching positions or other responsible appointments because they could not govern themselves at university. Let, therefore, no student make bold to sharpen his sword, shout or otherwise be noisy in public, or provoke or otherwise challenge others and engage in fighting . . .

3) No student shall be seen on the street after 9 p.m. unless it be absolutely essential for him to be about, in which case he is to proceed quietly and with circumspection . . .

. . . .

5) It shall be understood that no student is permitted to use firearms within city limits or to break windows and damage lights on public or private buildings, on pain of imprisonment and expulsion.

6) Whosoever on being arrested offers resistance or provocation to the proctors and patrols or otherwise affronts them in word or deed, shall be liable to imprisonment or expulsion.

7) Any student who dares to hatch plots and affixes a notice to the board for this purpose, or otherwise causes a public dis-

turbance, shall be expelled *cum infamia* or punished yet more severely.

8) Punishments decreed for such students shall be carried out without remission, with the proviso that those of noble extraction shall pay a fine for their misdemeanors while those of lesser birth shall be imprisoned . . .

9) Students are forbidden to engage in betting or other games of chance, and cautioned against incurring unnecessary debts.

. . . .

12) It is HIS MAJESTY'S desire that students continue to be given the privilege of relaxing and of diverting themselves in the same fashion as that granted to other persons of good conduct. They must, however, observe the necessary decorum and avoid all excesses, scandals, and other actions that are obnoxious to good citizens. Faculty and students will bear this in mind, and the rector and professors will be held accountable if these regulations are not carried out with the necessary force and vigor.

FRIDERICH

Winckelmann is unlikely to have been involved in these misdemeanors, or in some others that the King neglected to castigate, such as the carefree whoring observed by an English visitor to Halle: "All round the town, there are neighbouring villages, where the inhabitants unbend themselves with drinking and dancing, on Sundays and festivals; and most of the public houses are provided with good agreeable wenches for the conveniency of the students, whose flames, 'tis thought, would be more pernicious in town, were they not quenched in this manner."[3] Constrained to take his meals at a *Freitisch* and to make ends meet by giving private lessons, Winckelmann belonged to those who in Frederick's words "proceed quietly and with circumspection." Bored with the lectures, which he said provided an academic food that "stuck in one's teeth," he spent his mornings reading at home until the library opened, at one in the afternoon and for only one hour. For its 1,500 students, the University of Jena then had some 10,000 volumes housed in a two-room building from which nothing could be taken out; Halle, newer and smaller, probably had even less. The holdings, in any case, increased only slowly and by such haphazard means as bequests from professors, small sums taken out of student fees, and the obligatory contribution of one book from every student who graduated with the degree of Doctor of Theology. As he had done in Berlin, Winckelmann supplemented this scant fare by frequenting a second library, that of Francke's orphanage, and by making hurried excerpts which he worked up at home and eventually incorporated, as was his custom, into his own hand-copied library. Whenever he had a few pennies left over he bought books at auctions, and on occasion borrowed a volume or two from friends with libraries of their own. Hardships of this sort were the common lot of scholars in the eighteenth century, and must of course be taken into account whenever we judge the depth and extent of their knowledge. Although these men had to overcome fewer distractions because "the world" was not so much with them in their small and sometimes isolated universities, they also lacked the amenities—from electric light to card catalogues—that we have come to take for granted. Two hundred years ago, many a writer and scholar literally had to walk farther for a footnote than his modern counterpart might care to drive for an encyclopedia. It was quite in keeping with this ambulatory side of scholarship that Winckelmann should have made a strong impression on a prominent Halle professor, the philosopher Alexander Gottlieb Baumgarten, not because he had faithfully attended lectures or submitted a brilliant term paper but because he once walked, shortly after graduation, all the way from Hadmersleben to Halle in order to look up a reference in the *Annals* of the Paris Academy of Sciences.

Baumgarten, to whose servant Winckelmann presented himself in the hope of finding the volume there, had his former student shown in when he heard that he had undertaken a two-day journey for this purpose. He talked to him at some length, tested his knowledge, and urged him to become a professor himself. This was the last thing that Winckelmann would have wanted. Although Voltaire may have been right when he later said that anyone wishing to see German intellectual life at its best should visit Halle, Winckelmann found that his own subjects were poorly taught. The faculty of theology was inadequately staffed, and his favorite subject of classics was so much the handmaiden of the university's leading disciplines, law and what would now be called political science, that the first professor who taught it at Halle was forever lamenting the fact that even his learned colleagues knew hardly any Latin: "*Ius, ius, ius—et nihil plus!*" What little encouragement Winckelmann received came from Johann Heinrich Schulze, the owner of a collection of antique coins which was eventually incorporated into the university's archaeological museum. If the study of numismatics seems to us a roundabout way to classical antiquity, it was a much-traveled road in days when many of the great works of Greek art had not yet been discovered. Schulze's lectures on Greek and Roman history, in any event, were based on this collection, which may have afforded Winckelmann, who is known to have been enrolled in the course, a first visual contact with the ancient world. He had no way of knowing that, from this point of view as from all others, he would have been better off in Leipzig, where a rudimentary course in archaeology was taught even then, or in Wittenberg, the home of a scholar who had actually set foot in Italy (as rare a distinction, at that time, as fluency in spoken Latin is in modern classicists). Paradoxically enough, it was Winckelmann's misfortune, and a factor which colored his opinion of German universities in general, that he saw a good deal of precisely the most prestigious professors in Halle: Baumgarten, author of a highly regarded *Aesthetik* in which he endeavored to apply Wolff's system to the arts; Wolff himself, whose homespun philosophy showed such ignorance of the ancients that Winckelmann came to dismiss it as "childish trifles, destined to be devoured by the mice"; and the most famous of them all, the diplomat and historian Johann Peter von Ludewig, in whose library he worked as an assistant in the summer of 1740, when Ludewig had just furnished the Prussian Court with the dubious legal claims advanced by Frederick the Great to justify his annexation of Silesia later that year.

We have already had occasion to observe Winckelmann's extraordinary loyalty to those of his teachers whom he respected. It is indicative of his weakness for the more colorful side of human nature that he should have reserved a particular accolade for a professor who became not only famous but infamous. Gottfried Sell, a jurist who lectured on a variety of non-legal subjects as well, had published in 1733 a fascinating if overly rationalistic bit of natural history in the form of a dissertation on *teredo navalis,* the shipworm which had caused so much damage to the dikes and navies of Holland that the sudden decline of Dutch sea power has sometimes been ascribed to the depredations of this lowly creature. Unable to pay the debts he had incurred in building up his library and collections, Sell later disappeared from Halle and turned up in Paris. On hearing a report that he had been caught and hanged as a forger, Winckelmann wrote in 1755 that he had read the book on the shipworm and come to admire the author's skill (the German term *Geschicklichkeit* may have been intended to reflect praise of Sell's manual as well as intellectual dexterity): "As a former student of his, I was touched by this news as much as by anything I have yet heard." As it turned out, the report had been false. Sell lived to

1. *Trieste: The Locanda Grande in 1810.*

11. *Winckelmann. Painting by Mengs.*

III. *Frederick William I.*
Painting by Weidemann.

IV. *Frederick the Great on his*
accession. Painting by Pesne.

v. *Burgkeller (Arminenhaus) in Jena.*

vi. *Panorama of Jena, in the early eighteenth century.*

VII. *The* Laocoön. *Vatican Museum, Rome.*

VIII. *Augustus the Strong. Painting by Louis de Silvestre.*

IX. *Etruscan intaglio, from Winckelmann's* Description des Pierres Gravées du feu Baron Stosch *(Florence 1760).*

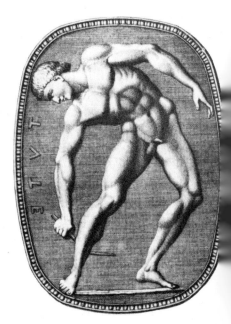

x. *Three views of eighteenth-century Rome. Paintings by Vanvitelli:
Trinità dei Monti, the Quirinal near Palazzo Albani, the Tiber with
Hadrian's Tomb (right) and St. Peter's (in background).*

(rear view)

(front view)

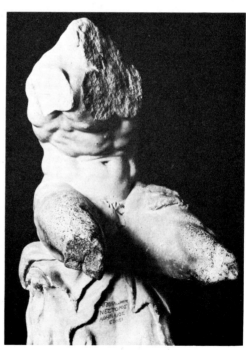

XI. *The Belvedere Torso.*

the eve of the Revolution, and was ungrateful enough to repay his admirer by mistranslating into French the latter's *Geschichte der Kunst des Altertums*, the *History of Ancient Art*.

Winckelmann seems to have belonged to those who in looking back on their university years discover that their chief gain consisted neither in the accumulation of knowledge nor in "good times," but in having laid the foundation of some lifelong friendships. Those he had with Marpurg and Guichard did not mature until these men, like Winckelmann himself, had made their mark in the world. His friendships with Berendis and Genzmer, fellow-students at Halle, and with his childhood companion Uden, are unique, however, in that they are reflected in a correspondence to which we owe many details about Winckelmann's life that would otherwise have been lost. Whereas Marpurg eventually became Director of the Prussian State Lottery and Guichard an intimate of Frederick the Great, the other three lived out their lives in obscurity—Uden as a country doctor, Genzmer as a parson, Berendis in the service of the Duchess of Sachsen-Weimar—and thus imperceptibly turned into foils, so to speak, against which Winckelmann saw his own progress set off. As he rose above his origins, these early friendships became charged with a tension of their own, subject to being strained at any time by arrogance on his part and resentment on theirs. Since most of their letters are lost while his have been preserved (a familiar constellation in cases where a famous man continues to correspond with the friends he had made in younger and humbler years), some moves in this game of one-upmanship can no longer be retraced. But it is clear that he played it to the end and withstood the temptation of cutting it short, for example by the kind of self-righteous remark with which he acknowledged the truth of the entry made after his name in the

C

records of the Cöllnisches Gymnasium: when a friend presented him with that document in Rome, he replied that if he had not been "an unsettled and capricious man," he would never have made his way to Rome in the first place.

All in all, then, the harvest of the two years at Halle was modest enough. He had gained some familiarity with academic life, made some friends, and in the end graduated in theology with an oddly understated citation to the effect that, although little was known about his religious beliefs, he had at least attended lectures and therefore presumably profited by his studies: *Quamquam autem ratione status animi, saltem quod satis est, nobis non innotuerit, tamen, cum praelectiones nostras eum frequentasse constet, speramus ipsum ex illis fructum nonnullum hinc secum esse reportaturum.* His knowledge of the world at large, of course, was still woefully limited. He had previously spent a few months in Berlin, briefly visited Dresden with friends, lived in Halle, and now had to return to the Altmark in order to earn enough money to continue his education elsewhere. The job was the familiar one of tutor, but the setting was new in that he found himself for the first time a member of a household that was neither academic nor clerical. He lived with the family of Georg Arnold Grolman, a Prussian officer who had served as a common soldier under Prince Eugene, distinguished himself at Malplaquet, and after his marriage settled in the village of Osterburg just north of Stendal. While Winckelmann instructed the oldest son in history and philosophy, the head of the family was away fighting in the Silesian campaign, from which he returned with a patent of nobility bestowed on him by Frederick the Great. The new tutor was meanwhile made to feel at home by Frau von Grolman, by all accounts a woman whose charms would have set aflame a more volatile man than Winckelmann.

Having replenished his funds, he enrolled in the University of Jena in 1741. Although spared the embarrassment of again having to masquerade as a *studiosus theologiae,* he had once more chosen the wrong institution. The student body, to be sure, was twice that of Halle, but the majority were fully as rambunctious as we saw them described by Zachariae, and no one could then have foreseen that Jena would be Germany's leading university by the end of the century. Far from pointing to the future, Jena was at this time a bastion of academic conservatism. It was, therefore, no coincidence that the professor whom Winckelmann credited with having taught him all he learned there should have been engaged in fighting a hopeless rearguard action. Georg Erhard Hamberger was in fact the last major representative of the mechanistic approach to medical science, in which all bodily functions and processes were mathematically analyzed and forced into line with the laws of physics. What Descartes had done in philosophy, Spinoza in religion, and Hobbes in political "science," Hamberger attempted to do in the very different field of medicine by applying mathematical or at least mechanical procedures to the explanation of the most varied biological phenomena. To him, the circulation of the blood resembled nothing so much as a machine subject to hydrostatic laws, and the bone structure with the musculature that activates it, a set of levers; the respiratory system was an arrangement of bellows, the intestines were sieves, and so forth. Beyond this, he reluctantly acknowledged the existence of an ill-defined vital force as the final causative instance of organic movements and changes, even though he was hard put to assign to it any definite location in the models that he constructed in order to illustrate the functions of various organs. Although physiological discoveries had long since begun to break up this rigidly systematized structure, Hamberger refused to change his views until the very end; indeed, he must have been the kind of man that Mérimée had in mind when he wrote, a century later in *Lettres à une inconnue,* that "there is nothing more irritating than a German professor who thinks that he has discovered an idea." In a deathbed repentance worthy of a bigger man and a better argument, Hamberger finally declared himself vanquished by Albrecht von Haller, with whom he had long been locked in acrimonious combat.

When summing up his experiences at Jena ten years later, Winckelmann said that he had studied physics, medicine, and anatomy with great application. The remark has a Faustian ring to it, and there do exist some similarities between his abortive foray into the natural sciences and Goethe's own, wider-ranging but in many respects equally frustrating excursions into those inhospitable regions. Incomparably the greater man, Goethe too was defeated in the end, not by science but by the scientific establishment of his time. In denying to mathematics its pivotal role in all advanced scientific endeavor (an attittude in which Winckelmann was confirmed by his temporal Bible, Bayle's *Dictionnaire historique et critique*), both men eventually came up against an unsurmountable barrier. Their scientific studies nevertheless helped counterbalance that conjectural stance which is the basis of all literary and aesthetic creativity. Their plastic way of looking at art and at the world about them, and their substitution of anatomical and other incontrovertibly scientific evidence for untutored enthusiasm, represent the tangible result of these interests, which were not haphazard in origin but an expression of their common belief in nature as the ultimate source of truth. Winckelmann, in particular, absorbed enough of this mentality to recognize in the mathematical proportions of a work of art a prerequisite without which beauty cannot be said to exist; at the same time, he never sought to define beauty on the sole basis of such proportions. With a foot in each camp, he thus came to occupy a position of informed neutrality in the struggle—so vehement in his time—between the experimental and the speculative points of view.

Instead of writing a dissertation, Winckelmann wanted to conclude his studies with the *erudita peregrinatio,* the academic journey that was then customary. It appears that he had intended to go to Paris, among other things in order to examine a collection of Greek manuscripts of which a catalogue had just been published, when the War of the Austrian Succession made traveling so hazardous for a man of military age that he found it the better part of discretion to turn back at Gelnhausen, and to proceed from there to Fulda. He is said to have stopped by a fountain outside the city gate, in order to shave, when he heard a woman scream. Turning around, he saw a young lady gesticulating from the window of her carriage. When he walked up to her, she told him not to be silly: he was too young even to be thinking of slitting his throat.

Apocryphal or not, the story illustrates the predicament in which he found himself at the age of twenty-three. Unwilling to enter the ministry, but penniless and educated far above his station in the Prussia of 1742, he could at best hope for an opening in a *Lateinschule* such as the one he had himself attended in Stendal. In the meantime he was fortunate to find, through the good services of a friend, a job that would tide him over until such a position fell vacant. He became tutor to F. W. Peter Lamprecht, the oldest son of the Dean of the Chapter of Magdeburg Cathedral, who had settled in Hadmersleben near Halberstadt. During this interval of over a year, he became very friendly with the young man, who later followed him to Seehausen, where they shared a room until Lamprecht left in 1746. Winckelmann lent him money which the other does not seem to have repaid, and to judge from his correspondence, passed through an emotional crisis when their friendship broke up.

It is quite possible that this relationship, paralleled by one into which Winckelmann entered at about the same time with F. U. Arwed von Bülow, the son of a former resident Prussian minister in Stockholm, was homosexual. This is suggested by its intimacy no less than by the violence of Winckelmann's reaction when it ended, for reasons which, like those of real lovers' quarrels, remain all but incomprehensible to the outsider. On what other basis, one is tempted to ask, would a man react to a friend's departure in terms like these: "With what endearments [*"Zärtlichkeiten"*] can I reply to your kind lines . . . I renounce all, honor and pleasure, peace and contentment, unless I can see you and enjoy you . . . my eyes cry for you alone . . . I shall love you as long as I live"? Lest the affective density of the German language be blamed for such hyperbole, the picture may be rounded out by an equally fervent letter in Latin addressed "*Ad delicias suas*," or the following effusion in the writer's own, somewhat willful French: "*C'est un coup mortel dont ta lettre me vient de percer. Grand Dieu ne reste-il point de ressource? Ah pût-on me prêter des ailes de l'Aurore, pour voler vers toi! . . . Mille soupirs sont des témoins que je me meurs pour désir de celui que j'aime éperdument . . .*"[4]

But *is* the picture complete? We do not know how Lamprecht felt about it all, or even how he looked at the time— although it may be inferred, from the very detailed notions of male beauty held by his mentor and friend, that he was handsome. We do know, however, that the cult of friendship flourished in that century as it had not done since the days of Periclean Greece. German literature, in particular, preserves numerous professions of undying affection, demands for greater intimacy, and the like, exchanged in some instances by correspondents who had never met in person. Winckelmann himself wrote in this vein to other men, among them Genzmer ("I love only you . . . I say: Love, you are mad" ["*Liebe du bist toll*"]), although the addressee was a man of almost oppressively normal tastes, if other witnesses are to be trusted who describe him as a generous host, fond of good wine and conversation, and married to a pretty young woman. Do these *billets doux* represent no more than excrescences of the epistolary art that was so highly regarded and skillfully practiced in the period of Richardson, Walpole, and Rousseau? In real life, Winckelmann may have been as unlikely to debauch young Adonises as his contemporaries among the German poets were to deflower the Chloës and Amaryllises at whose adorable little feet they, portly, middle-aged *Bürger* for the most part, lay all the ardent if stylized lover's plaints that are now gathering dust in anthologies of rococo verse. It is a sobering thought that while the poetic gaze of Christoph Martin Wieland, the greatest of these writers in the manner of Anacreon, seems to have been forever fixed upon the enchanting bosom of some Arcadian nymph, he unfailingly returned from these reveries to the tired arms of his wife, in which he begot a quite extraordinary number of little Wielands.

There are other reasons as well for believing that at this stage, at least, Winckelmann's aberration, if such it is, was no more than a latent tendency. Any proof to the contrary, at any rate, will not be found in his correspondence. If that contains only one letter addressed to a woman, it is not because the author was a homosexual but because he happened to be a scholar and a man of affairs in an age in which women were rarely educated, let alone trained in the academic as well as practical matters that are discussed in these letters. John Wilkes, Winckelmann's friend in later years and surely the most heterosexual of men, once described his mistress Gertrude Corradini as having "a perfect Grecian figure, cast in the mold of the Florentine Venus, excepting that she was rather taller, and more flat about the breasts . . ." but was ungallant enough to add: "Impartial heaven had not bestowed on her a common share of understanding or wit." This is not the place to discuss woman's role in the eighteenth century, but it is safe to say that for every Mme du Deffand there must have been a hundred Corradinis. For a man like Winckelmann, then, liaisons like those with Lamprecht and Bülow may have represented the only available outlet for the scholar's particular brand of friendship, which Voltaire defined as "*la passion du sage.*" As a man of classical erudition, furthermore, Winckelmann knew from Plato's *Phaedrus* and Xenophon's *Symposium* what heights such relationships, in which a young man acquires virtue and wisdom from an older one who is in turn ennobled and rejuvenated by this contact, had attained precisely in the historical period whose values he had absorbed and was destined to revive. Knowing his Plato, he readily believed that physical beauty should also be the home of spiritual and moral excellence; and he need not have read much Shakespeare (although he is known to have read Pope, Dryden, and Cowper *on* Shakespeare) to have rejoiced as he did in the expectation that his friend would in time become the father of beautiful children who bore his beloved traits. The marked pedagogical trait in these relationships is a reflection both of the didactic temper of the times and of his own inclinations and training, which had convinced him early in life that he had been "born to instruct the young"—"*ad iuventutem erudiendam natus.*"

If this was indeed his vocation, it was to be put to a severe test in the permanent position which he now accepted in the Prussian school system.

IV

When Winckelmann presented himself to the school board of Seehausen in 1743 in order to give his introductory lecture, on the dogma of the Redemption, the scene before his eyes must have reminded him of his childhood. Seehausen, like Stendal, had been founded in the Middle Ages and lived on agriculture, stock farming, and beer brewing. It, too, was a sleepy country town in the Altmark, with a population so indifferent to schooling that advanced work in Latin had had to be discontinued altogether for lack of student interest. His predecessor, Friedrich Eberhard Boysen, had arrived in Seehausen with all the enthusiasm of a recent university graduate, and Winckelmann, acting as *Konrektor* or vice-principal to the *Rektor,* Gottfried Nikolaus Paalzow, also started out with the determination to make a go of things. However, the demands he made on his pupils were too great for these placid farm lads, who had no academic interests of their own and resented being made to study such impractical subjects as Latin and Greek. The new teacher, on his part, was overworked and underpaid, at 120 *Taler* a year (in purchasing power, perhaps equivalent to $600), a niggardly

C*

sum that had to be pieced together from church funds, the proceeds of local collections, and the honorarium for such incidental tasks as preaching at funerals, giving private lessons, and performing marriages. All of this, of course, was in addition to his regular schedule as classroom teacher of Hebrew, geography, logic, history, and classics. If he made ends meet at all it was by living on bread and cold cuts for dinner, and taking his lunch in the house of a local merchant who prided himself on having such a learned guest at his table.

It was not long before the differences between Winckelmann's way of life and that of the town came out into the open. Polite and considerate to everyone, he nevertheless kept to himself and took little part in the affairs of his fellow-citizens. He read voluminously, and in his autodidactic fashion made excerpts not only from the ancients but from the French, English, and Italian authors whom he had meanwhile taught himself to read in the original. In short, he marched to a drum of his own, and the good people of Seehausen would have shaken their heads in disbelief if they had known how he spent his free time. "Since I lived only a mile away at the time," Uden recalled, "I visited my old school chum, who was very glad to see me. His erstwhile pupil Lamprecht had joined him . . . from Hadmersleben, and slept in Winckelmann's room. The latter, however, had not used his cot all winter, but sat in an easy chair in a corner by the table, flanked by bookshelves. He spent the day teaching in school and afterwards instructed Lamprecht, who went to bed at ten while Winckelmann continued to study until midnight. He then put out the lamp and, sitting in his chair, slept until 4 a.m. At that hour he roused himself and studied until 6, when he gave another lesson to Lamprecht until it was time to start the day's work in the classroom. This is how I found him on my visit, and this is how he spent the period in Seehausen."[5] Since that period lasted over five years, from April

1743 until August 1748, Winckelmann must have been un-commonly resilient in body as well as in mind. "He himself re-marked," according to Uden, "that he had so toughened his spare and rather tall frame that he could get along on no more than two or three hours' sleep." In later years, there was to be no love lost between Winckelmann and Frederick the Great. But if he had been aware of his existence at this time, the King of Prussia would have been proud of this subject of his who was, like himself, a living embodiment of the motto of that monstrous if fascinating country: *Toujours en vedette* (Ever On Guard). Yet it is no wonder that Winckelmann's equanimity gave way on occasion, as it must have done in November 1744 when "a quarrel broke out at the end of the exam period between the learned *Konrektor,* who feels himself capable of more demand-ing work, and the students who are deficient in comprehension and devotion to learning."

The innuendo makes one suspect that this report came from the pen of Valentin Schnakenburg, the school superintendent and first preacher at St. Peter's Church in Seehausen, who had be-come disillusioned with his young assistant when he found him unwilling to take a hand in minor parish business like giving instruction in the catechism or holding the occasional sermon. The disappointment turned to hatred when he preached in church one Sunday morning and caught Winckelmann sur-reptitiously reading Homer, from a copy he had hidden in his prayer book. After this, Schnakenburg went about declaring that the *Konrektor* lacked all faith and devotion, in lamentable con-trast to his predecessor, Boysen (who later claimed to have done more for the school in the short time he had spent there as vice-principal than Winckelmann did in the several years of his tenure). The latter took all this in his stride, but became furious when Schnakenburg assigned him to teach the elementary classes, implying that his Latin also left something to be desired.

Winckelmann might have been dismissed then and there if Friedrich Rudolph Nolte, the superintendent of schools for the whole Altmark, had not taken an interest in him. A cultured and influential man, Nolte was the author of the catechism from which Frederick had been instructed as a young prince. More recently, the scholar and school administrator in Nolte had come to be impressed by Winckelmann's self-discipline and by the single-mindedness with which he pursued his studies in the face of almost insurmountable odds. It was Nolte who had suggested him for the *Konrektorat* at Seehausen, and who was to recommend him again when the time came for Winckelmann to turn his back on Prussia once and for all. "It has proved impossible," the superintendent wrote on that occasion, "to offer him in this country the rewards to which his uncommon knowledge entitles him."

Indeed, the thought of leaving Seehausen must have presented itself to Winckelmann almost as soon as he arrived there. The place clearly held no future for a man of his abilities or, for that matter, ambitions, which being strong but unchanneled made him restless without providing him with a specific aim to the realization of which he could devote his energies. The most that he could hope for in the normal run of things was eventual advancement to the dignity of *Rektor,* by stepping into Paalzow's shoes when the latter retired in the fullness of time. With luck, he might even end his days as principal of a *Gymnasium* in one of the larger Prussian towns. It would have been a respectable attainment for a man who had started out in life at the very bottom, but it seemed so depressing a prospect to Winckelmann that he never seriously entertained it even in his darkest hours. Although he had no idea what the future held in store for him and therefore expected nothing specific, an inner voice told him that it would be more than his present existence, more than this "servitude," as he later called it, that

forced him to "teach the ABC's to scabby-faced children."
Yet it was one thing to harbor such faith in oneself, and quite
another to give it concrete expression.

The next few years of his life are thus marked by attempts to
escape, alternating with periods of desperation at seeing himself
rebuffed on all sides. It was in such moods thát he exclaimed:
"I cannot leave my sphere of life. Fate has condemned me to
laborious studies of which I shall not see the results," or, more
bitterly still because he possessed the gift of looking at himself
as dispassionately as if his life represented a case study: "Living
in localities far removed from courts and untouched by the
events of the time, and being limited to contacts with one's own
kind and condemned to unending travail and financial worry,
has the effect of narrowing one's outlook." It is not surprising
under the circumstances that his growing revulsion against
teaching ended by making him dislike his native country, which
he rightly or wrongly considered responsible for his misery. His
republicanism dates from this time, and soon took on an anti-
Prussian tinge which suggests stronger and more personal experiences than his readings in the libertarian writers of antiquity;
it is, in any case, remarkable that his later exposure to other,
non-Prussian forms of absolutism should have elicited from
him no censure of tyranny as such. In these years, however, the
idea of striking his tents (*"decampieren"*) and leaving Prussia
altogether led him to consider moving to England, where he
hoped to find work as a copyreader, or of returning to university
in order to prepare himself for the more mobile calling of a
history professor. He had barely discarded these plans, the very
impracticability of which was a measure of his despair, when
he heard that a teaching position was open in a Pietist institution, the Schule zu Kloster Berge near Magdeburg. When his
application was turned down, Nolte urged him to contact the
school board at Salzwedel, where a *Konrektorat* had become

vacant. Winckelmann rode across from Seehausen on the appointed day, only to find that the job had just been given to a local candidate.

The most stinging of these defeats and rebukes was administered in 1745 by Johann Friedrich Wilhelm Jerusalem, the principal of the newly founded Collegium Carolinum in Brunswick, to whom he had previously presented his respects through Bülow. A combination of *Gymnasium,* polytechnic institute, and university which offered professional training in law, medicine, etc., along with the standard liberal arts curriculum, this school had just been established by the Duke Charles of Brunswick-Wolfenbüttel and entrusted to his court preacher, a widely traveled pedagogue of great social and administrative talents who also acted as tutor to the hereditary prince (who, in turn, after a great many years became the hapless commander of the allied army that invaded Revolutionary France in 1792). Had he been given the position he now applied for, Winckelmann would have become a colleague of Zachariae and joined the faculty of one of the country's most progressive schools. As it was, Jerusalem refused to receive him. Winckelmann never forgot the insult, if such it was, although the other is not likely to have been half as wretched a man as the frustrated job seeker made him out to be; in fact, he was generous enough eventually to praise Winckelmann's contribution to German letters. Goethe, who was not overly fond of clergymen, nonetheless called Jerusalem a "liberal and sensitive divine," and Boswell found him to be "a learned, agreeable man with a pleasing simplicity of manner."[8] Winckelmann, in any event, henceforth affected to have forgotten his very name. When he wrote a friend in 1758 that Benedict XIV lay dying in Rome, he could not forbear asking: "And how is the Pope of Brunswick? What did he call himself? Bethlehem, wasn't it?" Stout hater that he was, even he might have relented had he lived long enough to witness the fortitude with which Jerusalem bore the suicide of his only son—a calamity that suggested to Goethe, who had known the young man, the idea of letting his Werther die in the same manner. Bruised and battered, Winckelmann resembled a man caught in quicksand, who flings himself about only to find that he sinks deeper with every frantic movement. When his deliverance did come, it arrived suddenly and from an unexpected quarter.

At a chance meeting in the school superintendent's office, an acquainance told him that he had just declined an invitation to go to Nöthnitz near Dresden, as librarian and secretary to a former Saxon diplomat, Count Heinrich von Bünau. Winckelmann applied for the job and got it. He resigned from the *Konrektorat* at Seehausen, sold all his belongings except his books, paid a hurried last visit to Stendal, and left Prussia for Saxony in the summer of 1748, after proudly giving Uden the address to which he wanted his mail forwarded: c/o *Son Excellence Monseigneur le comte de Bünau, Ministre d'État de Sa Majesté Impériale.*

V

After delving into the minutiae of Winckelmann's life as a student and rural schoolteacher, we must come up for air and briefly orient ourselves in the world outside Halle, Jena, and Seehausen. From the seminal events of the decade 1738–48, which encompasses his university years and those of his "servitude," we might note the following: in England, philosophy had reached a peak with Hume's *Treatise of Human Nature*, lyric poetry with Young's *Night Thoughts*, and the sentimental novel with Richardson's *Pamela* and *Clarissa;* although Rousseau and Diderot had only just begun to write, the Enlightenment was already in full swing in France, where Voltaire had established himself as a social critic with *Zadig* and as a dramatist with *Mahomet* and *Mérope,* while Montesquieu was getting ready to publish *L'esprit des lois;* except for Klopstock's *Messias* at the very end, it was a barren decade in German literature, but an important one for architecture, with Sanssouci being built in Potsdam and the Frauenkirche in Dresden. Bach was still active, Handel composed the *Messiah* and *Judas Maccabaeus,* and the opera had lately found a home in Naples as well as in Venice;

the Industrial Revolution was getting under way with the perfection of crucible steel, the blast furnace, and the spinning jenny; while the Pope combatted freemasonry from Rome and the Stuarts lost their last bid for power in Scotland, the center of the political stage was occupied by three formidable ladies who were coming into their own—Madame de Pompadour had been declared *maîtresse en titre,* Maria Theresa was valiantly if unsuccessfully defending her patrimony against Frederick the Great, and Catherine had just been betrothed to the man by whose murder she was to ascend the throne of Russia. A minor but highly symbolic event was the publication of *Rule Britannia:* England was girding herself for the final test of strength with France, in India and North America as well as on the Seven Seas.

While these and other developments took place in the world at large, Winckelmann, as we saw, taught and read. His intellectual life at this time may be dissected like a sphere, by proceeding from the periphery toward its core and center of gravity. First, we find a surface layer of frenzied and all-ingesting reading done in the polyhistoric fashion of the eighteenth century, which treasured the ideal of man as a "walking encyclopedia" as much as the twentieth extols the contrasting figure of the expert. Characteristic of this layer are the extracts he made from the *Acta Eruditorum* of Leipzig, a learned publication issued in imitation of the Paris *Journal des Savants.* It contained nuggets of solid scholarship (such as Leibnitz's first presentation to the public of samples of his differential calculus) interspersed with the loose gravel of reviews, digests, progress reports, and other items of merely topical interest. From his notes, it is clear that Winckelmann had to rely on this secondary source for his knowledge of many basic works of classical philology, of which he had evidently not been able to secure a copy. While reading in this journal about the latest develop-

ments in literature and science, he did not pay any especial attention to reports on the discovery of antique monuments or works
of art. If any concentration on a particular topic is discernible
in the excerpts, it is on the title, format, and type of the most
recent books: in a word, he seems to have read on this level not
like an antiquary or classicist, but like the librarian he had been
in Ludewig's house and was to become again in that of Bünau.
Equally eclectic in nature but more formal in arrangement, as
befits their source, are the many notes he made in Osterburg
and Seehausen from Bayle's *Dictionnaire.* The four huge volumes must have appealed to him not only as an ideal reference
work for purposes of self-instruction, but because their author's
way of looking at things resembled his own. No doubt the
Frenchman's religious tolerance and attitude of *nil admirari,* his
weakness for the anecdote and critical but amused acceptance
of every human folly, and above all his gift for presenting a
learned argument lucidly and wittily, complemented similar
traits and talents that lay dormant in his reader. Since the
Dictionnaire is no longer used, its impact on Winckelmann can
best be assessed by substituting in one's mind for the *Encyclo-
paedia Britannica*—with its many contributors, each of whom is
an expert in his own field—a work compiled by a single universal scholar who offers all this heterogeneous information
from A to Z in the shape in which it appears refracted in the
prism of his own personality.

A deeper and more concentric layer is represented by
Winckelmann's historical studies, in which one detects several
substrata: readings in the history of the Holy Roman Empire as
seen from the constitutional viewpoint, such as it was taught at
Halle; readings in more original accounts like De Thou's *History
of my own Times* and Grotius's *Annals of the Low Countries,*
i.e., in reports by men who had themselves taken part in the

events described; and readings in the works of De Rapin-Thoyras and of Louis XIV's court historiographer Gabriel Daniel. Such studies in what was then modern if not contemporary history were doubly useful because Winckelmann had not only to instruct himself, but to prepare some of his charges for the eventuality that they might become diplomats—young men like Grolman and Bülow who qualified for that calling by birth if not talent. A still more immediate concern of his, for idiosyncratic as well as professional reasons, was the study of the ancients and especially of Greek literature, a discipline which was then in danger of dying out altogether. The decline, during the Thirty Years' War and later, of the schools which Melanchthon had brought to such efficiency in the early sixteenth century, coupled with the ruling French taste and the supremacy which Latin enjoyed as the language of diplomacy, scholarship, law, and the Church, had so reduced the standing of Greek that many German classicists had left home and preceded Ruhnken to Holland. The resultant vacuum led to a scarcity of the raw material of scholarship, the texts themselves. Try as he might, Winckelmann could not find in 1747 an edition of Sophocles comparable to that which Thomas Johnson had published in England. The last German edition of Plato dated from 1602; between 1606 and 1759, Homer was published but once. Given this lack of texts, let alone commentaries, Winckelmann saw himself obliged once again to make up an anthology of his own, by copying from borrowed books the passages that appealed to him. The surprising feature of this activity is not the lack of any overriding considerations of a philological or historical nature in his excerpts, but the fact that he did not attempt to help fill the vacuum by editing a text or two himself. In view of the depth and extent of his reading, the textual emendations we have from his hand are few in number and indifferent in quality. The reason is not hard to find: although he knew languages well, he possessed little philological technique and training. Languages and literary texts interested him less as subjects in themselves than as bridges to the understanding of ancient civilization, and eventually as corroboration of the visual evidence of ancient art. The most concentric layer consists, therefore, of his studies in Greek literature, in which his favorites, next to Homer, were Sophocles, the historians Herodotus and Xenophon, whom he admired for their plasticity and stance of "This is what I saw," and Aristophanes, to whom he may have felt attracted through the same feeling of kinship that drew him to Bayle: that penchant for "types" which forms such a puzzling contrast to his preferences in art, where he abhorred everything that smacked of the bizarre, the caricaturing, even the individualistic.

At the very core of his thought during this decade stood Homer. Much had happened, in Homer studies as in all classical scholarship, since Erasmus had declared that everything worth writing had been written long ago in Greek and Latin, and that ancient Greece was the fountainhead of all human wisdom and science. Geographical discoveries had enlarged man's knowledge of the earth far beyond the confines of the ancient world; scientific advances had similarly revolutionized his concept of the universe; and the rise of national literatures in the various countries of Europe had further detracted from the veneration in which the ancients had once been held. The writers of France, in particular, were not only highly respected in themselves and because they represented that nation; they had also gone further than other modern authors in viewing life through the eyes of contemporary society, and in turn drawing their subject matter from the preoccupations and predilections of that society. To the French public of the seventeenth and eighteenth centuries,

Homer seemed embarrassingly crude, bloody, primitive: altogether too stark for the stage and the salon. This diminution
of his stature had begun with Scaliger and been continued by
the brothers Perrault and others, who faulted the poet because
his characters failed so signally to live up to the ideal of the
honnête homme and *gentilhomme*. Even Voltaire considered the
even-numbered books of the *Aeneid* superior to anything
the Greeks had written, and Tasso the equal of Homer. Superim-
posed upon these aesthetic valuations was the general tendency
to scorn the ancients by indirection, in looking at them from
the present rather than within the context of their own civilization, about which little enough was known at this time when
Herculaneum had barely been discovered and Troy, Cnossos,
and other buried cities still slumbered undisturbed. The prevailing attitude of the period may be summarized in the form of a
rhetorical question: If man was perfectible and progress inevitable, did it not stand to reason that literature, too, must
have made great strides since Homer?

It was said of one of the Perraults that, although he condemned much of Greek literature, he did not have a single
Greek book in his library. By way of contrast, Winckelmann's
achievement in extricating Homer from the accumulation of
scholastic dust and rococo powder under which he had all but
disappeared from view was based first of all on a very thorough
knowledge of the Greek text itself, which he read three times
in the winter of 1743–4 alone, "with all the application that such
a divine work commands, and with quite a new insight." While
this insight did not come to fruition until later, one aspect of it
can be traced in the excerpts he made from Homer at this time.
They are so eclectic in nature that one cannot escape the conclusion that he turned to the poet as a Christian turns to the
Bible: for solace and guidance. One can, if so inclined, conjure

up the shades of Schnakenburg and other tormentors, and of Seehausen itself, in quotations like these:

Ah me, what are the people whose land
I have come to this time . . . ?

and

Yet here is a man who wishes to be above all others,
who wishes to hold power over all, and to be lord of
all, and give them their orders . . . ;

or even find therapeutic values in statements like:

He should not sleep night long who is a man
burdened with counsels.[7]

It is unwise to make too much of such instances of self-identification, on the part of a reader suffering in solitude, with an author who has given exemplary expression to these sufferings. Yet the frequency of quotations of this kind suggests the existence of a very personal tie, akin to that which later bound Beethoven to Homer. More important in the long run is the fact that by reading the poet without the variously tinted glasses through which the Greeks, the Romans, the Italians of the Renaissance, and the French and Dutch scholars of his own period had viewed him, Winckelmann learned to penetrate not only literary, but all works of art to their very essence: to the point where aesthetic impression and spiritual reality merge until there is only "experience" left, instead of "feeling" or form on the one side and "thinking" or content on the other.

Throughout these years, one of his biographers says on taking leave of him in Seehausen, Winckelmann had, "like a slave, only half belonged to himself in the day. His real life began at night, when he invited the ancients to be his guests. There he sat, the pale and lean man, in his narrow, bare, ice-cold monk's cell behind the cemetery, with his . . . dark, sparkling eyes over the aquiline nose peering out from the depths of his cloak into a parchment copy of Plutarch or Sophocles, dreaming, in the midst of impenetrable, snow-covered fields, of the Mediterranean and its people, while the northeast made the small, round panes rattle in their rotting frames and the moon set in the west, behind the massive and gloomy steeples of St. Peter and Paul."[8]

SAXONY

I

Winckelmann's new home was so close to Dresden that he lost no time in familiarizing himself with the social and moral topography of the Saxon Court. "Corrupt as they are," he informed Uden in February 1750,

they are nevertheless always looking for honest men. One of the most distinguished court physicians in Dresden . . . furnishes a striking example of this. He lives very simply, always dressed in the same shabby clothes, and arrives on foot wherever he is called. He had been introduced at court by Count Sulkowski, who fell from power some time ago; and even though a Lutheran, he acted as personal physician to the King and Queen, which enabled him to set aside some 20,000 *Taler*. But he had never enjoyed court life, and thus went one day to his benefactor, the Count, thanking him and asking to be relieved of his duties. Given permission to do so, he henceforth avoided both the Court and Sulkowski . . . The latter, however, had no sooner been forced to resign and retire to Poland than he fell dangerously ill and called our physician. Although he was old by then, the man jumped into the saddle and rode all the way to Warsaw. On being ushered into his patient's room, he declared that he

would not have come at all if he had still been a court physician;
in that capacity, he added, he had looked after Sulkowski not as
a doctor but as a courtier. He charges nothing for his services
now, which he can afford to do because he is rich and has no
family.

Winckelmann is not likely to have related this parable merely
in order to cheer Uden on his daily rounds among the sick people
of Stendal. The context and matter-of-fact tone suggest, rather,
that he had his own patron and benefactor in mind. For Heinrich von Bünau had also achieved some prominence at court,
and would have risen far above the rank of Gentleman of the
Bedchamber and Overseer of the University of Leipzig if he had
not been unable or unwilling to cope with the machinations of
Augustus III's favorite, Count Brühl, who appointed him governor of the county of Mansfeld and thereby practically sent
him into the wilderness. Too honest a man to intrigue his way
back into the royal presence and yet bored with the provincial
setting of Eisenach, Bünau withdrew from affairs altogether
and lived on his estates at Nöthnitz, busying himself with the
historical work for which he had engaged Winckelmann as a
research assistant. Although he later became a minister under
the enlightened Duke Constantine of Sachsen-Weimar—the
father of Goethe's Charles Augustus—Bünau's upright character and sense of *noblesse oblige* had in effect blunted the
career that should have been his, both by virtue of his administrative gifts and as the scion of a family that is documented in
the history of Thuringia as far back as 1166.

The headlong pursuit of power undertaken by Bünau's rival,
Heinrich von Brühl, was not impeded by any such considerations of fitness or propriety. The son of a minor court official, he
had advanced rapidly under Augustus II, and when that monarch died in Warsaw (Saxony and Poland being then joined in
personal union) in 1733, ingratiated himself with his successor

by gathering up the crown jewels of Poland and hurrying to lay them at the feet of his new master in Dresden. Augustus III, or Frederick Augustus II in his capacity as Elector of Saxony, rewarded Brühl by allowing him to climb the ladder of court and civil service appointments so quickly that he became Prime Minister in 1746, after having disposed, by fair means and foul, of Sulkowski and several other potential rivals. One would in fact have had to travel all the way to Saint Petersburg to find, in the person of Grigori Grigorievich Orlov, another court favorite who had risen so fast. But, whereas Orlov made history by going to bed with the Empress of Russia, Brühl did so by taking the Elector of Saxony and King of Poland to the art gallery in order to admire the latest acquisition of a Correggio, Titian, or Raphael. *"Cela amuse le maître,"* he used to say with a knowing wink whenever more responsible ministers reproached him for such extravagances.

Uneducated though he was, Brühl got together a library of 70,000 volumes merely in order to outshine Bünau with his collection of 42,000, just as he had himself appointed a general although he had not served a day in his life. Indeed, his vanity was such that he united in his person the following titles and perquisites, whose recitation would fill a whole aria in the musical comedy that alone could do justice to rococo Dresden: at one and the same time, Brühl acted as *Premier-, Kabinetts- und Konferenzminister, Wirklicher Geheimer Rat, Oberkämmerer, Kammerpräsident, Obersteuer-, Generalakzis-, Oberrechnungsdeputations-, Berg-, auch Stift Merseburger und Naumburger Kammerdirektor, Oberinspektor der Porzellanmanufaktur, Chef der kurfürstlichen Parforcejagd, Kapitular des Stifts Meissen, Propst zu Budissin.* With a monthly income of 65,000 *Taler,* he loved to act the part of the humble and pious Christian— Protestant in Saxony, Catholic in Poland—and arranged the schedules of visiting dignitaries in such a fashion that they would "surprise" him at his devotions. He was, in short, a consummate scoundrel, who held on to power by artfully indulging every whim of Augustus III, a weak and diffident man who took so little interest in affairs of state that he once asked whether his troops had given a good account of themselves in an engagement (the Battle of Chotusitz in 1742) in which they had not taken part at all.

The sovereign and his servant died within a few months of each other in 1763, at the end of the Seven Years' War, which had begun with the calamitous defeat of Saxony, itself a direct result of their anti-Prussian policies. Their deaths marked the dissolution of the union of Saxony and Poland, the Electorate being passed on to Augustus III's son Frederick Christian while the Kingdom of Poland, soon to undergo its first partition, was given to Stanislaus Poniatowski. A commission of inquiry appointed after his death found Brühl guilty of having embezzled the staggering sum of five million *Taler,* or close to $25,000,000, some of which had gone into his collection of several hundred rings, snuffboxes, and wigs—the last-named item prompting Frederick the Great to remark that the collecting of wigs was an odd hobby for a man who had no head worth covering.

One can readily sympathize with Bünau's decision to retire to Nöthnitz rather than rub shoulders with a man like Brühl. The sympathy, however, tends to evaporate as one examines the result of his enforced leisure, the *Teutsche Kayser- und Reichshistorie,* which remains the main achievement of his life. It had been his intention to write a history of Germany from its beginnings to his own time, for a public not limited to fellow-scholars. It was therefore written in German, and designed to cover more than the murky details of constitutional law that had until then been the historians' main bill of fare. If this *History of the German Empire and its Emperors* was, nonetheless, a still-born work, the fault lay not so much with the author's pedantic if honorable personality as with the lack of any viable historiographic tradition in eighteenth-century Germany—or for that matter, the lack of any viable history. For unlike that of France, Spain, and England, the history of Germany represented not the growth of a homogeneous people that was forged into a nation and eventually spread its customs, laws, and language over much of the globe, but the slow disintegration of an artificial structure that had already ceased to function in the Middle Ages. If such poets as Lessing and Goethe could distill from it no more than the setting of plays like *Minna von Barnhelm* and *Götz von Berlichingen,* then the dullish Bünau must be excused for failing to make these centuries of internecine strife come to life. It was inevitable that his opus should have made tedious reading and remained a largely unpublished fragment. He could not possibly have found, in the Empire's crumbling masonry, a great figure that could be used as a peg on which to hang the tapestry of an entire age, in the manner in which Voltaire displayed that of the *Siècle de Louis XIV* as a dimension of the Sun King himself.

Bünau needed assistants because it was his habit to dictate the descriptive passages with an approximate version of quotations, spellings, and dates. These were then checked by the secretaries: Johann Michael Francke, who had been in his service since 1740, and now Winckelmann, who was first put to work documenting his employer's account of the reign of the Frankish king Clovis. Totally inexperienced in methodical research, Winckelmann found himself hard put at first to do what was demanded of him. He discovered to his dismay that he had to delve into dusty tomes dealing with church history, military tactics, and other fields of which he knew nothing, including constitutional law, which he studied from a four-volume encyclopedia—*"monstrum horrendum"* he calls it in a letter—written by a professor at Leiden. It was deadly dull work, the kind of chore that even graduate students can tolerate only in the knowledge that they will be released from it on acquiring their doctorates. For Winckelmann, it was a daily task much as teaching the ABC's had been, and one that for all he knew would continue to the end of his days. He had originally been hired for one year, but the Count thought so highly of him that the job was for all practical purposes a permanent one. Once he had found his bearings, he was sent on still more recondite errands. When Bünau, for example, remembered having read somewhere that Sidonius Apollinaris had spoken of Toulouse as the "Gothic Rome," it fell to Winckelmann to track down the reference. It was not to be found in that author or in several other early historians of France; after leafing through thousands of yellowed pages, he eventually came across a mention of Toulouse as the "Rome of the Goths" in some long-forgotten *Histoire générale de Languedoc*. He took the volume to Bünau, and yet another footnote was added to the *Reichshistorie*. Later on, when the reigns of the Emperors Otto I and II came up for consideration, his share of the work transcended the mere checking of trivia. It became a joint enterprise, Winckelmann being allowed to prepare the actual text while Bünau reserved for himself the right to edit the final version.

The sensation of "languishing in durance vile" that had gripped Winckelmann in the Prussian civil service was so strong that his relief at having escaped lasted throughout the first year in Nöthnitz. "This is the calmest period of my life," he confided to Uden in 1749, and in December that year he still felt like "thanking the kindly fate that has transported me here from the slavery of the classroom." What made his new job bearable, despite its essential sterility, was first of all the environment in which it was done: one of the best private libraries in all Europe, with every volume handsomely bound in English leather and Bünau's coat of arms with the legend *Ex bibliotheca*

Bunaviana imprinted in gold on the back, the whole tastefully arranged in a spacious, high-ceilinged salon that had a staircase leading up to the gallery—which in turn could be closed off by means of a door decorated, in the *trompe l'oeil* fashion of the time, to look like yet more bookshelves. The new secretary had been given a room of his own in the same building, a manor house that looked out on the vineyards along the banks of the Elbe, just beyond sight of the steeples of Dresden.

The social milieu was equally agreeable, in comparison at least with that of Seehausen. Although differences of age, rank, and condition precluded any familiarity between them even if they worked side by side, Bünau and Winckelmann got on well enough to take the harsh edge off the fact that in the *ancien régime* setting of Nöthnitz, one was in fact the master and the other the servant. "The manner in which I deal with my boss [*"mit meinem Herrn"*] is without pretense or affectation, as free and straightforward as if I had to do with a friend, although I behave in this manner only when I am alone with him. This makes my colleagues and the others a little jealous; since I do not ease up in my work, however, and even insist that I have no wish to make my fortune through the Count and would not care if he chose to dispense with my services altogether, I give them no real cause for envy. I am satisfied. At least I am glad to be in a place where I can think and speak freely, and would actually be blamed less than others if I uttered a harsh word, for example at the dinner table. It is left up to me when I work, and how."[1] It is unlikely that Winckelmann really deluded himself into believing that he was a sort of permanent house guest who now and then feels an urge to make himself useful. The freedom to say unpleasant things at dinner may well have been mere indulgence on Bünau's part, shown to a man who was in reality a newcomer to polite society. (Once he had moved to Dresden, Winckelmann was to find, as Doctor Johnson did

D

in London, that "a man who has not been in Italy is always conscious of an inferiority." Winckelmann overcame these feelings even before he went to Rome. He knew that he had a propensity for committing faux pas, a shortcoming which he corrected so successfully that he was soon able to hold his own in any company.) Much of the above may therefore be discounted as bragging, since it is addressed to a friend on whom he wanted to impress his good fortune. At the same time, he must have had a measure of influence in the household because it was on his recommendation that Bünau now hired Berendis as tutor for his youngest son. Although their relationship was destined to undergo severe strains, the tensions that arose between them were muted by the old gentleman's fondness for Winckelmann and by the respect in which the latter continued to hold Bünau even after he had left his service. In the end, it was Winckelmann himself who caused a break, by an action that the other man could not accept; even then, Bünau dropped but did not openly censure him. It remained for Herder to ask, long after the principals had died: "What would Winckelmann have become if he could have followed from the beginning the call of the Muses, rather than that of the magistrate of Seehausen or of Count Bünau?"[2] and for Goethe to add that if Bünau had only purchased one expensive volume less for his library, he would have had the money to send his secretary to Italy and launch him that much earlier on his life's work. But Winckelmann himself, although no stranger to self-pity, does not seem to have seen it in this light.

He had, in fact, little cause for complaint when he compared his lot with that of two other secretaries and librarians whose acquaintance he made in this period: his colleague Francke, with whom he corresponded to the end of his life, and Christian Gottlieb Heyne, who was on the point of starving to death when Winckelmann first met him in 1753. His contacts with Heyne were conditioned by the circumstances of the time, which dictated that the few men who rose above their station should regard one another diffidently as potential competitors: after all, the other fellow was equally unlikely to be held back by the niceties and hesitancies observed by those who had grown up secure of their place in society. Until they had both made their way to the top of their profession, Winckelmann and Heyne accordingly treated each other with a gingerly reserve, which, one suspects, stemmed from the shared realization that they simply could not afford to be either friends or enemies. For Heyne, too, had been raised in extreme poverty, as a linen weaver's son in Saxony; he too had studied theology because it was the only thing he could afford to study, and had become a private tutor. By chance, an elegy which he had written on the death of a friend was brought to the attention of the all-powerful Brühl, who among his many other roles liked to play that of patron of the arts. He summoned the budding poet to Dresden, but as was his wont had forgotten all about him by the time young Heyne presented himself among the sycophants who were awaiting their turn in the antechamber. Left to cool his heels for a whole year while he struggled to support himself as a substitute teacher, Heyne eventually got himself appointed a cataloguer in Brühl's library, at a yearly salary of 100 *Taler,* the sort of sum that the minister normally spent on a snuffbox. It was at this time, in the winter of 1753–4, that he and Winckelmann occasionally met on the latter's visits to Dresden; but like their masters, the rival collectors Brühl and Bünau, the two librarians do not seem to have had a great deal to say to each other.

Heyne later became a professor at Göttingen, where he reigned, as an iron-fisted academic tyrant, until his death in 1812. Much of his influence derived from his tenure as secretary of one of the most prestigious learned societies in Europe, the

Königliche Gesellschaft der Wissenschaften. Although his scholarly work has been forgotten long ago, he was a power to be
reckoned with in his own time, when a professorship was the
highest distinction that a man of *bürgerlich* or non-aristocratic
origin could attain, when the *Rektor Magnificus,* or president
of a university, took precedence at court over a baron, and when
even young Goethe—who was to say so many nasty things about
professors—confessed to his sister that the glamor of a university teacher had so blinded him that he yearned for no honors
other than those of an academic chair. It was only after they had
become established, the one in Göttingen and the other in Rome,
that Heyne and Winckelmann dropped their guard and felt free
to do what a less rigidly structured society would have permitted, if not encouraged, them to do in the first place: to help
each other. Winckelmann recommended Heyne to various academies in Italy, and Heyne in turn saw to it that Winckelmann was
made a member of the Königliche Gesellschaft. Much later again,
in 1779, when another learned society issued a call for essays
to commemorate the tenth anniversary of Winckelmann's death,
Heyne submitted the prize-winning entry while Herder went
away empty-handed.

Winckelmann had two distinct responsibilities in Nöthnitz: providing the documentary scaffolding for the *Reichshistorie,* and
cataloguing Bünau's library under such general headings as fine
arts, history, etc. He therefore read extensively as well as in
depth, and came in contact for the first time with the great historians of his own age, men who differed favorably from the
parochial chroniclers whose works he had to consult in his
capacity as a research assistant. A whole new world now opened
out to him. He read Bolingbroke, who showed that historical
studies have a moral dimension in that they make the reader a

better citizen by freeing him from religious and national prejudices. From Voltaire, he learned that the history of a given
period is not limited to battles and dynastic alliances, but encompasses the interplay of economic and cultural with political
and military developments. Montesquieu taught him that the
rise and fall of nations is the result of changes that take place
within the set of more or less constant factors—from the degree
of political freedom to the relative severity of the climate—
which govern a nation's life. Having made these convictions his
own, Winckelmann was to draw on them in later years when
working on the *History of Ancient Art*. His early readers were
struck by the close causative connection that he postulated between political liberty and the flourishing of the arts in Greece.
They would have been less surprised if they had known that
he had not only studied these historians and such independent
political theorists as Grotius, Bishop Burnet, and Clarendon,
but expressed all along in his correspondence (which of course
was not available to them) strongly held political views of his
own. While never systematized as an organic body of thought,
these were of a libertarian if not democratic nature.

It was in Nöthnitz that he discovered not only the historians,
but the writers of his time. Having taught himself enough English to help in the preparation of the catalogue of Bünau's holdings in that literature, he made excerpts for his own use from
Milton, Dryden, Congreve, Otway, Thomson, and others. He
knew by heart entire passages from Pope's *Essay on Man*.
Giving in to his penchant for satire, he studied, and extravagantly
admired, Butler's *Hudibras*. When he came across it ten years
later in Florence, he also treasured Cleland's *Memoirs of a
Woman of Pleasure,* better known as *Fanny Hill*. A very mixed
bag, compared to his orthodox familiarity with the newer Italians and his clear-cut preference, in French literature, for such
aphoristic distillations of worldly wisdom as the maxims and

reflections of Queen Christina of Sweden, Pitanal, La Roche-foucauld, and La Bruyère. As might be expected in view of the low regard in which German writers were then held, he read them last of all. When a friend recited passages from Gessner's *Idylls* to him in Italy, he claimed to be astounded to find that these poems were enjoyable, and explained that his early con-centration on philological and historical studies, and his subse-quent residence abroad, had kept him from reading as much German literature as he would have wished. It was a lame ex-cuse, not improved by being reiterated when he sought to reason away, after reading *Laokoon,* his near-ignorance of Lessing's other works. The truth of the matter is that Winckelmann had grown up at a time when there *was* little in German that was worth reading, and that while remaining attached and in fact indebted for some of his own imagery to the only German poetry he knew well—the Protestant hymns of his youth—he suffered from the same hardening of the literary arteries that afflicted Frederick the Great. The one removed himself in spirit to ancient Greece, the other to Paris; both henceforth remained deaf and blind to the writers of Germany. Thus there is no evidence that Winckelmann knew any of Bodmer's work or even Klopstock's, although he had read *Paradise Lost,* which had been translated by the former and served as a model for the latter's *Messias.* The first two cantos of that epic had been greeted with such enthusiasm, in 1748, that it must have taken as much effort to avoid reading them then as it costs to read them now.

II

The outwardly placid pattern of Winckelmann's life in Nöthnitz, with its routine of cataloguing Bünau's library, looking up
material for the *Reichshistorie,* making occasional visits to
Dresden, and pursuing his own studies, masked a crisis which
culminated in his conversion to the Roman Church. No other
action of his cost him so much soul-searching, and none was
more commented upon and yet misunderstood by his contemporaries. Some professed to see in it the slaughter of an unwary
Protestant lamb by the wicked wolf of Papacy, others took it
as an instance of a turncoat's unprincipled ambition. The truth
was rather more complex.

Winckelmann had been raised in the Lutheran Church, but
was not really a believer, even in his youth. Such religious impulses as he occasionally felt seem to have led him in the direction of Pietism, which appealed to him on account of the privacy
of its communion with God and because its practices offered an
alternative, within Protestantism, to the stark doctrinairism that
had overtaken much of the Lutheran Church. Yet there was little
common ground between the Pietists, devout and contrite souls,

and Winckelmann, on whom fate, having withheld so much else, had bestowed a generous measure of self-reliance. One cannot quite imagine him beating his breast in the fashion epitomized by a much-sung hymn of the period:

> *Just as a fiend of Hell doth moan,*
> *Do I lie here in sinful mire,*
> *And smitten with myself do groan*
> *Much as I would for sweets expire;*
> *Just like a raging cur gone mad,*
> *Body and soul turn'd rank and bad,*
> *Thus lie I here and cry and cry.*[3]

As it was, he had gone along with such standard acknowledgments of faith as church attendance and choir singing. But he had denied the immortality of the soul even as a student, and remained a freethinker all his life. "True religion," he wrote in 1754, "is to be found only in a select few among any group of believers. No man can be bound by obligations that transcend all reason." His essential indifference to such matters had become more marked since his arrival in Saxony, where he found himself for the first time beyond control of the Lutheran hierarchy under whose auspices he had been educated and by whose temporal arm, the Prussian school administration, he had lately been employed. Although eminently an inner-directed person, Winckelmann was by no means impervious to his surroundings. The influence of the men who set the moral and religious tone of these surroundings, and the influence of the sovereigns under whom he lived, may be likened to that of the stars. It was no less powerful for being symbolical rather than tangible, and if Winckelmann had acquired his self-control and unpretentiousness under the "sign" of Frederick William I and Frederick the Great, he now changed religion under that of Augustus the Strong. It is a constellation that deserves a closer look.

After John Sobieski's death in 1694, the Polish nobility, unable to agree on the succession of a ruler chosen from among
their own ranks, considered the candidature of several foreign
princes who were known to covet the crown of this kingdom,
which persisted in calling itself a republic because it was in
effect ruled by an assembly of nobles. Given the country's unsettled condition, the proverbial fractiousness of its ruling class,
and the fact that the kingship was elective, the prestige of that
crown outweighed the largely ceremonial power that devolved
upon its wearer. Years before, when Sigismund III had so far
forgotten himself as to threaten force during an assembly of the
Diet, an aged senator had warned him: "Do not draw the sword,
so that later generations may not give you the name of Caesar,
and us that of Brutus. For we elect our kings, and annihilate
those who would become tyrants. Govern, Sire, but do not
command!" Even though it thus symbolized the titular rather
than factual dominion over the vast lands from the Oder to the
Dnieper and from the Baltic to the Black Sea, the crown of
Poland was still a glittering prize pursued by a galaxy of pre-
tenders. These included the Prince Louis François Conti, a
nephew of the great Condé and the candidate favored by Louis
XIV; the Elector Max Emmanuel of Bavaria; the last king's
son, Jacob Sobieski, who also happened to be related by marriage to the Emperor Joseph I; and the Margrave of Baden,
Ludwig Wilhelm, whose reputation as a general who had been
victorious against the Turks particularly commended him to the
ever-embattled Poles. Partly because the great powers were dead-
locked and partly because he was willing to pay an exceptionally
high price, the man who won out in the end was one whose
candidacy had not been taken very seriously when the bidding
began: the Elector of Saxony, Frederick Augustus I. He turned
Roman Catholic in order to fulfill the most stringent of the
conditions that went with the kingship. By selling to Branden-

D*

burg and Hanover his claims to certain disputed territories within the Empire, he was also able to raise the huge sums required to assure himself of the necessary votes.

By personality if not political influence, Frederick Augustus was the only sovereign of the age who could hold a candle to Louis XIV and Peter the Great. Popular with his Saxons on account of his joviality and accessibility, he was a man's man who seems to have actually performed many of the feats of strength and daring that gained him the epithet of "Augustus the Strong." He was also such a ladies' man that he broke innumerable hearts and sired innumerable bastards. According to the malicious Margravine of Bayreuth, there were 365 in all, or one for every night of the year—which is perhaps not as preposterous as it sounds because the birth of the Crown Prince in 1695 was followed, a few days later, by that of a boy (the future Maréchal de Saxe) born to Aurora von Königsmarck, the first of his official mistresses. Augustus was diplomatic enough to staff his seraglio with Polish as well as Saxon beauties, and a statesman of sufficient skill to preserve for Saxony the right to furnish the doyen of the *corpus evangelicorum,* i.e., the senior among the Protestant electoral princes within the "Holy Roman" Empire (by the device, simple in concept but difficult of execution, of declaring that his conversion was a personal matter which had no bearing on his hereditary privileges as Elector of Saxony).

Augustus's change of religion was an extraordinary event at a time when the principle of *cujus regio, ejus religio,* according to which the subjects took their religion from the ruler, was only beginning to be discarded and the tolerance of the Enlightenment had yet to take firm root. It was nonetheless received without much protest by the Saxons, even if these remained overwhelmingly Lutheran. Augustus assuaged their concern by solemnly confirming the Protestant clergy in its prerogatives, by a covenant that he honored throughout the remainder of his reign. As for the rest, he trusted that their habitual levelheadedness would make them appreciate the advantages that accrued to the relatively small Electorate of Saxony from being made the tail that wagged the huge Kingdom of Poland: not only a gain in prestige and influence for the court of Dresden, but the opening up of a large market for the manufactures of Saxony, into which, in turn, the agricultural surplus of Poland could henceforth be imported duty-free. Besides, had a famous French monarch not proven, in times gone by, that such a step could actually redound to the nation's as well as the ruler's benefit? And had the manner of his own change of faith, so clearly unburdened by the weight of conviction, not lent to the whole embarrassing procedure a touch of mundane if not spiritual grace? If the French had not only tolerated but in the end applauded a king who cynically observed that Paris was well worth a Mass, could the Saxons really censure their elector who had called out in Cracow, when he was made to kiss the paten holding the bread in the Eucharist during his coronation as King of Poland: "First they make you eat and drink, and then they make you lick the plate"? Augustus, strongman and charmer, was just the man to carry it off. This he did so well that the personal union outlasted his own reign and continued through that of his son, Augustus III, who had quietly been converted, in far-off Bologna and without informing his piously Protestant mother, while still a young prince. (Sobieski, it will be remembered, had not been able to secure the succession of his own son, a Roman Catholic Pole.) Out of deference to this greatest of its rulers, the House of Wettin remained Catholic even after the union with Poland had been dissolved. From 1763 to the last king's abdication in 1918, Augustus the Strong's Catholic descendants peacefully ruled over Saxony, the cradle of the Reformation.

Although the Saxons had declined to follow Augustus into

the arms of Rome, it is obvious that this instance of an unchallenged and patently pragmatic conversion did not pass unnoticed among those of his subjects who were themselves deficient in religious steadfastness. Winckelmann, no subject but a recent immigrant, was soon confirmed in his cold-blooded appraisal of such problems: "The last time the Maréchal de Saxe [the sovereign's illegitimate half-brother] dined in the Brühl gallery," he observed in August 1749, "some 1000 onlookers crowded around the table and broke numerous glasses. He looks like the most honest man in the world, like any ordinary citizen, at ease with everyone. They make much of the fact here that he attends Lutheran services. Those who know better realize that he has no more religion than other prominent men. Appearances are the only thing that counts."

His religious indifference and latent dissatisfaction with his job made Winckelmann particularly susceptible at this time to the influence of a man whom he first met when he had to show him, a visiting dignitary, through Bünau's library. Count Alberigo Archinto was the Papal Nuncio to the Court of Saxony. As member of a long-established Lombard family—an Archinto had founded the Abbey of Chiaravalle in 1135, two others had been archbishops of Milan—and a gout-ridden man in his fifties, he did not relish what he called his "Babylonian exile" by the banks of the Elbe. No matter what the natives might say, Dresden was not Rome or even Milan, but the upstart residence of an upstart king who, although himself recently converted to the true Church, ruled over a population made up of Lutheran zealots. The food was vile, the climate abominable, and the company tedious because the vaunted scholars of Leipzig and Dresden were little more than pedants, whose boorishness made him yearn for the conversation of the mercurial Italian abbés among whom he had spent his youth. Archinto especially dreaded the long voyages to Poland, when he had to accompany into the wintry wastes of that land the court to which he was accredited. "I will not be happy," he complained on such occasions, "until I see before my door the horses that will carry me back to a Christian country." He seemed delighted to discover, in Bünau's house and later when he invited him to his own table in Dresden, that this underpaid librarian was not another Saxon "bear"—"*orso*"—but a sensitive and learned man with whom it was a pleasure to discuss books and antiquities.

Archinto soon began to wonder, no doubt aloud and in his presence, what a man like Winckelmann was doing in a place like Nöthnitz, running errands for an amateur historian whose work, if it ever saw the light of day, would serve to enhance the author's reputation and not that of his assistant. A man of his ability should surely be in the center of things, rather than bury his light under a bushel among all these rustic *"orsi"*! Archinto's own friend, Cardinal Passionei, just happened to be looking for an able librarian to whom he could entrust his collection of 300,000 volumes. Had Winckelmann ever considered moving to Rome? He must have; it was inconceivable that a man of such knowledge, that a classical scholar of his distinction should not have figured out for himself that the Eternal City, in fact the Papal Court, was the only setting in which he could readily unfold his wings, the more so as he had recently been observed examining and measuring the antique sculptures in the Dresden museum. If he was interested in the arts, then there was of course no place like Rome for him. As a matter of fact, he, Archinto, had heard so much about Winckelmann that he had taken it upon himself to write to Passionei, and had received two letters in reply in which the Cardinal—did Winckelmann know that he was *Secretarius Brevium*, charged with the promulgation of all papal briefs?—in which His Eminence had urged him to send his young protégé to Rome forthwith. He would be given a room in Passionei's own palace in the Vatican and expected to go about in black, as did all those who belonged to a cardinal's staff; but his duties might be nominal, and he need not fear that such semi-clerical garb would disqualify him from participating in the gayer side of Roman life. He—Archinto—and Passionei did not dream of demanding in so many words that Winckelmann embrace the Roman faith, although it would surely be to his own advantage to do so. Not only did the Church directly administer, in the Vatican and elsewhere, most of the great collections of manuscripts and art; through its dignitaries abroad, the Holy See was also able to further many a scholarly career and to dispense stipends, privileges, letters of introduction, and other bounties of the sort. And anyway, now that the subject had been mentioned, what was a conversion among men of the world? *"Changer la religion,"* they said, *"c'est changer la table, mais non pas le Seigneur."* A mere formality for Winckelmann, and an honor for himself, Archinto, who could then take pride in having brought into the Church a great savant, much as Bossuet had done in converting the mathematician Saurin. Besides, it could all be done privately, in the presence of only a handful of friends, like that nice Father Rauch whom they had both known for some time. . . .

One can imagine how earnestly Winckelmann reflected on these possibilities, which were suggested to him not by some bare-footed friar but by a veritable Prince of the Church, who had the ear of His Holiness and was himself *papabile*—of sufficient stature and prospects to be reckoned among the candidates for the Papacy. It was common knowledge that Archinto was an intimate not only of the legendary Cardinal Passionei, through whom Voltaire had dedicated his *Mahomet* to Benedict XIV, but of Count Brühl, to whose country estate he liked to retire whenever the gout became unbearable. The prospective convert may be forgiven for wondering whether it was Providence herself that had now caused this man to take an interest in him, Johann Joachim Winckelmann, the cobbler's son from Stendal. The gift of proselytizing is so unevenly distributed among the clergy that the human factor looms large in most conversions. Besides, Winckelmann was no fool. He knew that something was expected of him in return for a trip to Rome, and he also guessed that the Church looked on his conversion as an investment: he was being courted not for what he was, but for what he had it in him to become. Yet he would have had to be blind if he had not also weighed, along with the pecuniary aspects of this transaction, the genuine solicitude of a man like Archinto against the callousness of such Protestant divines as Jerusalem and Schnakenburg, who had barely given him the time of day.

The remarkable thing about Winckelmann's conversion, in retrospect at least, is not the step itself but the fact that he was so slow in taking it. He had met the Jesuit Leo Rauch, Chaplain to the Elector and King, in 1748, and Archinto shortly thereafter; yet he was not received into the Roman Church until June 11, 1754 (a year almost to the day after another rediscoverer of antiquity, Edward Gibbon, had taken the same step in London). The pros and cons were so evenly matched in Winckelmann's mind that he advanced to the edge several times, only to hesitate, stop, and withdraw before advancing once again. He was so far removed from any state of grace and illumination that he wrote Berendis as follows: "I have not turned my coat yet—*den Pelz gewendet*. It is, however, a *conditio sine qua non*. His Excellency the Nuncio gave me to understand that His Eminence not only demanded it, but that it would be to my own advantage if I made my conversion in the former's presence. For example, if His Eminence or His Holiness were to die (don't laugh), much attention would be paid to this in Rome, and my future would depend on [having been converted]. I do believe that [Archinto] wants to claim the honor of having made a convert. Unless I am mistaken, he thinks as sensibly as I do. He has a beautiful mistress, whom I happen to know."[4] If Winckelmann had not been much of a Protestant, he clearly would never make a model Catholic either! This show of cynicism notwithstanding, he was whistling in the dark because there remained in him, along with such ostentatious irreverence, a residue of shame at the thought of selling himself and taking part in a ceremony which in this case would amount to a farce in dubious taste. He knew very well in his innermost heart that the step which he was about to take was dishonorable because it was motivated by expediency rather than conviction. In the final instance, however, it was not this consideration that held him back so long, but two others: the fear that he might be short-changed in the bargain, and his reluctance to disappoint his family and friends. The first concern is understandable because he had taken on, in dealing with the Vatican, a formidable partner with whom to do business; and the second may even be counted to his credit—for it is pleasant to find in him, at this time when the kaleidoscope of his personality was shaken so violently that one despairs of ever seeing the pieces settle down again in their accustomed pattern, that regard for others which had belonged to the pattern as much as had the colder qualities of ambition and self-control.

Winckelmann had lost his mother several years before he left Prussia. Another obstacle to his conversion was providentially removed in 1750 when his father, whom he had supported during his last years, died of epilepsy in the old age home at Stendal. Martin Winckelmann would not have found peace if he had suspected that his son would desert the Lutheran church, which had helped him acquire the very skills that now made him so desirable in the eyes of its rival, that of Rome. But there remained his employer, Count Bünau, who had so firmly put principle before expediency in his own life; there remained his long-time benefactor Nolte, and there remained his friends, Uden and Berendis and Genzmer, as well as Bülow and Lamprecht, both of whom he visited at this time: men who knew him well enough to realize instantly that this was not a genuine conversion, which would have been bad 'enough in their eyes, but an act of prostitution. Friendship in all its shadings formed his main, at times his only emotional tie with the world; his temperament and the circumstances of his life being what they were, it had taken the place of marriage, country, and religion. It is touching to see how anxious he was to soften the impact that his change of faith was bound to have on these men. Using Berendis as a go-between, he tried to prepare Bünau for the news, and when it had become public, addressed to him a pathetic appeal for understanding if not approbation: "I cannot and must not keep it from Your Excellency: I carried out my resolution and have, alas! taken the plunge . . . I have made myself unworthy of Your Excellency's continued forbearance, but I implore Your Excellency's heart full of goodness and grace to hear me out at least. May God, the Lord of all tongues, peoples, and sects, restore in Your Excellency the feelings of charity . . ." Bünau did not reply, and in fact took little further notice of his secretary, who had resigned from his service by then and was on the point of moving to Dresden. Already much earlier, Winckelmann had informed or misinformed Uden that "His Majesty has graciously accorded me an opportunity of going abroad at His expense, especially to Italy . . . My chief destination will be Rome, where I shall spend at least a year, with the understanding that I will be able to preserve my complete freedom of conscience . . . I cannot deny that they may have certain designs on me in Rome, but I rely on the above assurance and on the King's generosity." One can almost see him squirm on his chair when he wrote these lines, which leave so much unsaid and misrepresent so much else, including his departure for Rome, which was then eighteen months away.

Winckelmann's hesitation only served to aggravate the predicament in which he found himself. He had been told that he would live in the Vatican as a member of Passionei's household, but when he pressed Archinto and Rauch for details, it developed that the salary that had been set aside for him was little more than pocket money. He had no desire to exchange his dependence on Bünau, whom he knew, for a like dependence on a cardinal he had never seen; and Heyne's experiences with Brühl warned him not to count his chickens before they were hatched, by lightly giving credence to promises of support extended by forgetful if well-meaning patrons. It was only after much arguing back and forth that he managed to extract, through the mediation of the court physician, Ludovico Bianconi, a yearly grant of 200 *Taler* from the Elector's privy purse. Other fears that tormented him were that Archinto might suddenly be recalled to Rome, or that Bünau might dismiss him before he had found his footing at the electoral court in Dresden or the papal one in Rome. As a man without means or marketable skills other than those of a librarian and teacher, he felt a practical as well as emotional need of friends. One misstep, such as a premature disclosure of his plans to Bünau or an inaccurate report to his contacts in Prussia or a denunciation to Passionei, and he would find himself shunned by both parties, without a job, connections, or prospects. It had become a question of timing rather than principle, and the constellation had to be just right before he could take the jump. Rumors had already got about that Bünau's secretary, the ex-theology student and former Prussian schoolteacher, had been seen in Dresden in the company of such unlikely people as the Papal Nuncio and the Elector's Chaplain. One such report had reached the pastor of the Lutheran Church which Winckelmann occasionally attended in the nearby village of Leubnitz, and this cleric of more zeal than discretion took it into his head to announce, one Sunday morning when he saw Winckelmann dejectedly sitting in his pew, that the congregation would now pray for "an errant sheep that wanted to convert to Catholicism, but had decided to return to the pure faith, and to bear public witness of this decision by taking Holy Communion in their presence." Winckelmann, who had felt every head turn in his direction, got up and walked out of the church, never to return.

Far from testing his mettle, as conflicts are said to do, this protracted inner struggle almost undid him. He had to admit to himself that he was not made for intrigues, and that his health was beginning to give way under the strain. "If you are well," he wrote Berendis, "I shall be happy to hear it, for I am not. They tell me that I am losing weight all the time, and I notice it myself. My old complaint, unusual nocturnal perspiration, returns even with the most rigid diet. I can see considerable changes in my constitution. My digestion is so weak that for some time now I have been able to eat meat only once a week . . . it is more than three months ago that I last had a glass of beer . . . I have been advised to go on a milk diet, which I did and intend to continue . . . I get my own in the morning, and drink it warm, as it comes from the cow, by itself or with tea; nothing but vegetables for lunch, often only a watery soup." These disturbances were accompanied by insomnia, fainting spells, and a form of paranoia peculiar to those who have trouble communicating: even while engaged in correspondence with a dozen friends who rarely failed to reply, he was forever waiting for mail. All in all one could, if so inclined, reconstruct from his behavior during this period an entire symptomatology of stress. Having once made his conversion, however, and rejected what the document unkindly called *"errores Lutheranae sectae,"* he immediately regained his habitual sense of physical well-being: "I eat with relish," he boasted in December 1754, "I shit well ["*ich scheisse gut*"] and sleep soundly, my night sweats seem to have gone."

Although the psychological fracture never healed completely, because he had, in a manner of speaking, forfeited his innocence as well as his self-respect, the change of religion was too superficial and came too late in his life to affect greatly the habits and preferences he had acquired in earlier years. A friend who visited him in Rome reported that the convert himself had told him that "even though he was a faithful servant of the Church, he had taken to singing, while making his breakfast in the morning—may the Saints in Paradise forgive him!—one of our good old Lutheran hymns."[5] The notion of Winckelmann brewing himself a cup of chocolate and launching into his favorite *"Warum sollt' ich mich denn grämen"* in the attic of the Palazzo Albani, while his friend the Cardinal was engaged in his own matins downstairs, goes far toward reconciling one to this particular and presumably inevitable conversion.

III

"Europe had not seen happier days than these," Voltaire wrote of the period between the Peace of Aix-la-Chapelle in 1748 and the Lisbon earthquake of 1755. "Trade and commerce flourished from Cádiz to Saint Petersburg, the arts were honored everywhere, nations were on good terms with one another. The continent resembled a large family that has buried its quarrels."[6] For Winckelmann, too, everything for once fell into place when he moved to Dresden, or at least it seemed to have done so in retrospect, when he recalled the "fanatical love" he had felt for Saxony at that time. Having changed his religion, he was now free to enjoy the benefits that this step conferred on him: a small pension, sufficient to let him live a few months without working; leisure to devote himself full-time to his new passion, the study of art; and access to the capital's museums and galleries and to the men who administered them. Life was good. He was in his mid-thirties, *"nel mezzo del cammin,"* and with the prospect of living a year or two in Rome once the arrangements had been completed, he knew that the best was still to come. In the meantime, here he was in Dresden, where the arts were indeed honored as nowhere else on German soil.

When Winckelmann prefaced his *Gedanken über die Nach-ahmung der griechischen Werke in der Malerei und Bildhauer-kunst* with the observation that Augustus the Strong had introduced the arts into Saxony as if they had been a "foreign colony," he was not only being diplomatic. After all, these "Reflections on the Imitation of Greek Works in Painting and Sculpture" (1755) were dedicated to that sovereign's son and successor. The statement was true enough even if there existed no geographical or historical reason why Dresden, rather than Karlsruhe or Berlin or any other major city, should have become an art center of such magnitude that it came to be called, until its destruction in 1945, *Elbflorenz,* or Florence-on-the-Elbe. The conditions favoring the importation of foreign and the en-couragement of native art were the same all over Germany. In every state there were those who felt that German painting, sculpture, and architecture were in a decline redeemed only by the vigor of the country's musical life and the first stirrings of its literary revival. Many of them shared Leibnitz's and Goethe's belief that what German culture needed was an infusion of Latin skill and wit, of *savoir faire* and *esprit.* But only the Electorate of Saxony possessed, in its dynasty which could look back even then on a tradition of supporting the arts, the catalyst that was required to activate these latent forces. The three Johann Georges who ruled successively from 1611 to 1694 had laid the foundation. On it, Augustus II and Augustus III now built a system of patronage and support which can truly be compared with that of the Medici in Renaissance Florence. As a young man, Augustus the Strong had been among the first European princes to go on the grand tour. Even after his accession to the throne, he thought nothing of spending hours watching a potter or a goldsmith at work, or of taking a hand himself in the design of decorations for a court fête. We have already noted that he had purchased, by barter for two regiments of infantry, the porcelain that the royal *Plusmacher*, Frederick William I, had wanted to sell on becoming King of Prussia in 1713. Having thus primed the pump, Augustus made his porcelain works at Meissen overtake their chief competitor, the factory of Delft in Holland. (The Dutch had been the first to fill the demand for chinaware created by the introduction, in the late seventeenth century, of such hot beverages as coffee, tea, and chocolate.) By welcoming to Saxony the inventor of true or hard-paste porcelain, Johann Friedrich Böttger, and later virtually holding him captive in a part of the Electorate whose soil contained the kaolin and other clays required for its manufacture, he gained a quasi-monopoly in the production of this commodity, which was so admirably suited to the economic conditions of the time. The relative lightness of the individual item, coupled with its high artistic and monetary value in relation to size, made Saxon porcelain a forerunner of the Swiss watch: the perfect product for a country in which skilled labor could be made to compensate for the lack of cheap mass transportation. Meissen porcelain eventually became a diplomatic as well as economic weapon in the Electorate's arsenal, in the supple hands of Count Brühl, who would discreetly send a service to a sovereign, statesman, or ambassador—men who would have indignantly rejected any notion of letting themselves be "bought" by a corresponding gift of money.

Besides the interest in porcelain and architecture that he shared with his father, Augustus III's taste also ran to painting and engraving. His greatest coup as a collector was the addition, to the famous Gemäldegallerie begun by Augustus the Strong, of some hundred pictures bought from the Duke of Modena in 1745, among them Correggio's *Night,* Rubens's *Saint Jerome,* Titian's *Tribute Money,* and a Saint Agnes by Guido Reni, who was so fashionable at the time. When the collection's *pièce de résistance,* the *Sistine Madonna,* was brought in and uncrated in 1754, the Elector and King is said to have pushed the throne out of the way with the words: "Make way for the great Raphael!" The story is quite in keeping with his nature, for he was so fond of painting that he frequently sent handwritten instructions to his court painter about the pictures he wanted hung on the walls of his private apartments. The most important among the many buildings erected in Dresden during the reigns of Augustus II and III were the so-called Zwinger, a "superb" edifice even in the jaundiced eyes of Boswell, who complained about having to pay admission to see the library and museum— "which is shameful when they are the property of a prince";[7] the Protestant Frauenkirche built by George Bähr, no architect at all, but a carpenter of genius, who insisted on giving it a stone cupola against the advice of all the engineering experts; and the Italianate Hofkirche, the consecration of which marked the official reintroduction, if only as the religion of a small but vigorous minority, of Roman Catholicism into Saxony. Architecturally speaking, the three buildings reflect a gradual rejection of the more playful features of the rococo, in favor of a simpler style which relied for its effect on proportion and on the material itself: wood was no longer painted to look like stone, or masonry twisted into shapes suggestive of wrought iron. Without putting too fine a point on it, this development may be likened to the growth of the Palladian fashion in England.

No one in all Saxony greeted this return to a soberer and more nearly functional art as warmly as did Francesco Algarotti, a much sought-after courtier and dilettante who dabbled in music as a reformer of the opera, and in literature as the author of an introduction to optical science which bore the disarming title *Newtonianism for the Ladies.* Having previously seen much of Italy, France, England, and Russia, Algarotti spent the years

1740–56 in Berlin and Dresden, imparting to both cities an air of cosmopolitan refinement which they had hitherto lacked. If he was a lightweight, an exotic butterfly fluttering from court to court, he knew nonetheless how to make this weight felt in a specific direction: his admiration for Palladio and his enthusiasm for the ancients made him a forerunner of neoclassicism. Among the artists of Dresden he found allies in Pietro Rotari, who went on to become Catherine the Great's favorite painter, and in Anton Raphael Mengs, whom we shall meet again as Winckelmann's friend and collaborator.

Winckelmann had arrived in Dresden in October 1754 thinking that the teaching of Greek would be his profession, and left the city in September 1755 knowing that the remainder of his life would be devoted to the study of art. He did not, of course, wake up one fine morning and decide that he would henceforth be an archaeologist and art historian. No enterprising publisher approached him with an invitation to "Write me a good history of art!" On the contrary: the precise circumstances of this conversion, deeper and more far-reaching than the religious one that had preceded it, remain hidden from view. His otherwise so eloquent correspondence was silent on this subject; his friends, so generous in other respects with their reminiscences of him, had little to add to it since he no longer lived with the ones he had made in his youth and had not yet found those of his Roman years. It is not even clear when and by what means he first gained access to the art world of Dresden. The few details that have been preserved—such as the fact that he was able, from 1752 on, to enter the gallery even on days it was officially closed, presumably through the good offices of Father Rauch—throw no real light on these winter and spring months of 1754–5. The difficulty of interpreting his metamorphosis chronologically and step-by-step is compounded by the lack of any visible connection between what he saw in Dresden and what he wrote in the "Reflections," on which he was working at the time. If he was impressed by the buildings that were going up all around him, the essay does not show it. Of all the paintings he is known to have studied, only the *Sistine Madonna* called forth much of a response. A particular case in point is the Antikensaal, the museum of antiquities that Herder and others credited with having opened his eyes to Greek art.

Established by Augustus the Strong with purchases from the Chigi and Albani collections in Rome, this museum had recently received a sensational gift in the shape of the *Vestal Virgins*. These were Roman copies of statues from the school of Praxiteles, representing two young women and a somewhat older one whose head covering should have identified her even then as a married woman; the figures are, in fact, not vestal virgins at all but funerary statues of Roman matrons in idealized Greek costume. They were remarkable because they formed a group (most previously discovered antique statuary having consisted of individual pieces), and on account of the unusual manner of their preservation and recovery. During the occupation of Naples by Imperial forces at the beginning of the century, an Austrian cavalry officer, Emanuel Maurice d'Elboeuf, had had a villa built on the beach at Granatello near Portici. When the peasants on his estate brought him some remnants of antique masonry and sculpture that they had found while tilling their fields, D'Elboeuf, a restless and inquisitive man, began to undertake some haphazard excavations of his own. In the course of these, he sank a shaft into what turned out to have been the amphitheater of Herculaneum, the city that had been overwhelmed, along with neighboring Pompeii, by the eruption of Vesuvius in A.D. 79. From this shaft he now extracted the statues, which he promptly shipped off to a restorer in Rome because complete sculptures were deemed more valuable than fragments, even of a masterpiece. From Rome he had them forwarded to Vienna—secretly, since the exportation of art objects from Italy was forbidden even then—in order to ingratiate himself with a distant relative, the Austrian general Prince Eugene, who also happened to be his commander-in-chief. The art-loving general, who does not seem to have taken the hint that the giver expected a promotion in return, was overjoyed, and proudly displayed the marble ladies in the belvedere of his palace. After his death, Augustus III bought them and had them shipped to Dresden in 1736.

As the first art works to have been discovered in Herculaneum, a site that together with Pompeii soon became an inexhaustible source of supply for the museums of Europe, the misnamed *Vestal Virgins* had an immediate and powerful effect on the artists of Saxony, among them the sculptor Lorenzo Mattielli, who created the statues of saints on the façade and bell tower of the Hofkirche. Here again, one would expect some reaction from Winckelmann. But he praised the *Vestal Virgins* only from the technical point of view, as an example of how the ancients rendered in stone the effect of drapery, and made no reference at all in the "Reflections" to a *Venus Anadyomene* in the Antikensaal, a work that Canova considered superior to the *Venus de' Medici*. Furthermore, the *Vestal Virgins* were at that time not exhibited, but housed in a shed where they huddled, as Winckelmann put it, "like herring in a box [so that] they could be seen but not examined"; this had not bothered Mattielli, who had been farsighted enough to copy them in clay while they were still in Vienna. Whatever influence these statues may have exerted on Winckelmann, they can hardly be said to have precipitated the transformation of this Saul among the classicists into the St. Paul of art historians. Like all acts of aesthetic cognition, this transformation remains at bottom a mystery. It forms part of the larger mystery of how

Winckelmann, Lessing, Herder, and Wieland, none of whom had at this time examined more than some second-hand reproductions, could have become so convinced of the exemplariness of Greek art that their praise of this art helped establish a cultural thralldom that has aptly been called "tyrannical."[8] All that they, not to mention Schiller and young Goethe, had actually *seen* of Greek works were some copies in the Dresden Antikensaal, in the Gypssaal in Mannheim, and perhaps in the mediocre collection that Frederick the Great had been assembling in Potsdam.

In Winckelmann's case, the mystery can be solved in part by working backward from his first work and from the circumstances under which it was composed. Even in this, the most opaque period of his life, he is best understood in terms of the work he did and the company he kept. Among this company we have already met the royal physician Ludovico Bianconi, whom Archinto, who had meanwhile been recalled to Rome, had charged with looking after their common protégé. Bianconi, however, had plans of his own. Years before, while serving as Resident Saxon Minister to the Holy See, he had begun to prepare an edition of Moschion's *De morbis mulierum*. Stymied by his poor command of Latin and Greek, he had taken the half-finished manuscript back with him to Dresden, in the hope of finding there some dupe who could do the actual translating without being in a position to claim a share of the scholarly laurels that would come with its publication. He approached Winckelmann, but found that he had come to the wrong man. When Bianconi called to ask what he could do to make his stay in Dresden more enjoyable, Winckelmann replied, "Nothing, I need nothing," and after an exchange of amenities showed his guest back to his carriage. Translating an ancient text on female disorders was not the kind of work for the sake of which he had changed religion. With a mixture of tact and gruffness that would have done credit to a far more experienced man, he managed to fend off Bianconi while yet keeping on the right side of this would-be scholar who was, after all, his chief contact at court. He had sold himself for a banquet in Rome, not a mess of pottage in Dresden.

Bianconi soon understood that Winckelmann wanted to be left alone to do his own work and choose his own friends, such as the painter Adam Friedrich Oeser, from whom he rented a room in Dresden and later in the suburban house in which he wrote the "Reflections." Oeser, born 1717 in Pressburg, had lost his parents early in life. Apprenticed to an itinerant artist, he was painting frescos in the country houses of Hungarian magnates when he heard that an academy in Vienna had organized a contest for promising young painters. He submitted a *Sacrifice of Abraham* and won a gold medal, an object which almost became his undoing when it disappeared in an unsuccessful competitor's pocket while being handed around the banqueting table. In attempting to retrieve it, Oeser got into a fight and was stabbed. Although it was a light wound, he nearly died of it because the surgeon who treated him had been "bought" by his rival. Having gained some notoriety as a result of this mishap, Oeser was eventually called to Dresden, and many years later to Leipzig as director of that city's Academy of Painting. He might have become Goethe's father-in-law if the poet, who as a student courted his daughter Friederike, had been the marrying kind. Oeser is forgotten nowadays as a painter, a member of the mediocre Viennese School which specialized in allegorical ceiling and cupola work depicting nymphs and *amoretti*, in large groups and sweeping motion. Yet he lives on in the praise of Goethe, whom he instructed in drawing; in that of Wieland, who credited him with possessing "the simplicity of the true genius"; and in that of Winckelmann, who undertook under his guidance his only excursion into the creative regions of art, in the form of a few drawing lessions. Above all, Oeser seems to have been a "character": lazy in his work, but an inspiring teacher and a moving force in the bohemian circles of Saxony.

Among the teaching aids by means of which Oeser impressed on his students the exemplariness of Greek and Roman art, cameos and intaglios played an important part. These engraved gems were second only to coins among the earliest art objects to have been methodically preserved and collected. Petrarch had owned a number of them, as had Lorenzo de' Medici and Pope Paul II, who once offered the citizens of Toulouse to have a bridge built over the Garonne if they would only let him have a valuable cameo that was kept in a local church (they turned him down, foolishly as it developed because King Francis I sequestered the stone shortly afterward without any compensation whatever). During the Renaissance and again in the eighteenth century, gem cutters and engravers took to imitating the antique models, and by 1750 the hobby had become so widespread that there existed no fewer than twenty-one large collections in England, France, Italy, Germany, and Holland. Glyptography was taken up by people of fashion, such as the Marquise de Pompadour, who engraved a winged genius of music in an onyx, and by humble tradesmen like Philipp Daniel Lippert, the inventor of a whole new technique of making pastes or glass imitations of precious stones. One of the most extravagant collectors of them all was Mengs, who once bought a cameo showing Perseus and Andromeda which had been too expensive even for the King of Spain; he had it set in a bracelet for his wife, the bewitching Margareta, on whose softly fleshed arm it so dazzled poor Winckelmann that he proclaimed it forthwith the world's most beautiful cameo. Among the last of those who used engraved gems for ceremonial purposes—as diplomatic presents—was Pius VII, who gave Napoleon an antique cameo which the Emperor in turn bequeathed to Lady Holland.

The more mundane collectors were captivated first of all by the beauty and value of the materials themselves: yellow topazes, blue sapphires, the striped onyxes and agates, dark-green emeralds, and the ancients' favorite stone, carnelian, with its many shades of red. The ease of handling and exhibiting cut stones also made them a desirable investment, much as certain paintings are in our day, while their smallness appealed to men and women whose taste was in any case attuned to the delicate and minuscule in art: to porcelain figurines, *petite poésie*, arabesque book bindings, miniature portraits. Those of more scholarly inclinations, on the other hand, treasured cameos and intaglios because they were as a rule better preserved than marble statues or fresco paintings, and in addition furnished mythological and historical details not always found in these larger-scale works. After reaching its high point about the middle of the century, the craze abated in measure as more antique statuary and painting was brought to light, in Campania and elsewhere, while the gem market became glutted with pastes and faked engravings. In its time, however, glyptography was a major branch of classical studies which engaged the attention of Lessing, the Comte de Caylus, and many other antiquarians. The names and styles of the major gem cutters—of Dioscorides of Samos, for example, who had designed the Roman emperor Augustus's seal, or of that Solon who was not recognized as an engraver at all until the Duc d'Orléans discovered that the name inscribed on a famous intaglio was the artist's and not that of the Athenian lawgiver supposedly represented by the portrait—were almost as familiar as those of Phidias and Polyclitus. A considerable fame was also enjoyed by the owners of great *dactyliothèques,* or collections of engraved gems, such as the Dukes of Devonshire and Buckingham or the "Roman Hogarth," Pier Leone Ghezzi, and by the leading scholarly specialists: P. J. Mariette, the author of a much-quoted *Traité des pierres gravées* (1750), or the

Baron Philipp von Stosch, whose collection was to be catalogued by Winckelmann.

Lippert, the doyen of Saxon gem collectors, had been a
draftsman in the Dresden ordnance depot when he chanced to
see some facsimiles of antique cameos that had been got together
by an acquaintance. Although thirty-six at the time and a family
man, he gave up his job and became a porcelain dealer in order
to have more time for what now became his real avocation, the
collecting and manufacturing of paste cameos. Since his way of
making facsimiles, from a compound of magnesium oxide and
isinglass, or fish glue, was cheaper than the concoctions of seal-
ing wax, gypsum, calcium sulphate, and other substances employed by his competitors, he soon acquired a collection of 3,000
items that were either self-made or had come to him as the
result of exchanges such as take place nowadays among stamp
collectors. He became a celebrity visited by travelers to Dresden,
among them Lessing, to whom he gave a cameo showing a
skeleton with a butterfly, a *memento mori* that the writer henceforth wore in a ring. The catalogue of Lippert's collection not
only confirmed Oeser in his belief that engraved gems represented a valuable commentary on the history of ancient civilization, but spread the fame of this particular *dactyliothèque* far
beyond the confines of Saxony. Feeling his lack of classical
erudition, the owner had enlisted the help of a professor at the
University of Leipzig, Johann Friedrich Christ, who provided
the learned framework for the catalogue by way of suitable
quotations from ancient authors and mythological explanations
(in general, cameos and intaglios from antiquity bear engravings
of legendary scenes, while those of Renaissance vintage tend to
show portraits). Christ, a firm believer in the classical languages
even while these were everywhere being displaced by French and
German, for good measure translated Lippert's whole scholarly
apparatus into Latin. His commentary was later revised by

Heyne, but in the end retranslated into German when Lippert decided that even though he was uneducated, he knew a great deal more about engraved gems than the other two were ever likely to learn. And he was right. His own workmanlike observations show a better insight into the principles and practices of this art than do those of the bookworms Christ and Heyne. Lippert's expertise was the more remarkable as he had to depend on drawings while making his pastes, and rarely saw in the original the cameos which he reproduced and described.

Algarotti's influence made itself felt at court, Oeser's among the artists, Christ's and Heyne's in academic circles, Lippert's among the collectors. The man who channeled these currents into the river of European neoclassicism, or at least into its Saxon tributary, was Christian Ludwig von Hagedorn, the director of the Dresden Academy of Art and younger brother of the poet Friedrich von Hagedorn. Although he had tried his hand at painting and engraving, Hagedorn amounted to so little as an artist that his very name was lost on the editor of a contemporary reference work, in which he appears listed under "Experiment"—"*Versuch*"—because he had modestly entitled his sketches *Versuche* rather than signing them with "Hagedorn."[9] Of far greater import than his creative work were his activities as a collector, academy official, and author. He endeavored to redress the balance between the Nordic artists—painters like Jan van Eyck, Holbein, and Dürer—and the French and Italians who had supplanted them in popular and critical esteem. His vindication of the Dutch, in particular, sprang from pedagogical as much as aesthetic considerations, because their realism seemed to underscore the function of painting as counterweight to the falsehoods which social life forces on the individual: "Only those who respect Nature," he writes somewhere, "can truly appreciate Art." In his capacity as museum official, Hagedorn encouraged businessmen to support the local building trades,

E

with a view to recreating in modern Saxony the collaboration that had existed, in ancient Greece and again in the Middle Ages, between the patron who commissioned a work of art, the artist who conceived and designed it, and the brassfounder or other worker who helped produce it. (It was this unglamorous but necessary preoccupation with the economic side of art that also prompted him to take up a collection for the artists and artisans whose studios and shops had been destroyed in the bombardment of Dresden in 1760.)

These didactic and physiocratic concerns show that Hagedorn was a true child of his time. Yet there were other sides to him that pointed to the future. In his *Lettre à un amateur* he interpreted painting not as an art form subject only to laws of its own, but as a reflection of a nation's total artistic endowment and of the social conditions under which it was created. It was hardly an original idea even then, but Hagedorn was in a position to put it into practice: instead of hanging pictures pell-mell or according to his own fancy, he was among the first museum directors to arrange them in such a fashion that they represented organically the unfolding of various styles and schools. While he preferred to write in French, his German was almost as good as Winckelmann's. The two were, in fact, so evenly matched in this regard that Gottsched at first credited Hagedorn with having written the *Sendschreiben,* or "Open Letter," the anonymous pamphlet in which Winckelmann attacked his own "Reflections" in order to give that work wider currency.

Winckelmann would not have been himself if he had been content to sit at the feet of Hagedorn, Algarotti, or even Oeser— minor oracles in the minor temple of neoclassicist Saxon art. In this winter of 1754-5 he not only struck out on his own in the essay that will presently be examined; he also had a number of practical problems to solve. There were errands to be run for others, such as the purchase of porcelain for friends in Prussia.

There were books still waiting to be sold in Stendal and See-hausen: a transaction he entrusted to Uden. With the proceeds, he bought himself a fur coat—an odd investment, at first glance, for an indigent scholar about to depart for Italy. Yet it was based on common sense as well as vanity. He had discovered that libraries were almost invariably unheated even in winter, and that the lack of warm clothes could be as serious as that of books. If self-indulgence played a role in this purchase at all, it took the form of a symbolic gesture that he was to repeat several times: like a snake shedding its skin and acquiring a shiny new one, Winckelmann bought himself a new wardrobe whenever he was about to enter a fresh phase of his life. Now that he was working for himself and no longer subject to a daily routine set for him by a school board or private employer, there was also the problem of husbanding his time. It was a hard thing to learn for a man entering middle age, and complicated in his case by the need to preserve good relations with Bianconi even while hold-ing him off. "I spend the whole morning at home," he informed Berendis in December 1754, "and occasionally go to the Royal Library at 11 in order to take out books, which they are willing enough to entrust to me. From noon until 1:30 I have my lunch, then take a walk across the river and go home. I do not as a rule leave the house again until 7 . . . Every day I draw for at least two hours. Oeser is my only friend here, and that is how it is going to stay." In the evening, he had a glass or two of wine in a nearby tavern, and, on very rare occasions, attended parties in houses to which he had been introduced by Bianconi.

The families he visited belonged to the lively circle around the Crown Prince Frederick Christian and his consort Maria An-tonia, a Bavarian princess who composed operas and wrote some passable poetry. We could probably dismiss as so much flattery Algarotti's description of her as a latter-day Vittoria Colonna, if she had not also been complimented by a man who had nothing to gain from doing so, Frederick the Great: "I see only one person in all of Saxony," the old misogynist would write shortly after the Seven Years' War, in which they had been enemies, "to whom I must express my admiration. *Il n'y a que vous, Madame, tout le reste ne m'est rien.*" Masculine in temperament and appearance, yet colorful and witty, Maria Antonia was a woman after Frederick's heart; perhaps she reminded him of a certain ballerina whom he had liked because she possessed, as the sharp-eyed Voltaire observed, *"les jambes d'un homme."* It was, in any case, a token of Winckelmann's willpower that he usually returned at an early hour to his room on the fourth floor of Oeser's house, and refused to let himself be presented to Maria Antonia even though Bianconi had offered to do the honors. He had been raised in a dwelling that was little more than a wooden shack, and when the time came would confidently break bread with princes of the blood and read from his works to cardinals and popes. But that moment had not yet arrived. In the meantime, and while the first of these works was being written, he paid no more heed to the call of social advancement than he had paid to that of spiritual salvation.

IV

⊒⊒

The "Reflections on the Imitation of Greek Works in Painting and Sculpture" is an essay of just over 50 pages, subdivided into 178 paragraphs varying in length from a single sentence to half a page. Its main argument is contained in the famous paradox: "The only way for us to become great, and, if possible, inimitable, lies in the imitation of the Greeks."[10] Among the reasons why ancient Greece became the home of an art characterized by a "noble simplicity and quiet grandeur," Winckelmann lists, in another key sentence, a temperate climate, a certain freedom from political constraints, and a number of customs and conventions that were peculiar to the Greeks and served to enhance their health, appearance, and athletic prowess. "The great contests," he states,

> were for them a powerful incentive to engage in sports, the laws prescribing a training period of ten months for the Olympic Games, in Elis, the very place where these were held . . . Through these exercises their physique acquired the grand and manly contour, free of fat and flabbiness, that the Greek masters imparted to their sculptures. Every ten days, the youths of Sparta

had to present themselves in the nude to the *ephores,* who subjected to a stricter diet those who had begun to put on weight . . . They shunned all bodily awkwardness, and when Alcibiades as a boy refused to study the flute because playing it would contort his face, the young men of Athens followed his example. The Greeks' whole attire was accordingly designed in such a way that it would not do the slightest violence to their natural development. The growth of beautiful forms and figures was not inhibited by the various modern garments that pinch and squeeze, especially about the neck, hips, and thighs. In Greece, even the fair sex would not suffer, merely for modesty's sake, clothing that was restrictive: the young Spartan women wore such light and brief dresses that they were called "those who display their hips." We also know how anxious the Greeks were to beget beautiful children . . . They went so far as to try to make blue eyes black. It was for this reason among others that they established beauty contests. These were held in Elis, the prize consisting of weapons which were hung up in the Temple of Minerva. There could be no shortage of experienced and learned judges in these contests, since the Greeks, as Aristotle tells us, had their children instructed in drawing, chiefly because they believed that this skill enabled them to discover and define physical beauty . . . Those diseases that wreck so much beauty and spoil the noblest features, were still unknown among them. There is no mention of smallpox in the works of Greek physicians . . . Venereal diseases and their offspring, the English malaise, did not ravage their beautiful forms . . . The gymnasia were the schools of artists, where the young, otherwise clothed in accordance with public decency, did their exercises naked. There they went, the philosopher and the artist: Socrates in order to teach . . . Phidias in order to enrich his art through [the contemplation of] these beautiful creatures.

After so much stress on beauty, one would expect to find a precise definition of that quality. But we are told first of all where beauty is *not* to be found: neither in the addition of individually pleasing traits nor in the morphological relationship of such traits to each other or to the whole. While there are features that may be considered exemplary in an individual model or sculpture (Winckelmann makes much of the wavelike contour of Greek statues and the omission, on the artist's part, of such realistic detail as dimples and folds in the skin), beauty is more than the sum total of such features. Any attempt to achieve it eclectically is bound to end in a short-circuit; the Greek profile, he admits, may have been "as peculiar to the ancient Greeks as flat noses are to the Kalmucks or small eyes to the Chinese." Eclecticism runs counter to his concept of beauty as a universal standard not subject to ethnic, temporal, climatic, or other variations. It leads to naturalism, as in Dutch painting, which Winckelmann disliked for this reason. Beauty, then, is not the end product of an anthropological or even an aesthetic chain of reasoning, but a Platonic idea formed in the minds of the best Greek artists. It stands in the same relationship to physical perfection as that in which Phidias' mistress Kratina stood to the *Aphrodite of Cnidus*, or Phryne to the *Venus Anadyomene*: they were merely the models from which the sculptors distilled an ideal that filled the beholder's mind and uplifted his soul as well as pleased his senses. The few artists of more recent times who attained this degree of sublimation did so not by slavishly imitating the ancients, but by looking at life with the same ethos that had animated the latter; in a word, through emulation rather than imitation. It was thus that Raphael painted his *Galatea* (not as a portrait of a beautiful woman but as a concept "raised above the common form of matter"), his *Retreat of Attila*, and above all the *Sistine Madonna*, with "a face so innocent and yet a more than feminine grandeur, in an attitude of blissfully serene calm, that calm with which the ancients endowed the images of their gods. How grand and noble is the whole contour of that figure!" This painting serves to illustrate the most striking thesis in the essay; namely, that the imitation or emulation of the Greeks represents a quicker and surer way to perfect beauty than does the imitation of Nature.

Winckelmann's Greece is a utopian society which enjoyed a sufficient measure of freedom, order, and wealth to enable its citizens to express to the fullest the artistic gifts that waxed and waned with the unfolding of their national life; for "the arts have their youth, even as man." Such gifts used in such a setting enabled them to create works of everlasting perfection, in contrast both to the somber art of the Egyptians who preceded and to the tense and self-conscious art of the various nations that followed them. Among these, the Romans left works which are at best second-rate and derivative, while those of the Italians, French, Dutch, English, and Germans all too often show traces of excessive realism and of a striving for effect. The classical art (and, though he mentions it only tangentially, the literature) of Greece sprang from, and in turn ennobled, a civilization which valued emotional restraint no less than physical beauty: it knew neither human sacrifices nor gladiatorial combats, and considered as altogether unbecoming the artistic representation of the extreme states of mind induced by these and similar "thrills." From the "mini-skirted" girls of Sparta to the noble simplicity and quiet grandeur of the *Laocoön*, Greece was a land in which there had once prevailed a state of preternatural beauty and harmony, a lost Eden that men must yearn for and strive to re-create, in modern times and on Nordic soil, through that emulation of the ancients which he considered the key to artistic perfection. It little matters that this vision, which was not original with Winckelmann but which he formulated more convincingly than anyone before him or since, has long ago been replaced in our minds by the contrasting one of the Greeks as a people that may have been more gifted, but was possibly no less neurotic than we are. Perpetuated in countless works of art and literature, Winckelmann's Greek ideal forms to this day a part of our collective historical consciousness.

Laocoön, the group that Winckelmann regarded as represent-ative of some of the finest qualities of classical Greek art, does not date from the classical period at all. Hellenistic in concept and execution, it was created in the first century B.C. by the Rhodian sculptors Agesander, Polydorus, and Athenodorus. Rediscovered in Rome in 1506, and examined by Michelangelo, who planned to restore the father's right arm, it was purchased by Pope Julius II and placed in the Vatican. In the eighteenth century, the sculptor Agostino Cornacchini restored the missing extremities, the father's and younger son's right arms and the older son's right hand. The subject is familiar enough: having warned his fellow-citizens against the wooden horse left behind by the Greeks during their sham retreat from the walls of Troy, the priest Laocoön is punished by the partisan goddess Athena (according to another version, by Apollo), who sends two sea serpents to strangle him with his sons as he was sacrificing to Poseidon on the shore. It is a subject that has challenged a num-ber of artists, among them Titian, who, surfeited with all the praise that had been heaped upon the group, drew a caricature in which he substituted monkeys for the men. Whatever the vir-tues and defects of Winckelmann's interpretation, there is no question but that he picked a worthy topic in this work which Pliny had already described, in his *Natural History*, as superior to any other in painting and in sculpture. One may share Winckelmann's admiration of the group or damn the latter as melodramatic to the point of exhibitionism, but one cannot dis-

E*

miss it as insignificant or uninteresting. Not the least of Winckelmann's achievements lies in his designation of the *Laocoön* as
normative at a time when examples of Greek sculpture were
exceedingly rare, as often as not wrongly identified and ascribed,
and held by many to be inferior to Roman work.

In the passage from the "Reflections" that Lessing cites in
the beginning of his own *Laocoön, or the Boundaries Between
Painting and Sculpture*, the "great and resolute soul" characteristic of the Greeks is expressed

> in Laocoön's face, and not only in his face . . . The pain that
> shows in every muscle and sinew of that body and which the
> onlooker, even disregarding the face and all the rest, can fairly
> feel for himself as he watches the painfully retracted pelvis—
> that pain, I say, is nevertheless not violently reflected either in
> the face or in the whole attitude. He does not raise an outcry,
> as Virgil has him do:

> > *"He screamed to make high heaven shudder—screamed*
> > *like a bloodied bull run roaring from the altar*
> > *to shake free of his neck an ill-aimed ax."*[11]

> The way in which the mouth is opened does not permit it. What
> he utters is, rather, a fearful and anguished sigh . . . Physical
> pain and nobility of soul are evenly distributed and, as it were,
> balanced throughout the entire figure. Laocoön suffers, but he
> suffers like Sophocles' Philoctetus: his misery touches our very
> souls, and yet we wish that we too could bear suffering as this
> great man bears it . . . The artist had to experience for himself
> the strength of soul that he imprinted on the marble.

This view of Laocoön as the innocent victim of divine wrath
was shared by many eighteenth- and nineteenth-century commentators: by Lessing and Herder and Goethe and Schiller in Germany; by Madame de Staël in France ("The most beautiful
statues of Greece are almost all pictures of repose. The *Laocoön*

and *Niobe* are the only ones which depict violent emotion; and
with both it is the vengeance of Heaven which they bring before
us, and not passions springing from the human heart"); by
Byron in England ("Or, turning to the Vatican, go see/Lao-
coön's torture dignifying pain—/A father's love and mortal's
agony/with an immortal's patience blending..."); and by Hawthorne in America ("... an immortal agony, with a strange
calmness diffused through it, so that it resembles the vast rage
of the sea, calm on account of its immensity...").[12] At variance
with this interpretation was that advanced by Wilhelm Heinse
and several others, who, while agreeing with Winckelmann on
the artistic merits of the statue, regarded it as a representation
not of a hero's martyrdom but of a transgressor's punishment: a
picture not of the good, but of the evil Laocoön who had
offended Apollo by engaging in sexual intercourse in his temple,
and now recognizes the justice of the god's retribution even as he
suffers it. "The whole group," Heinse wrote,

shows a man ... with whom the long arm of divine justice has
finally caught up. He sinks into the night of oblivion under this
awful verdict, and an acknowledgment of his sins may still be
read on his lips ... His whole body shakes and trembles and
swells with fire from the tormenting, deadly poison which wells
up as from a fountain. His facial structure with the beautifully
curled beard is utterly Greek ... and represents a clever man
more concerned with his own advantage and enjoyment than
with the law ... Here suffers a mighty enemy and rebel against
society and the gods, and it is with a sense of painful relief that
we watch the terrifying downfall of this magnificent criminal ...
The flesh is marvelously alive and beautiful; all the muscles
issue from the body itself, like so many waves from a stormy sea.
He has finished crying out and is about to draw breath ... even
his private parts are thrown in relief by the general tension:
scrotum and penis are contracted [the statues in the Vatican were

not equipped with fig leaves until the latter part of the eighteenth century] . . . The left flank ranks among the highest achievements of all art.[13]

These and other physiological details lead us to a third interpretation, according to which Laocoön, neither hero nor villain, is the archetypal example of man as the plaything of forces so overwhelming in nature that there is no room left for an emotional response on his part, let alone for the noble restraint which that response was said to epitomize. If this is so, we have before us not an ethical symbol but a clinical case study, an aspect that Boswell stressed when he wrote: "*Laocoön* supreme; equal to all ideas. Nerves contracted by it, so that beautiful *Apollo* [which stood next to it] could not be felt."[14] The convulsively tensed musculature and the beginning paralysis that Bernini thought to detect in the father's left leg seem to bear out this existentialist interpretation, which is rendered more plausible still if the group is "read" from left to right. The youngest son is *in extremis*; he sinks back, his glance is directed upward, he is no longer of this earth which he barely touches with one foot. The father is seen in the precise moment in which his resistance is being overcome; he struggles with every last ounce of his strength, but the outcome is not really in doubt: the serpents have bitten him and hold him firmly entwined. The older son, to the father's left and on our right, is relatively untouched. Neither tense like his father nor faint like his brother, he is the only one who relates with the others by looking at them rather than out into space; one suspects that he might even be able to escape, as he does in one version of the legend. Despite these and other contrasts, the group retains its architectural unity through the triangular and pyramidical form of the composition (gained, to be sure, at the cost of foreshortening the sons so that they appear dwarfish in relation to the father), through certain correspondences among the three figures (the right hand is raised in each case while the left attempts to pull away the serpents: a unifying motif in themselves), and through the artist's choice of this particular moment in Laocoön's struggle.

"If a work of sculpture is to become truly alive before our eyes," Goethe wrote, "it must represent a transitory moment. No part of the whole can have been in this position before, and every part must have given it up immediately afterward . . . In order to grasp the intention of the *Laocoön*, stand before it at some distance, with closed eyes. Open and shut them again quickly. You will see the group in motion, and fear to find it changed the next time you look."[15] In describing the work as if it were a *tableau vivant*, Goethe came much closer to the truth than even he could have guessed with all his prophetic gifts. For between his time and ours, the whole group has indeed been "in motion." In 1905, the German art dealer Ludwig Pollak made a sensational discovery: while browsing through a Roman stonemason's shop, he came upon the marble fragment of a man's right arm entwined by a serpent. Obviously, the arm had at one time belonged to a statue, but the *Laocoön* seemed out of the question because the arm was of a different color, and bent at the elbow rather than outstretched. After exhaustive scientific analyses, however, experts proved that this was indeed the arm that had once been Laocoön's, and that its discoloration had been due to the chemical properties of the soil in which it had rested during the centuries of its separation from the trunk. Determined to restore the work to its pristine stage once and for all, the experts took it apart in 1942 and again in 1960, and in reassembling it stripped off all later additions, including the restored arm for which they now substituted the original. As a result of this latest and presumably definitive restoration, the group has lost some of the pathos that had distinguished it in the eyes of its earlier admirers. This trend toward the prosaic is reinforced by the current de-emphasizing of the originality of the father's facial expression. Many art historians see in the tortured mouth and the eyebrows knotted in pain merely another example of the Greek penchant for the stylized rendition of emotional states. Laocoön's face, according to them, may be no more than a variant of the well-known mask of Tragedy.

While these developments might have made the hypotheses of lesser critics collapse like so many card houses, they have not affected the validity—limited as it has always been—of Winckelmann's interpretation. It is a one-sided interpretation because it over-emphasizes the ethical factor, and applies to a work that was actually three centuries more recent and far less original than he believed it to be. Nonetheless he glimpsed, behind this misdated and faultily restored sculpture, a part of the essence of Greek art and of the Greek spirit. Even in the classical period to which he ascribed the *Laocoön*, the Greeks were neither "great and resolute" to the exclusion of all else, nor invariably committed to the ideal of Noble Simplicity and Quiet Grandeur. But regardless of whether the arm is raised or bent and whether Laocoön's expression is individual or generic, the work does exemplify the value the Greeks had once assigned to these elusive virtues.

We have looked at the *Laocoön* in some detail because it is the first major Greek work that Winckelmann interpreted. His analysis, and indeed the whole essay of which it forms the core, may strike the modern reader as arbitrary and old-fashioned. Can one really define not only a period in cultural history, but concepts such as art or beauty so largely on the strength of one damaged sculpture? Is the naked human figure carved in stone the only subject worthy of an artist's skill and a critic's acumen? Did Winckelmann not endow this particular work with a set of ethical and aesthetic standards that may well be irrelevant in our time? Most of us, after all, are no longer willing to grant an artist—let alone a critic—the right to make binding pronouncements on the basis of such slender and subjectively viewed evidence. In the final analysis, however, this is beyond the point. There are no ultimate answers to questions such as "Is it beautiful?" or "What does it mean to *us?*" There are only approximations to such answers, and even these must be found anew by every generation, which in turn tends to dismiss those found by its elders. What matters is that both the particular method of legislative art criticism that Winckelmann initiated and the conclusions at which he arrived were *not* dismissed for some 150 years. Until the end of the nineteenth, and in some instances well into the present century, his inductive method remained the compass most often used by art historians; and the definition of Greek art which that compass registered, true North.

All Western art, whether Romantic or Pre-Raphaelite or Impressionist or whatever, used to be judged first of all by the number of degrees by which it deviated from the classicist meridian that Winckelmann had done more than anyone else to establish as the basis of all good taste. The opening statement of the "Reflections," "Good taste, which is beginning to spread through the world, was born under the sky of Greece," was to be echoed by the most diverse men under the most diverse circumstances: by Boswell when he informed Rousseau that he had studied art in Rome and "acquired taste to a certain degree"; by Lord Elgin when he prayed that his marbles would reach England in safety, "where they must prove of inestimable value in improving the national taste"; by Hawthorne when he confessed in Italy that "some unwritten laws of taste" had made their way into his mind and that "all this Greek beauty has done something toward refining [him]"; and by countless others. In Germany, not only art but much of literature came to be judged in the terms set forth by Winckelmann, thanks to Lessing, whose *Laokoon* (1766) was in part inspired by the "Reflections." While praising the essay in general terms, Lessing pointed out many inaccuracies in Winckelmann's quotations from the ancients, and took issue specifically with the latter's censure of Virgil. Lessing maintained that the poet had been as justified in having Laocoön scream as the sculptors had been in showing him as merely sighing. While the idea of a hero crying out in pain would not have been unbecoming in itself, since stalwarts like Achilles and Philoctetus had been so described in ancient literature, its representation in marble would have violated the very spirit of sculpture, by giving a false permanence to the moment of extreme emotion and by introducing an unsightly motif into an art the supreme law of which—and, in this postulate, Lessing and Winckelmann were of one mind—is the immortalization of beauty. From these considerations, the author proceeded to draw up a whole list of characteristics separating the literary from the visual arts.

Compared with his pages on sculpture, Winckelmann's observations on Greek painting are humdrum and flat, even if one bears in mind that so few examples of that art had then been recovered. This did not prevent him from castigating later painters for their failure to hew to the "narrow and not always tangible line between the pleasantly full and the superfluous," which made them err now on the side of fleshiness, now on that of emaciation (he mentions Rubens but not El Greco). Although he takes them to task for the paucity of their subject matter, which consisted almost entirely of sacred and mythological motifs, the remedy he recommends, allegorical painting, was both unpopular and unoriginal. It had been suggested to him by Oeser, at a time when the contrasting tendency of using historical events as symbolizations of moral forces was just coming into its own. Winckelmann's closing remarks, on the methods by which sculptors measure the proportions of a statue and on the supremacy of line over color, show him beholden to the very notion that he had just finished disproving: that of the mathematical reducibility of aesthetic effects, as propounded by Le Brun, De Piles, and other lawgivers of French academic art.

The "Reflections on the Imitation of Greek Works in Painting and Sculpture" is an uneven work, as remarkable for what it leaves out (any reference to classical architecture, for example, or to Christian painting other than the *Sistine Madonna*) as for what it contains: the most persuasively argued case yet made for the exemplariness of classical Greek sculpture. Even after two centuries, one is impressed by the incisiveness with which Winckelmann, a newcomer both to art criticism and to writing, proclaims his belief in the normative function of this sculpture. The authority that he claims, and that was readily granted to him by his readers, is based on qualities that are already fully evidenced in this first work: on his profound knowledge of the Greek language and literature, and his ability to reach out from this to an understanding of the entire cultural life of that people; on his infectious enthusiasm for the subject, and his gift for discussing it in a manner equally far removed from the speculative lucubrations of Germans like Baumgarten and Heyne, who were jumping from branch to branch in the dark forest of metaphysics and destroying much foliage in the process, and the mathematical calculations of Frenchmen like Testelin and Claude Perrault, who had tried to unlock the secrets of beauty not with their minds and souls but with a slide rule. Last but not least, the respect in which he held Greek art—a respect conveyed by his elevated style as much as by the argument itself—restored to the discussion of that art a dignity that it had lost in the beginning of the eighteenth century, when the Olympian gods and Homeric heroes had been trivialized beyond recognition by the makers of porcelain figurines, the authors of Anacreontic poems, and the purveyors of other frivolities *à la grecque.*

The extraordinary effect of the "Reflections" on the contemporary public was due less to the novelty of Winckelmann's arguments, some of which had been in the air ever since Montesquieu had first spoken of *"le grand et le simple"* as characteristics of ancient art, than to his style and the manner of the essay's publication. The short sentences and paragraphs read as if they had spurted out of a man who had too long kept them bottled up in his mind. Anxious to avoid the verbosity of academic writing, and accustomed by now to expressing himself as a *philosophe* rather than as an *érudit*, he reduced to a pithy remark everything that he relates: quotations from the ancients (which he rarely bothered to document), statements of a general nature, anecdotes, local allusions to the Dresden scene. So strong was the impression of spontaneity made by this essay that as seasoned a critic as Herder referred to it as "the first fragrant blossom of Winckelmann's youth." In reality, however, Winckelmann had come to the task after as solid an apprenticeship as that undergone by any writer. He was no youth, but a man of thirty-eight who had always been an avid and exceptionally retentive reader, and had accumulated in his books of excerpts a vast storehouse not only of ideas but of images, metaphors, and similes culled from various sources.

Even though they were thus nourished by reading, seasoned by age, and honed to the proverbial fine edge by the most rigorous self-discipline, Winckelmann's talents might not have borne fruit if the literary constellation had not been so favorable just then. In England and especially in France, mundane literature had invaded the library and the salon, providing the writer with a new audience to which he could appeal and by which he would be judged: the urban middle class. Even in Germany and

Italy, countries that had not yet achieved political unity, the modern idiom's victory over Latin had given the writer a nation-wide public. If this public now made greater demands on him because it forced him to eschew all legal, theological, and other technical terminology, it also held out to him a greater reward: that of becoming a "classical" author, an epithet that now ceased to be applied exclusively to the ancients. Once Montaigne had addressed himself to a lay public in the *Essays*, men and women began to draw their information about political science from Montesquieu, penology from Beccaria, natural science from Buffon, philosophy from Shaftesbury, and to turn for their entertainment to Voltaire, Pope, and others who wrote urbanely and in their native tongue about matters of general interest. What had been lacking until the publication of Winckelmann's "Reflections" was a German writer of this caliber, and a man who could discuss, for an educated but non-expert public, a field that had hitherto lain fallow: art history and aesthetics.

(Digressing for a moment while we raise our eyes to the larger picture, we might add that while the discussion of these subjects has become a popular pastime in our own days, when art appreciation is taught to college sophomores and the most unlikely cities vie with one another in opening museums, the German language, in which much of this discussion was initiated, has fallen into disrepute because it is thought in some quarters to be connected with the checkered history of modern Germany. Yet most of the basic tenets of *Kunst-* and *Kulturgeschichte* were established precisely by those German writers who stand in the direct line of descent from Winckelmann: Herder, Goethe, certain Romanticists, Nietzsche, Burckhardt, and, in that part of their work which may justly be called *Kulturkritik*, Marx, Spengler, and Freud. Even as he protests against traditional forms by "creating" a work out of the entrails of automobiles and other offal of the industrial age, the modern artist is beholden to these men who first defined, with the conceptual and linguistic tools designed by Winckelmann, the aesthetic, moral, and social dimensions of all art.)

The leanness of thought and word and the great tensile strength that distinguish the essay were as much a reflection of necessity as of the author's literary skill. Obliged to pay the printer out of his own pocket, he so pared and trimmed the manuscript that a leading critic of the period judged that, while the style was "very lively and pleasing," and so succinct that "not a single unnecessary word is used," its very conciseness detracted at times from its clarity.[16] In the belief that economy, even if forced, can be made to provide its own compensations, Winckelmann had his publisher, Georg Conrad Walther of Dresden, restrict the first edition to fifty copies, and cannily withheld a second printing until some desperate would-be readers had begun copying the "Reflections" by hand. He thus created an artificially tight market for this essay, which, although humbly dedicated—on Brühl's advice—to Augustus III, was accurately rumored to contain a devastating if oblique attack on the baroque vogue at court and the sovereign's own preference for painting over sculpture. And it is true that everything that Winckelmann disliked in the baroque—its grandiloquence and monumentality, its emphasis on motion and on startling effects of light and space, its use of one material to simulate another, its stress on the supernatural, its interest in individual psychology and in ecstatic and enraptured states of mind, and all the other sins with which he rightly or wrongly charged his *bête noire* Bernini —is castigated here by indirection: in Winckelmann's praise of the very opposite artistic principles and practices.

But he went further. Whether or not he was a born writer, he did exhibit from the very beginning of his career a flair for publicity that would have aroused the envy of such inveterate self-advertisers as Boswell and Voltaire. For there now appeared an anonymously published pamphlet, the *Sendschreiben*, or "Open Letter on the 'Reflections,' " in which that essay was ridiculed and its author taken to task, among other things for having failed to provide chapter and verse for his quotations from the ancients. It was a hoax perpetrated by Winckelmann himself, for the sole purpose of whetting the public's curiosity. Although his strong sense of the scurrilous did not as a rule extend to his own person and work, he now felt sure enough of his arguments to reduce them playfully *ad absurdum* through sheer exaggeration. "I do not believe," he says tongue-in-cheek, "that facial disfigurement by smallpox is as gross a bodily imperfection as that which someone noticed in the Athenians. No matter how well their faces may have been cast, their rear ends left much to be desired. Nature's parsimoniousness in this respect was, however, made up for by its generosity to the Enotocetes of India, who are said to have possessed ears of such size that they used them for pillows." True to the pamphlet's style, the statement is buttressed by two learned footnotes, referring in this case to Aristophanes. The passage may have made some readers smile and think of Swift's "learned commentator" William Wotton, and it may have sent others scurrying to their copies of *The Clouds*. But nobody is likely to have fallen asleep over it.

This is not the kind of tissue out of which contributions to knowledge are woven, and Winckelmann himself soon tired of the game. Before giving it up, he unfortunately published yet another pamphlet, an *Erläuterung*, or "Commentary upon the 'Reflections,' etc., and Reply to the 'Open Letter' on these 'Reflections,' " in which he enlarged upon his original theses. Dialectics and irony, however, were not his forte, and the "Commentary" consists of little more than the shavings pared off the

"Reflections." It is of interest only as a token of his awareness that it is not enough to have something to say, and to say it well: one must also see to it that it is read by others.

The "Reflections" were well received even before the dust stirred up by these sequels had settled. The little essay was translated into French and Italian, and praised not only by Nicolai but by Gottsched, by Mendelssohn—who recommended it to Lessing's attention—and in due course by Herder, Diderot, Goethe, Schelling, Friedrich Schlegel, and a host of later writers. In the context of Winckelmann's life, its publication at this time was more than a success. It was a stroke of luck because it gave him, on the eve of his departure for Italy, enough of a reputation to ensure that he would not arrive as a nameless pilgrim. His friend Oeser had embellished the "Reflections" with some engravings, including a dedicatory vignette which showed the Persian Sinetas offering water in his cupped hands to the King of Kings, before whom nobody was permitted to present himself empty-handed. It was a fitting symbol for the man who set out from Eger on September 24, 1755, on the first leg of his journey to Rome. He, too, came bearing an offering of first-fruits that would make him pleasing in the eyes of the mighty.

ROME AND HERCULANEUM

I

"To prevent the inconveniencies of a bad lodging," an English traveler to Italy advised his readers in the 1750's, "those that do not carry a complete bed with them, ought at least to make a provision of a light quilt, a pillow, a coverlet, and two very fine bed-cloths, that they may make but a small bundle . . . However, if this should appear troublesome, 'tis advisable at least to travel with sheets, and upon coming to an indifferent inn, where the bed may happen to look suspicious, you may call for fresh straw, and lay a clean sheet over it.—A traveller should be very cautious," the writer continues,

of pulling out money or valuable things before strange company on the road or in public inns; for almost all the robberies and murders that are committed on passengers, are occasioned by such imprudences. If this be a salutary advice in all countries, 'tis especially so in Italy, where though the public roads are not much infested with highway men, yet there are a great many villains who are ready to murder or assassinate a stranger in private houses, when they happen to have a prospect of some considerable prey. For this reason a traveller should always be furnished with some iron machine to shut his door on the inside, which may be easily contrived, and made of several sorts; for it frequently happens that the doors of the lodging-rooms have neither locks nor bolts, and opportunity, according to the old proverb, makes the thief. 'Tis proper also to travel with arms, such as a sword and a pair of pistols, and likewise with a tinder-box, in order to strike a fire in case of any accident in the night.[1]

On this and on subsequent journeys in Italy, Winckelmann was spared all such "inconveniencies," so much so that it may be argued that in moving about the country as safely as he did during the next thirteen years, he ran up a debt that he eventually had to pay with his life. In 1755, at any rate, nothing could have been further from his mind than swords, pistols, and tinderboxes. If he suffered at all, it was from a surfeit of protec-tion. After leaving Dresden in a diligence hired by a Jesuit priest ("a somewhat embarrassing company," he writes, "which I could not very well refuse"), he found himself handed on from convent to convent all the way to Bologna, where he stayed a few days as house guest of Bianconi's brother, who served as honorary Saxon consul in that city. From there he continued to Ancona, Loreto, and Rome, which he entered through the Porta del Popolo on November 18, 1755. The stretch from Bologna to Rome alone, half a day's drive on the *autostrada del sole*, had taken him twelve days. If his journey, like that of Wilhelm Meister in Goethe's novel, seems to have been watched over by invisible if benign powers, the reason is likely to have been not only humanitarian concern on the part of the Society of Jesus but also the fact that he carried on his person the sum of 150 *Taler*, which had been entrusted to him in Regensburg for delivery to the order's College in Rome. Ten years later, another budding author and Roman Catholic sym-pathizer, James Boswell, would find *his* road to Rome similarly smoothed by the Dominicans.

For a man who had yearned so long to see Italy, Winckelmann's first reaction to the promised land was curiously tepid. Like other travelers, he was impressed by the prosperity of the countryside around Bolzano, and appalled by the squalor he encountered on entering Italy proper, near Trento. Like Rousseau, he gave short shrift to Venice. Like the Président de Brosses, who jested that Romulus must have been drunk when he obeyed the dream that bade him found a city in "so ugly a region," he passed through the Roman *campagna* unaffected by that most evocative of landscapes, which was only discovered a generation or two later when Shelley, Byron, Madame de Staël, and Chateaubriand devoted to it some of the most eloquent pages in all travel literature. In short, Winckelmann, who enriched immeasurably our understanding of ancient art, added little to our appreciation of the natural setting which, according to the Romantics, forms the proper background for much of that art. It is indicative of his tourist's naïveté that he once remarked that he had eaten, in some Tyrolean inn, with a large company whose every member had brought his own silver cutlery. Like his claim that he had been granted a clown's freedom to say what he pleased at Bünau's table, the statement was intended to impress with his good fortune the friends that he had left behind in obscure Prussian village schools. But he quite missed the point. Silver was then widely held to possess sterilizing qualities, and the remarkable feature of this meal was not the wealth of his traveling companions, but the primitiveness of their accommodation. For the twenty or so guests seem to have been helping themselves out of one large bowl placed in the center of the table. This was still an occasional practice in eighteenth-century country inns, where people who ate with their fingers excused themselves by arguing that it was no worse than putting a fork or spoon into one's mouth between helpings from the communal dish. Whatever the reasons for

Winckelmann's lack of enthusiasm—whether it was the company in which he found himself or his age, which would no longer let him be swept off his feet easily—disappointment in the Papal States as such is not likely to have figured among them. Impatient as he was to see Rome, he cannot have harbored any illusions about the state of which it was the capital. He did not even bother to protest when the set of Voltaire's works that he was carrying in his luggage was confiscated at the border. It was only too evident that nothing had changed since Montaigne had been forced to hand over, on a like occasion but as long ago as 1580, a copy of his own essays.

Bordering on the Kingdom of the Two Sicilies in the south and on the Republic of Venice and the Grand Duchy of Tuscany in the north, the Papal States were among the poorest and most backward countries of Europe. They encompassed not only Rome, with just under 200,000 inhabitants, but the cities of Bologna, Ferrara, Ancona, and Ravenna, which had been annexed by the great popes of the Renaissance. Much of the land was fertile and the Adriatic provinces of Emilia and Romagna could even then be called prosperous. Yet the few centers of manufacturing and industry (wool in Matelica, soap in Spoleto, silk in Iesi, glassware in Forli) did not develop, for lack of roads and capital, and in any case the clergy, which made up almost a tenth of the population, produced in convents and monasteries many of the goods required for its own use. These intrinsic economic weaknesses were exacerbated by the prevalence of malaria in the low-lying areas, by the brigandage that had long been endemic to that part of Italy, and above all by the absence of a professional and entrepreneurial middle class. As a result, there existed such a sharp division between wealth and poverty that 113 absentee landowners and 64 ecclesiastical corporations owned between them 475,000 of the 500,000 acres comprising the *agro romano,* or Roman plain.

The attempts at reform launched by progressive popes like Clement XI (1700–21) and Benedict XIII (1724–30) had ended in failure because they proved incompatible with the social order that made the Papal States unique among the world's nations. While a pope exercised absolute power on two levels, as chief of government and as supreme pontiff of the Roman faith, his authority was at the same time limited by two characteristics inherent in the Papacy as a political institution: the fact that the sovereign was not hereditary but elected; and its corollary, that his reign tended to be brief because he was usually an old man when elected. Despite their conservatism in ideological matters, the Papal States represented in the political arena a mercurial force unencumbered by the long-term dynastic aims whose patient furtherance gave a sense of continuity to the policies pursued by the Spanish, French, and Austrian monarchies. Whereas Louis XV and Frederick the Great reigned 59 and 46 years respectively, the period from the former's accession in 1715 to the latter's death in 1786 saw no fewer than eight different occupants of the Holy See. Overhauled and inaugurated anew every few years by a man on the verge of senility, who had to rush through his program if he wanted to see it implemented at all, papal policy accordingly proceeded on the one hand by fits and starts and on the other, in the day-by-day administration of its territories, at the snail's pace dictated by its unwieldly system of government-by-congregation. Some of these entities, staffed by ill-trained clerics and as a rule presided over by a cardinal, looked after purely canonical affairs, while others, like the Congregation of Good Government and that of Accounts, corresponded in function but not in efficiency to the Ministry of Trade and Commerce in worldlier states. These sluggish organs further inhibited the metabolism of a body politic that was already straining to heal the scars left by the Jesuits' struggle against the Jansenists and

Gallicans, and to throw off the virus of Rationalism. "The Pope gives the orders," it used to be said in those days, "the cardinals refuse to obey, and the people do as they please"—"*Il papa comanda, i cardinali disobbediscono, e il popolo fa quel che gli pare.*" It is no wonder that there emanated from this state an aura of sloth and corruption that was commented upon by visitors from the well-governed Grand Duchy of Tuscany and Kingdom of Sardinia, and by practically all foreigners. "The government is so bad," De Brosses wrote in 1740, "that one could not imagine a worse one if one tried. Whereas Machiavelli and Thomas More amused themselves by devising utopias, one finds here the opposite notion turned into reality. Imagine, if you will, a population made up in equal parts of priests, of men who hold no steady job, and of others who do no work at all; [a country] without agriculture, commerce, or industry, and that in the midst of a fertile region and on the banks of a navigable river; a ruler who is invariably an old man with but a few years left, as often as not incapable of undertaking anything on his own, and surrounded by relatives whose only thought is to look after themselves while there is yet time, in a place where every change of government is marked by the arrival of new thieves to replace the old ones who have filled their pockets."[2]

More restrictive intellectually but more easygoing in its daily routine than elsewhere in Europe, life in the Papal States had a texture all its own. In Potsdam and Dresden and at other temporal courts, careers were for all practical purposes made and unmade by the sovereign. Ideological and even personal factors could if necessary be brushed aside by a wave of the royal hand, as they were in the occasional employment of Protestants and Jews in Catholic courts or in the appointment and dismissal of official mistresses. In eighteenth-century Rome, however, the roads to failure were many, and the traps along them nicely camouflaged. One did not have to be on the wrong side of the great gulf that separated the *papabili* from the *non-papabili*, or the Jesuits from the members of lesser orders, or even those who had been mending their fences at home from those who were sent on missions abroad, in order to fall afoul of an establishment which replenished itself, in striking contrast to temporal monarchies, from the ranks not only of the well-born but of the pious, the scholarly, and the merely harmless. When the conclave of 1740 had lasted several months and the candidates supported by Austria, France, and Spain, respectively, had fought each other to a standstill, someone remembered that Prospero Lambertini, hitherto not considered *papabile* at all, had jokingly recommended himself to his fellow-cardinals with the words: "If you are looking for a saint, take Gotti; if you are looking for a politician, take Aldroandi; if you want a good fellow, take me!" (The term he actually used, "*un buon coglione*," was much cruder.) Lambertini, who did a perfectly creditable job as Benedict XIV, was neither the first nor the last pope elected not for what he could do, but for what he would presumably leave undone. In this respect, being a candidate for the Papacy was not unlike running for President of the United States: one had to be not only a competent man, but a man able to hide his ambition and competence from a section of the electorate.

Some of the most influential Romans who became Winckelmann's friends were precisely such men who had failed to hide their light under a bushel. After meeting Michelangelo Giacomelli in 1756, Winckelmann wrote with unwonted modesty that he had just made the acquaintance of a "great mathematician, physicist, poet, and Greek scholar, by whom I gladly acknowledge myself vanquished in these fields." A strikingly good-looking *monsignore*, blue-eyed and blond and with an ease of manner gained in various diplomatic posts, Giacomelli had given free rein to his profane inclinations by publishing a translation of Aristophanes. Taken to task by his superiors, he cited St. Jerome and other Church Fathers in his defense, but was nonetheless forced to make amends by translating St. Chrysostom's treatise on the priesthood. Benedict XIV made him Secretary of Papal Briefs on account of his knowledge of canon law and his fine command of Latin. Giacomelli might have received a red hat if he had not stumbled again in letting himself be persuaded, by a flattering appeal to his scholarship, to become Cardinal Fabroni's librarian. That cardinal had been one of the zealots responsible for a number of measures which so heightened the tension between the Holy See and the Catholic powers that it had to be relieved, in the end, by the suppression of the Jesuits sixty years later. By allying himself with the intransigent Fabroni, Giacomelli incurred the enmity of the moderates, who were about to gain the ascendancy in the inner councils of the Vatican. In the course of time he became as reactionary as his master, whom Winckelmann's friend Wilhelm Muzel-Stosch once characterized as "a persecutor if ever there was one; by persecutor, I mean that he is ignorant, pigheaded, inhuman, and evil in every sense of the word." Giacomelli died in 1774, an embittered and forgotten man who had joined forces with the wrong man at the wrong time. Although his hobby had brought him only grief, he remained fond of classical literature, and passed on to Winckelmann many astute observations on the languages he had studied. Among these was the remark that Greek is so dignified and yet pliable a tongue that writers could express in it both the sublimest thoughts and the earthiest details, while Latin and Italian tend to blur at the extremes, becoming rhetorical at the highest and flat at the lowest end of the semantic spectrum. "Imagine posterity," Winckelmann quotes him as saying, "acquiring any knowledge of our customs, way of life, clothing, etc., from *our*

XII. *Corpse of a Pompeiian (plaster-of-Paris cast).*

XIII. *Casa dei Vettii, Pompeii, partially restored.*

XIV. *Hercules as a boy, Pompeiian fresco.*

xv. *Casa dei Vettii, Pompeii: the kitchen.*

xvi. *Greek vase, showing the fall of Troy.*

XVII. *Villa Albani (front view), Rome, showing typical eighteenth-century garden.*

XVIII. *Villa Albani, detail of façade.*

XIX. *Villa Albani, sculpture gallery.*

xx. *Villa Albani, Galleria Nobile, with statuary, reliefs, and mosaics on wall.*

XXI. *Winckelmann in his fur coat. Painting by A. von Maron.*

poets, as we have come to know those of the ancients from
theirs!" The two hundred years which separate Montale from
Metastasio have, if anything, sharpened the contrast.

Another case of an intelligent and ambitious priest mis-
reading the signs was that of Winckelmann's employer. The
scholarly scion of a noble family of Fossombrone near Naples,
Domenico Passionei as a young man had been sent on diplomatic
errands to The Hague, Lucerne, and Vienna, and brought back
from these missions so many books and manuscripts that his
library came to be second only to Bünau's. He took to calling
himself the "Head Librarian of Europe," and bibliophiles
everywhere were delighted to see him appointed Director of the
Vatican Library in 1756. Like so many collectors, he had a number of endearing foibles, including that of "forgetting" to return
borrowed volumes (as a cardinal, he was allowed to borrow
from the library of any religious order, even those in which the
Apostolic injunction *"de non extrahendo"* was otherwise enforced). The grand-seigneurial poise that was his by birth and
position enabled him to brush off like so many flies those authors
whom he disliked for personal reasons or on account of their
works. When the Canon Alexius Mazzocchi, whom we shall
meet again among the would-be archaeologists who made such
a mess of the excavations at-Herculaneum and Pompeii, inquired whether a book of his had been purchased by Passionei,
the latter replied that if Mazzocchi wanted to see his book in
the library, he would have to spare the owner the trouble of
going out to buy it. Having heard several such tales about the
"Pasha of Fossombrone," Winckelmann looked forward with
some trepidation to his first meeting with this man who had been
so instrumental in bringing him to Rome. When the confrontation could no longer be postponed, he was taken aback to discover in the Cardinal a courtly old gentleman "who received
me," as he reported to Bünau, "with an exquisite politeness . . .

F

and as a guest, that is to say, with a scholar's consideration for a fellow-scholar. Roman ceremoniousness does not extend to the domestic life of these gentry. Although his library is not public, all visitors have been told by His Eminence himself not to doff their hats or rise when he enters the room. He informed me of this rule even as he led me to the shelves and showed me his manuscripts." It is not recorded whether Bünau, who had mistrusted Winckelmann ever since the latter's change of religion, really believed him when he wrote that Passionei regretted not having learned German as a young man, if only because it now deprived him of the pleasure of reading the *Reichshistorie*. Winckelmann's flattery of Bünau, in any event, was no more ingenious than Passionei's courtesy to Winckelmann, whom he invited to table and took on drives about Rome, at the conclusion of which, having been returned to his own apartments in the Vatican, Passionei would order the coachman to take his guest home. The former schoolteacher admitted that the sight of the black carriage stopping before the house in which he lived on the Pincio, with the liveried servant awaiting his pleasure, made him wish that the school superintendent of the Mark Brandenburg could see him now.

Passionei was a collector's collector, who refused to have books catalogued because he considered it a point of honor to know where each volume was shelved, and who received visitors in person rather than have them referred to the librarians in his employ. However, his idiosyncrasies began to get the better of him when he allowed his hatred of the Jesuits (which caused him to veto, for the fifth and final time, the canonization of Cardinal Bellarmin, the great pamphleteer of the Counter Reformation) to affect his acquisitions for the Vatican library. His detestation of the order was such that he refused to have delivered to the palace any book printed under its auspices. He liked to begin his day by leafing through recent acquisitions, and had accordingly instructed his valet Giacomino to put all new books on a table, where they lay arranged in the order in which they arrived from the various European presses. The Pope, who knew of this habit, wanted to tease his friend one day, and had Giacomino smuggle in a certain Jesuit publication, telling him to make sure that it would be prominently displayed on that table. The Cardinal had no sooner seen the imprint *S.J.* the next morning than he rang for the valet and had him open the window. Passionei grabbed the book, and although by then a stoutish man in his sixties, rushed to the window and with a mighty curse heaved out the offensive object. His Holiness, whose chambers were situated across the courtyard, had been watching the scene and made the sign of the cross over the crumpled volume.

It was the kind of joke that the Pope could better afford to play than the Cardinal, whose star began to wane in measure as his hostility to the Jesuits, his Francophilia (a trait that Voltaire admired and Winckelmann disliked in him), and his numerous other prejudices became known. He was intelligent; unfortunately, he was also an intellectual, who shared the breed's frequent inability to repress a witticism even though he knew that it was imprudent as well as unkind to indulge in it. He therefore made many enemies, and when the conclave of 1758 met to select a successor to Benedict XIV, Passionei received only eighteen votes although he was, on the face of it, far and away the leading contender. No other candidate could match his first-hand knowledge of foreign countries, his scholarly reputation, his irreproachable way of life, and his record as a proselytizer who had not only helped convert Winckelmann but had shown the path of righteousness to an intimate of the great Leibnitz, the historian Johann Georg von Eckhart. Faced with the end of his career because he was too old by now to be considered a contender in future conclaves, Passionei threw off the caution that was worn like a cloak by those who still nurtured aspirations to the papal tiara. He reverted to his natural stance of a liberal and somewhat catty cleric, pretending occasionally to be a Jansenist merely in order to shock the faithful. It is sad to relate that Winckelmann, who had been in Rome several years by then, disengaged himself from this protector as soon as the latter's prospects began to dim.

II

Indeed, the man who now learned to walk the tightrope of ecclesiastical politics bore little resemblance to the rustic youth who had offered his services to the school board of Seehausen. It is a pity that he could not have read, while taking the measure of his new environment, the comments of an acquaintance of his who had also made his way in Rome. "The man fit to make a fortune in this ancient capital of Italy," Giacomo Casanova explained when writing his memoirs toward the end of the century, "must be a chameleon sensitive to all the colors which the light casts on his surroundings. He must be flexible, insinuating, a great dissimulator, impenetrable, obliging, often base, ostensibly sincere, always pretending to know less than he does, keeping to one tone of voice, patient, in complete control of his countenance, cold as ice when another in his place would be on fire; and if he is so unfortunate as not to have religion in his heart, he must have it in his mind, and, if he is an honest man, accept the painful necessity of admitting to himself that he is a hypocrite. If he loathes the pretense, he should leave Rome and seek his fortune in England."[3] Winckelmann would have agreed wholeheartedly. He might even have realized, with a shock of self-recognition, that his whole previous life could be seen in the light of an apprenticeship in just these skills—even if he would apply them not to his own advancement, but in the service of what had become his mission in life: proclaiming the exemplariness of classical Greek art to a world awed by the baroque and enchanted by the rococo. Doubtless it was such a flash of insight that now prompted him to write to Bianconi that if the Good Lord continued to grant him life and health, he would be able to exclaim: "Fate, I have mastered you!"—"*Superavi te, fortuna!*" Proud words, quoted from Cicero. But they could well have been uttered by the athletic-looking man who, a copy of the *Iliad* in his right hand, gazes out at us so calmly from the portrait that Mengs painted of him at this time. Although he complained that his hair had lately begun to thin and that he needed glasses for reading, he was in excellent condition for one who had lived through so much anguish. Agile rather than powerfully built, he had avoided, by dint of hard work and sensible habits, the excess weight and the slackening of mental alertness that frequently mark the onset of middle age. And it was well that he had done so, for he needed steady nerves in order to convert this brief sojourn in Rome into a permanent residence, and to guard his hard-won independence against encroachments from whatever side.

It was threatened above all by Archinto, now a cardinal and Governor of Rome—a position which combined the job of chief of police with that of supreme judge of the criminal court. Believing, as Bianconi had in Dresden, that he had a legitimate claim on the time of this man whom he had helped convert, Archinto now urged Winckelmann to enter his own or Passionei's service forthwith as a librarian. His recalcitrant protégé insisted, however, that he first had to familiarize himself with the city. Without bothering to ask Archinto's advice, he took a room in the Palazzo Zuccari, in the artists' quarter, which was still under the Spanish ambassador's jurisdiction (a connection preserved in "Spanish Steps" and Piazza di Spagna). It was a wise choice for a writer and art critic. Salvator Rosa lived around one corner in Via Gregoriana; Piranesi around the other, in the building that now houses Eleanora Garnett's boutique in Via Sistina; Mengs was practically across the street; Goldoni not far away in Via Condotti. By instinct or plain good fortune, Winckelmann had settled in one of the most desirable locations in all of Rome, near Trinità dei Monti, from where he could overlook the whole city, within a stone's throw of what is now the Hotel Hassler. The region's artistic center was the Villa Borghese, and, closer by, the Villa Medici, which had just been redecorated by the Baron de St. Odile and still contained the *Niobe* which is now in the Uffizî in Florence. Its social center was the Café Greco, frequented in these and later years by Casanova, Goethe, Keats, Leopardi, Schopenhauer, Gogol, and Berlioz, not to mention countless others who merely came to look and listen.

Winckelmann was just about to give in to Archinto's urgings that he begin work, when providence came to his aid in the form of a papal audience that the indefatigable Bianconi had arranged through a letter to the Pope's physician. On January 17, 1756, he was received by Benedict XIV, in a private audience during which he asked permission to examine the Greek manuscripts in the Vatican Library. It was a modest request, readily granted by Benedict, who was not only a jovial man with the gift of putting at their ease all who approached him, but himself a scholar of considerable achievement. But since only he and the Pope knew what had been discussed between them, and the latter was unlikely to divulge it because he had more important matters to think about, Winckelmann cagily let it be known only that their talk had been long and cordial and that His Holiness had dispensed him, as a mark of special favor, from kissing his slipper. It was just the sort of thing that Benedict might do, the self-styled *buon coglione* who was as popular in his time as that other favorite of the non-Catholic world, John XXIII, was to be in ours. Even so, Winckelmann's version of what had transpired between them was a heady concoction of insolence and cunning, brewed by a recent convert who had only arrived in Rome eight weeks ago with fifty or a hundred *scudi* to his name. But it worked: "They have to treat me with kid gloves," he gloated in a letter to Francke, who was still cataloguing books in far-off Nöthnitz, "because they have no idea of what we talked about and what the Holy Father promised me."

Archinto and Passionei backed off and let him alone. In fact, the finesse had worked so well that Winckelmann was now emboldened to play trump: "I belong to those," he loudly protested when being kept waiting on one of his rare visits to Archinto, "who value the one treasure that is shared by all rational beings: time. I have no intention of wasting it by counting the tiles in the floor of this room, and I am telling you"—it was in the antechamber of the Governor's palace, and one can fairly see the shocked petitioners and hangers-on trying to shut him up—"that I will not come back." In reality, of course, it was not he but Archinto who held all the high cards, and it did not take Winckelmann long to realize that he could not afford to make an enemy of so powerful a man. His bluff was unwittingly called by an old nemesis, Frederick the Great, who in 1756 invaded and quickly occupied Saxony, in what turned out to be the opening campaign of the Seven Years' War. Winckelmann was disturbed. He had not only grown fond of Dresden, but had every reason to believe that the Saxon treasury would no longer be able to pay the modest stipend that had enabled him to preserve the fiction of not needing a job. To make matters worse, Archinto, for whose benefit the game was being staged, was now appointed Papal Secretary of State. About to be hoist on his own petard, Winckelmann was tempted to make peace with Archinto and accept the job that he and Passionei had so long held out to him. But his nerves held. Although so short of money that he considered taking orders and entering a monastery, he continued to deal with Archinto as if he were his equal, by offering to look after his library, provided that he were given an apartment in the Secretary of State's official residence, the Palazzo della Cancelleria.

With a somnambulist's sureness of foot, he had again taken the right step. Against all probability, Rauch and Bianconi managed to send him some money after all, and Winckelmann was now able to play the comedy through to the end. Refusing to accept a salary from Archinto ("in order to show him what I think," as he put it, "and have him be obliged to me rather than placing myself under an obligation to him"), he only requested that a new bed be put in his room because the old one was too hard. It was an odd stipulation to make for someone as indifferent to creature comforts as he had trained himself to be, but was symptomatic of the calm, to use his own favorite metaphor, that he had preserved in the midst of the storm. It is not clear whether Archinto, who with all Europe aflame had other worries on his mind, accepted this offer at face value or whether the old diplomat was merely amused at the speed with which the sheep had donned wolf's clothing. Perhaps he was even big enough to realize that Winckelmann's intransigence was partly motivated by the desire, conscious or otherwise, to erase the embarrassing memory of a nameless schoolteacher-turned-librarian who had once shown a Papal Nuncio through Bünau's library. Winckelmann, in any event, who had left the Palazzo Zuccari by then and moved in with the Danish

F*

sculptor Hans Wiedewelt, now settled in a five-room apartment in the Cancelleria, with the mellifluous title of "Librarian to His Eminence the Cardinal Secretary of State," which he earned by making a few perfunctory inspections of Archinto's library.

Winckelmann's introduction to the art world of Dresden, which had taken place under Oeser's auspices, is paralleled by the guidance he received in Rome from a very different but no less flamboyant mentor: Anton Raphael Mengs, to whom he would pay tribute in the *History of Ancient Art* as he had once acknowledged his debt to Oeser in the "Reflections." Anton Raphael was the son of Ismael Mengs, a Danish-born miniature painter, who must have been an extraordinarily tyrannical father even for that authoritarian century, because he forced all three of his children to follow in his footsteps. Juliana Charlotte became a miniaturist and eventually entered a convent; Theresa Concordia, also a painter, married the Austrian portraitist Anton von Maron; their brother Anton Raphael, who once stated matter-of-factly that he had been thrashed until he became an artist—*"zur Kunst geprügelt"*—continued the tradition by making a painter of his own daughter Anna Maria. He was, at any rate, the only member of the family whose talents were equal to the career on which they had all been so forcibly launched.

Born near Dresden in 1728, Mengs had been instructed in the rudiments of drawing by his father, in Rome, where the teen-age boy was on one occasion locked up in the Vatican *stanze* in order to make him copy the frescos of the Raphael after whom he had been named. After his return to Dresden, he did portraits of Augustus III and of the castrato Domenico Annibali, who sang the contralto parts in the court opera; these commissions, in turn, led to Mengs's appointment as the King's painter while still in his early twenties. On his second stay in

Rome, in 1748, he was casting about for a model for his *Holy Family* when he chanced one day to see a pretty girl on the street. "There is the Madonna I have been looking for!"—"*Ecco la Madonna che tanto cerco*"—he exclaimed, and invited the startled creature forthwith to visit him in his studio. Coming from a handsome young foreigner, it was not the kind of flattery that passed unnoticed in eighteenth-century Rome. Margareta Guazzi, eighteen and beautiful but poor, came the next morning with her mother and duly sat for him. Mengs married her a few months later and took her to Dresden, where he had been offered a salary of 1,000 *Taler*, five times the stipend later granted to Winckelmann. When various panels and ceilings were assigned to local artists during the inauguration of the Hofkirche that year, the place of honor above the high altar was reserved for Mengs, who had submitted the sketch of an *Assumption*. Declaring that he had to go to Rome in order to execute the work in the manner of his masters Raphael and Correggio, he left Dresden for good in 1752, with the Elector's promise that his salary would continue to be paid. As *Premier Peintre du Roi de Pologne,* he had no difficulty in establishing himself as the city's leading portraitist. By the time Winckelmann presented to him the letter of recommendation that he had been given in Dresden, Mengs had become a member of the Academy of Saint Luke, or painters' association, and a professor in the Capitoline Academy founded by Benedict; Lord Percy had commissioned him to copy Raphael's *School of Athens* for Northumberland House; and Frederick the Great was thinking of purchasing some of his originals.

Although preordained to some extent by their common dependence on the Court of Dresden and by the fact that they were both converts, Winckelmann's friendship with Mengs was enhanced by personal and professional considerations as well. Mengs's was the only Roman house in which the other, who had to step so warily between the conflicting claims of his own ambition and those made on him by his clerical patrons, could relax and feel at home. He was accepted as a member of the family by Mengs himself, by Margareta, by the painter's sisters, who were permanent house guests, and even by the irascible Ismael, who had followed his talented son to Rome. "Without Mengs," he wrote, "I would have been as in a desert in this place, where I had no addresses. I spend most of my time with him, especially in the evenings . . . It is only with him that I have coffee, and I even leave my books and manuscripts at his place." During his first Roman winter while he still lived in the Palazzo Zuccari, these informal daily contacts were facilitated by a wooden archway, long since taken down, that connected the palazzo with Mengs's house. Even after he had moved in with Wiedewelt, Winckelmann said that whenever he felt like enjoying himself and drinking in company, he would visit Mengs (perhaps a dubious blessing for the latter, bestowed on him by a man who as time went on often went to bed "loaded"—"*beladen*").[4]

It was Mengs who introduced Winckelmann to Giacomelli and other lights in the city's artistic and scholarly circles. More importantly, it was he who helped Winckelmann decide what he would do in Rome. The ostensible reason for his journey had been to continue his study of art while working as a librarian, and to keep the Court informed about the discoveries at Herculaneum, in which the Saxon royal family had taken an interest ever since its purchase of the so-called *Vestal Virgins*. Bianconi, who in order to strengthen his own position in Dresden insisted on personally presenting to Frederick Christian and Maria Antonia the archaeological news items that Winckelmann sent from Italy, had planned to have him and Mengs travel to Naples together. The one was to examine the excavations, the other to paint a portrait of Maria Amalia, a Saxon princess until her marriage to Charles III, King of the Two Sicilies. When this excursion continued to be postponed by his chronic lack of funds, by Mengs's inability to finish the *Assumption,* and in the end by the war which temporarily severed all connections between Saxony and Rome, Winckelmann began to concentrate on his own projects. His instinct and interests drew him to the study of art; in view of the uncertain political situation, however, he kept for some time a second string to his bow by continuing his work in the ancient literatures. But he soon found that "there is nothing original left to do in the field of Greek letters." Thwarted in his desire to see Herculaneum, and reluctant to be a librarian except to the extent required for his financial survival, he began to collaborate with Mengs on essays dealing with the aesthetics of the Greek sculptors and the restoration of antique statues. His reading, accordingly, shifted in emphasis from literature to the examination and collation of what the ancients had written on painting and sculpture.

Winckelmann's decision to concentrate on art was reinforced by a discovery he made very soon after his arrival, namely, that the Romans among whom he had come to settle knew very little about the treasures deposited in their museums and galleries. Believing that these included some of the finest examples of Greek sculpture, of inestimable value both as records of the past and as models to be followed by living artists and others yet to be born, he began to compile an inventory of these works. From this material he created, haphazardly at first and later with ever-increasing purposefulness, the comprehensive analysis of Greek civilization contained in the *History.* What made his task more formidable was his conviction that the ethical function and timelessness of great art can be grasped only by a beholder who is able to rise to a level of receptivity analogous to that attained by someone who is vouchsafed divine revelation. Whereas Bernard de Montfaucon in *L'Antiquité expliquée et représentée en figures* (1719) and Jonathan Richardson, Jr., in his *Account of the Statues, Basreliefs, Drawings and Pictures in Italy, France, etc.* (1721) had merely described these objects without any reference to their authenticity, value, or chronology, Winckelmann emphasized that the works of men like Phidias, Polyclitus, and Praxiteles produce in the viewer more than a vaguely pleasing impression. They affect him as an educational, indeed as a moral force in cleansing him of imperfections of the soul and the impurities of ephemeral fashion. In the young, in particular, the examination of these works establishes a lifelong receptivity to what is genuine and great. Classical art raises the beholder to an altogether higher sphere, and Winckelmann's reaction to the *Apollo Belvedere* —"I forget all else over the sight of this miraculous work of art, and assume a more exalted position myself in order to be worthy of this sight"[5]— has since been echoed by others who similarly felt the obligation placed upon them by Perfection Beheld. Thus, Rilke has the poem *Archäischer Torso Apollos* end in the reflection "You must change your life"—*"Du musst dein Leben ändern."* This didactic function of great art presupposes the existence of a rather precise scale of aesthetic valuation. Clearly, one cannot formulate and hand down to posterity an ideal without first defining its components: simplicity and grandeur, a harmony based on the avoidance of extremes, or whatever else they may be.

No one could have been better qualified to help Winckelmann in this work than Mengs: a practicing artist, an informed admirer of the ancients, a fellow-resident of Rome, and a friend with whom he could speak in his native tongue. Yet the task that Winckelmann set himself was a heady one to be assumed by a young foreigner—he was not yet forty, Mengs barely thirty —who set out to challenge the prevailing fashion of his time and, specifically, the style-setting influence of Paris. It demanded the best that he had to offer, and he knew it. "I am working on a little manuscript now," he told a friend, "which is destined to be the precursor of a larger one. This little work, however, requires six months in order to reach the greatest possible perfection. I am endeavoring to create something original, something of my own." To another, he confided that he could give all sorts of miscellaneous news of Rome, "pages of it, with no effort at all. But I want to wait until I have done something that may be worthy of being transmitted to future generations. I shall weigh every expression, as on a scale." There is a new tone in these statements, a sense of mission if not destiny. To this mission Winckelmann subordinated all else until his departure for Naples in 1758. He sacrificed to it his comfort, walking many miles a day between his apartment and the great Roman libraries to which he had gained admission: the Vaticana, Passionei's on the Quirinal, that of the Jesuits' Collegium Romanum, and, the most rewarding of all in the field of art history, the Corsini Collection of engravings and paintings housed in Christina of Sweden's former residence, the Palazzo Riario. He sacrificed to it his good name, being taken for a necromancer when caught disturbing some graves in his search for ancient inscriptions, and his physical safety: on one occasion, he narrowly escaped injury when the head of a statue he had been examining broke off and landed crashing at his feet. He sacrificed to it his financial security, precarious at best and now endangered by book orders placed with Italian and foreign publishers, and even the sartorial freedom normally granted to tourists: from the middle of 1757 on, he wore a wig and went about in clerical garb—black silk cloak with white-edged blue bands, and dark velvet trousers.

In fulfilling Passionei's wishes that he don this costume, he also took on the proper protective coloring for someone who was enough of an insider to be invited to dinner by the Cardinal Secretary of State, and yet enough of a free agent, since he had not taken orders, to attend the ballet if he felt like it. Nor were these sacrifices merely external. Learning to curb his temper, he became a mediator who defused a number of potential quarrels. He maintained amicable relations with the two Mengses, father and son, although he lamented that it cost him great effort to do so; he praised Passionei's library to Bünau and Bünau's to Passionei without offending either; and he cheered up Hagedorn, who wanted Mengs to review the *Lettre à un amateur,* while calming the latter, who resented the request because he had barely been mentioned in the work. Winckelmann even managed such specifically Roman feats of adaptation as sleeping despite the nocturnal singing and arguing in the street, taking along his own cutlery and napkin when eating in public places, and distinguishing between good wines and the adulterated ones that go by the euphemism of *vini sofisticati.* In short, he so ordered his life that all possible sources of friction with his environment were reduced to a minimum, not from timidity or lack of interest, but because he needed to conserve his time. What little remained of it after a day's work was spent with friends like Father Contucci of the Jesuits' Museum of Antiquities; the papal chaplain Antonio Baldani, who corrected his Italian (forceful and increasingly picturesque as time went on, but never perfect as he had only begun to speak it in his late thirties); and the Marchese Gian Pietro Locatelli, custodian of the Capitoline Museum and host at these learned *conversazioni.* Besides all this, there were commissions to be executed for others, such as Oeser, who wanted to know how many copies had been made of Raphael's *Holy Family.* Perhaps it was on one of these errands that his eyes were opened to the natural glories of Rome: "This is the time to see the gardens in and around the city," he wrote Francke in the spring of 1756; "You have no idea, my friend, how beautiful nature is in this land! You walk through shady laurel woods, down avenues of tall cypresses and along latticed orange groves a quarter of a mile long . . . The better I get to know Rome, the more I like it." There was old business to be taken care of in his correspondence with Bünau and Walther, and there were new contacts to be made with such men as Johann Georg Wille, a Swiss who had become engraver to the King of France and published a translation of the "Reflections" in Paris, and the Baron Philipp von Stosch, owner of a famous gem collection to whom Winckelmann had sent a complimentary copy of that essay. Finally and most important of all, there were fences to be kept mended vis-à-vis his two cardinals, whom he played off one against the other even as he busied himself sporadically in their libraries.

He had agreed to be a guest at Archinto's table once a week and twice weekly at that of Passionei, whom he preferred as a person although he could not afford to be too closely identified with him because the Eminences had lately taken a dislike to each other. Even so, he accepted Passionei's invitations to his summer retreat above the ruins of Cicero's Tusculum, on a hillside near Frascati where the whole Roman plain lay at his feet and the sea, a sliver of silver, could be seen glittering on the horizon. The guests stayed in cells dispersed among the greenery—each with his name on the door—and met in the main building, where they assembled for dinner as they happened to be dressed, sometimes in shirt and slippers. Although they were presided over by a Prince of the Church, no conversational holds were barred at these reunions, which occasionally included Voltaire's friend Madame du Boccage, as well as Paolo Maria Paciaudi, a fashionable preacher who was fond of reminiscing about the high point of his life—when he had traveled to Paris in order to present the red hat to Cardinals Rohan and

Choiseul. It was, in fact, the company's Francophilia, as much as the fear of antagonizing Archinto, that eventually caused Winckelmann to renounce these rare occasions.

"I can be satisfied with my life," he informed Berendis at this time, in a letter which lays bare much of the gold and the dross in the man's soul, his humility and ambition, his common sense and otherworldliness, his cosmopolitanism and intolerance, and that curious blend of comradeship and homosexuality which characterized the emotional side of his nature. "I have no worries other than my work," he continued,

and have even found someone with whom I can speak of love: a good-looking, blond young Roman of sixteen, half a head taller than I am; but I only see him once a week, when he dines with me on Sunday evening. Now I only wish that you were here with the young Count [Bünau's son]. I could show you the beauties of ancient and modern times better than all the anti-quaries of Rome, who are ignoramuses, and your stay here would cost you less than in a German university town, except for a hired carriage, which is essential because the place is so big. See if you can't find the means [to join me here]. Compared to Rome, all else is nothing. You don't know half of it. Until this point we have followed one another: I always went ahead [i.e., from Seehausen to Halle and thence to Nöthnitz], now it is your turn to catch up once more. I thought I knew it all, and lo and behold! when I arrived here, I found that I am ignorant and that all the scribes are fools and asses. I am a smaller man now than I was when leaving the school for Bünau's library. If you want to understand humanity, this is the place in which to do so. Incredibly talented minds, men of the highest gifts, beauties of great character, such as the Greeks had formed them . . . Since freedom such as it is known in other states and republics is a mere shadow compared to what it is here (paradoxical as that may seem to you), there is even a different way of thinking in Rome. But people like these have little regard for foreigners who rush through the city, and as a result, the French are laughed at everywhere . . . I am saying this only because I know that you have been bitten by the French bug, an evil that is not easily exorcised in German courts, where a French clown is esteemed higher than a genuine German . . . Everything that I am setting down here will be demonstrated in a special work, in the future, when my reputation in the world will be more solidly founded than it is now.[6]

III

Winckelmann had no way of telling that this work on which he concentrated, to the exclusion of so much else, would turn out to be the *History of Ancient Art.* It grew under his hands so quickly that it soon absorbed the essays—then in various stages of completion—on which he had begun to collaborate with Mengs. Only two of these, the series on the statues in the Belvedere and the "Treatise on the Restoration (of Antique Statues)," were actually finished, and in the latter case published separately as *Abhandlung über die Ergänzungen.* The other essays, including that on the aesthetics of the Greek sculptors, were eventually incorporated into the *History.*

Designed by Bramante, the Belvedere is a terrace in the Vatican which contains an octagonal courtyard with a fountain and much greenery. Of the many statues with which the popes beginning with Julius II had adorned this courtyard and the adjoining rooms, four so fascinated Winckelmann that he devoted a few pages to each. The first of his *Beschreibungen,* or "Descriptions," that of the *Apollo,* was ready to be sent to Stosch and other correspondents as early as the summer of

1756. There followed those of the *Laocoön,* a variation on the theme first played in the "Reflections," and of the so-called *Antinoüs,* too cloyingly lyrical in its praise of youthful male beauty to fit this particular statue (which, as the author himself began to suspect before long, does not represent Hadrian's favorite but perhaps a Hermes or Meleager). The most rewarding for us is the "Description of the Belvedere Torso," first published in a German journal as *Beschreibung des Torso im Belvedere zu Rom* (1759), and later reprinted in the *History.* In any event, both the statue and Winckelmann's interpretation of it have stood the test of changing times and tastes better than the magnificent, but irredeemably antiquated prose hymn devoted to the *Apollo Belvedere.*

"I offer you here a description of the celebrated Belvedere Torso, commonly called the Torso of Michelangelo because that sculptor thought especially highly of this piece. It is known to be the fragment of a seated Hercules, made by Apollonius, son of Nestor, of Athens." After some preliminary remarks culminating in the statement, so characteristic of Winkelmann's no-nonsense approach to the study of art, that "it is not enough to say that something is beautiful; one should also know to what extent and for what reason it is so,"[7] he takes us—by the hand, so to speak—to the

much-lauded and never yet sufficiently praised torso of a Hercules, a work that is the most perfect of its kind and should be reckoned among the greatest of those that have come down to us. But how am I going to go about describing it, seeing that it has lost its most beautiful and significant portions? Like a magnificent oak that has been felled and stripped of branches and foliage so that only the trunk is left, the sculpted hero sits here maltreated and mutilated, with head, arms, legs, and the upper part of his chest gone. The first glance may show you no more than a misshapen stone. But if you can penetrate its secrets, you will discover a miraculous example of art, provided that you contemplate it calmly. Then Hercules will appear to you as if in the midst of his labors, and the hero will become visible along with the demigod. The artist began at the point where the poets left off. *They* fell silent as soon as the hero had been admitted to the Olympians and betrothed to the goddess of eternal youth. *He* presents him to us in deified shape, with an immortal body as it were, which has nonetheless preserved the strength and suppleness that he needed for his great deeds.

In the powerful outline of this physique, I see the matchless strength of the conquerer of the mighty giants, who had risen up against the gods and were subdued by him on the Phlegrean Fields; and at the same time the smooth contours of this outline, which render the body's structure so flexible, remind me of how supple he was in the fight with Acheloüs, who could not escape his hands no matter what shape he took . . . Each part of the body shows the hero engaged in a particular labor . . . I cannot look at what little remains of his shoulders without remembering that their tensed strength supported, like two mountains, the whole weight of the universe. [While Atlas went off to fetch the Apples of the Hesperides, Hercules, in what is generally considered as the eleventh of his Twelve Labors, took on the task of carrying the Heavens.] How magnificent is the arching of that chest! . . . It must have been against a chest like this that the giant Antaeus and the three-headed Geryon were crushed . . .

Ask those who know the best in mortal perfection whether they have ever seen a flank that can compare with the left side of this statue. The motion and counter-motion of its muscles is suspended in marvelous balance by a skillfully rendered alternation of tension and release. Just as the hitherto calm surface of the sea begins to stir in the fog, with wavelets playfully swallowing one another and giving birth to new ones, so does one muscle softly swell here and pass into another while a third one, issuing from between them and seemingly enhancing their motion, disappears again and draws our eyes after it beneath the the surface . . .

If it seems inconceivable that the power of reflection be shown elsewhere than in the [missing] head, you can learn here how a master's creative hand is able to endow matter with mind. The back, which appears as if flexed in noble thought, gives me the mental picture of a head filled with the joyful remembrance of his astonishing deeds, and, as this head full of wisdom and majesty arises before my inner eye, the other missing limbs also begin to take shape in my imagination . . . The manner in which our thoughts are directed from Hercules' feats of strength to the perfection of his soul constitutes one of the mysteries of art; and the perfection of that soul is recorded in the torso as in a monument that could not have been equaled by a poet who limited himself to celebrating the strength of the hero's arms. Yet the artist surpassed the poets. There is no hint of violence or sex in this portrait [as there was in the literary treatments of Hercules as murderer of his teacher Linus, or as abductor of Iole and lover of Astydamia, Omphale, *et al.*] Rather, the body's stillness reflects a great and resolute soul, that of a man whose love of justice made him face the greatest dangers in safeguarding the security of whole lands and the peace of their inhabitants . . . The world of art weeps with me in seeing this work . . . half destroyed and cruelly maltreated. Who does not lament, on this occasion, the loss of hundreds of other masterpieces? Yet art, in wishing to instruct us further, recalls us from these sad thoughts by showing us how much might still be learned from this fragment, and how an artist should look at it.

From beginning to end, from his admission that the Torso may have little to say at first to the casual observer (as was the case with Tobias Smollett, who saw the statue in those same years and confessed that he "had not taste enough to perceive its beauties at first sight"[8]) to his belief that the modern artist can still draw inspiration from it, the passage illuminates both the factual basis and the didactic purport of Winckelmann's interpretation of art. Clearly, the concluding exhortation had been taken to heart by the author himself, when he examined this "misshapen stone" with a sculptor's feeling for perspective and tactile effects, a philologist's familiarity with the cultural and literary coordinates, a poet's command of imagery, and a psychologist's knowledge of the cerebral and affective processes involved. It is no wonder that Diderot, accustomed to the dryly enumerative tone of Richardson's *Account* and Jean-Jacques Barthélemy's *Voyage en Italie,* should have been astounded by Winckelmann's imaginativeness: *"Que ne voit-il pas,"* he asks when comparing the author with Rousseau, *"dans ce tronçon d'homme qu'on appelle le Torse . . . ?"*[9] The novelty of Winckelmann's approach lies in the fact that he not only looked, and invariably looked closer than others, but entered into the spirit of the work, in this case by reliving in his own mind those of Hercules' fabled deeds that the statue evoked in him. In so doing, he eliminates the distance that normally separates the work from the viewer, so that the former is no longer seen from without, passively, but activated through being experienced from within. Once again, we are reminded of Rilke, of the *Auftrag* presented by the *Ding,* the creative challenge issuing from the object. Generally speaking, this is no longer our way of looking at a work of art, although we cannot but respect his determination to get at its essence rather than patting it on the head with more or less felicitously chosen adjectives. But then, Winckelmann would no doubt have been equally nonplussed by a "meaningful dialogue" held on the merits of a heap of twisted iron. In its own time and place, at any rate, the little essay, borne by an enthusiasm that can still be felt across the language barrier and the gulf of two centuries, must have been irresistible.

Here, a word is in order about an aspect of Winckelmann's writing that tends to discomfit the modern reader: its exuberance. It has many and varied roots. He was a pioneer in the rediscovery of Greek sculpture and painting, and as such sometimes pointed with a discoverer's pride at works with which we have meanwhile become yawningly familiar. As the first German to write in the grand manner on art, he had to create his own critical vocabulary as he went along; inevitably, his instrument case held blunter tools than the finely calibrated ones that were already available to French and English authors. He was a frankly partisan judge, who not only praised the Torso and its companion pieces for themselves, but used them as arguments against the fashion of his own time. Like many neoclassicists, he was a Puritan at heart, who combatted the rococo not only on aesthetic grounds but because he believed that art, no longer the preserve of wealthy patrons who wished to indulge their hedonistic and often licentious inclinations, should serve to extol the pristine virtues of frankness and moral rectitude. He was an inspired teacher, not a footsore tourist, and the sentimental denizen of a century that laughed and cried more readily than ours. Lastly, he was a homosexual in inclination if not action, whose effusiveness on behalf of these male statues must be weighed against the silence that he observed, in the "Descriptions" at least, on the *Aphrodite of Cnidus,* which then stood in a niche right next to the *Apollo.* In short, the discrepancy between his attitude and ours lies less in his vision than in the position from which he viewed.

Mengs shared with Winckelmann a knowledge of anatomy and workmanship, gained as a creative artist. Much the calmer of the two, he also tried to bring Winckelmann back to earth whenever the latter's imagination threatened to take wing in disregard of the evidence. An example in point was his insistence that the *Apollo* was not, as Winckelmann believed, a Greek original (it is, in fact, a Roman reproduction of a bronze figure by Leochares, dating from about 330 B.C.). Mengs also provided technical data for the "Treatise on the Restoration," in which his friend took issue with those who had arbitrarily restored the missing parts of rediscovered statues. The art historians eventually put the restorers to flight, but the din of this long-forgotten battle, which had been joined as long before as the Renaissance and was to be fought all over again in the building of the Villa Albani, still resounds in the "Treatise" and elsewhere in Winckelmann's work. At the time, Mengs was held to have been the chief beneficiary of the collaboration. Yet the philosophical grounding of Mengs's own *Reflections on Beauty and Taste in Painting,* published anonymously in 1762 and dedicated to Winckelmann, shows that the indebtedness was mutual. The former's neoplatonic metaphysics parallels the latter's belief that the material of an art work detracts from our perception of its beauty, representing but a phase through which that beauty must pass before it becomes pure. As a living artist, however, Mengs probably resented Winckelmann's preference for antique over modern works, just as the court painter in him must have blinked at the connection, so forcefully stated in the *History,* between political democracy and artistic excellence. Their collaboration was, in any event, recognized as having been so intimate that long after their death, one Nicola Passeri of Faenza published, in 1795, five fictitious dialogues that had supposedly been held between the two in Rome.

IV

When the opportunity to visit Naples and Herculaneum finally came in early 1758, Mengs was too involved in his painting and teaching to leave Rome. Winckelmann accordingly went by himself on this, the first of four journeys he was to make to the Campanian cities. In defiance of chronology, these journeys will be considered together here as one major stage in what he had begun to call, with his newly acquired sense of mission, the "pilgrimage" of his life. He had long wanted to do field work, to observe and perhaps take a hand in the excavations that had been sporadically undertaken ever since D'Elboeuf had first begun to dig in Herculaneum. The impatience of his sponsors in Dresden, and the desire to check his theories about Greek sculpture against the evidence of recent finds made in Herculaneum, rendered the matter even more urgent.

Determined to make the most of his Neapolitan debut, he contracted with a *procaccio,* or agent, to travel in comfort, with only one other passenger, instead of taking the regular coach that left every Saturday and took five days to cover the 120 miles to Naples. The price of ten ducats included dinner and a sin-

gle room every night, the other meals and amenities being supplied by the passengers themselves. A weightier sum and one
that he could ill afford to spend was invested in new clothes,
including, as he earnestly informed Berendis, an English travel
outfit and a coat of the latest fashion, of coffee-colored Abbé-
ville cloth with gold frogs. August Wilhelm von Schlegel, who
some fifty years later accompanied Madame de Staël over the
same route, was to make fun of these sartorial preparations.
But Winckelmann, no fop despite the frequent rejuvenation of
his wardrobe, had been in Italy long enough to appreciate the
necessity of making *bella figura*—which he did so convincingly
that the King of the Two Sicilies promptly addressed him as
"M. le baron de Winckelmann." No doubt he also felt that he
owed something to the standing he had meanwhile acquired
in Rome, and to his friends, Wille in Paris and Johann Jakob
Bodmer and Hans Caspar Füssli in Zürich, who had taken up a
collection to help him defray the expenses of this trip even
though they knew him only by correspondence. Besides, he
came so well recommended that he may be pardoned for believing that he would have some entrée to court and academic
circles. Frederick Christian had written to his sister, the Queen
of the Two Sicilies, whose ambassador to Rome had in turn
alerted Bernardo Tanucci, the Prime Minister in Naples;
Archinto and Passionei had announced his impending arrival
to Count Karl Joseph von Firmian, the Austrian envoy and a
collector of antiquities, who had long wanted to meet the author
of the "Reflections"; Bianconi and Rauch had sent letters on
his behalf from Dresden, and Mengs from Rome.

Instead of opening doors, these letters of introduction caused
them to be shut in Winckelmann's face. Like many men who
have to live by cultivating those in power, he had neglected to
neutralize, by some propitiatory gesture of comradeship, the
resentment that his familiarity with the high and the mighty

was bound to provoke in his equals. It was a lesson that he had learned in Nöthnitz, and successfully applied to his relationships with such men as Francke and Heyne. His failure to observe it now, whether occasioned by forgetfulness or over-confidence, was to cost him dearly. He proved to be too well-connected a visitor to be turned away at the gate, and at the same time too prestigious a man to be admitted to the excavations and to the little museum in Portici, where the more valuable finds were being kept. His fame had preceded him, and the courtiers and scholars, incompetent to a man, who were in charge of the work quickly closed ranks and kept him at arm's length in order to protect their sinecures. He breached the first line of defense in being admitted to court, but the museum staff, citing royal prohibitions against would-be thieves, refused him admittance until he obtained from Tanucci at least a temporary permit. Even so, he was specifically forbidden to make sketches or take notes. Thus, he found himself in effect sidetracked, on this first visit, to a particular aspect of the excavations: to the deciphering of the manuscripts that Camillo Paderni, the museum's director, had found in Herculaneum on October 19, 1752. These were papyrus rolls, so badly charred by the hot ashes that had fallen on the city in A.D. 79 that they disintegrated into dust at the slightest touch. It was quickly established that they were written in Greek, but only one roll, somewhat less carbonized than its fellows, could be partially read; it turned out to be a copy of an already known treatise on music, by the Epicurean philosopher Philodemus, a minor savant who had lived in Julius Caesar's time.

Having heard rumors of this sensational discovery, scholars all over Europe had meanwhile begun to wonder what the other manuscripts might contain: Sophocles' lost dramas, perhaps, or the works of an author whose very name had disappeared beneath the sands of time? Since Paderni—"an impostor," if

Winckelmann is to be believed, "foolish and ignorant, who struts about calling himself 'Doctor of Antiquities' "—had no idea what to do next, the King called in Antonio Piaggio, a former Vatican librarian who had constructed a nightmarish contraption of pigs' bladders (on which the wafer-thin material could be unfolded and glued), winches, and silk thread, with which he proposed to unroll at a snail's pace the 1800-odd scraps of manuscript that had accumulated in the museum vault. All suggestions as to speeding up the procedure, including one advanced by Winckelmann which involved the use of chemicals in order to obtain an etched reproduction of the letters, fell on the deaf ears of the Canon Mazzocchi, who had procured for himself the privilege of translating whatever texts might be deciphered. He had no intention of letting younger and abler men, and least of all a foreigner with court connections of his own, undercut this monopoly by presenting them with copper plates, which once reproduced could of course be read by anyone with a knowledge of Greek. (He need not have worried. Other and better minds, including that of Sir Humphrey Davy who spent some frustrating months in the museum in 1819, have since struggled with the papyri, only to find that it was not worth the bother—while Baudelaire, on the other hand, based his tale *Le jeune enchanteur* precisely on the fictitious deciphering of one of these documents. It was only in the early 1960's that Anton Fackelmann of Vienna devised, in the regeneration of the sheets through the sap of the papyrus plant, a method that promises to bring results.)

Rebuffed on all sides, Winckelmann made friends with Piaggio and watched him at work. He had meanwhile surreptitiously examined a sufficient number of exhibits, among them the statues of the Balbi family and some mosaics, vases, and candelabrae, to resolve some of the questions that he had been asking himself about the sequence of various phases of

Greek and Hellenistic art. Through his association with Piaggio, he now became an expert in the technical aspects of ancient writing, and in a brilliant feat of scholarship retraced in his mind the function and development of the *stylus:* the materials of which it was made, the possible shapes it could take, and the exact manner in which the ancients had used it for writing and erasing.

It was, perhaps, because he was thus forced to make the best of a bad situation that Winckelmann proceeded so eclectically in his first survey of the art works discovered in Herculaneum. After all, he had not been allowed to examine them in any detail. With the exception of two or three pieces, the sculptures in the Portici museum were in fact inferior variants of those that had already been brought to light in Rome, and Winckelmann did not know that one of the better ones, the so-called *Head of Seneca,* no more represented that philosopher than the many busts of Homer represent the poet; these busts are not portraits but types, stylizations of the Worried Thinker and the Blind Poet, respectively. More to be regretted is his early failure to appreciate the uniqueness if not the quality of the Herculanean frescos, the only major examples of antique figure painting to have been found since the discovery of the *Aldobrandini Marriage* in 1606. He praised *Achilles and Chiron,* but, lacking any organ for naturalism, disliked the *Theseus,* whose countenance struck him as rustic rather than heroic. The architectural frescos with foreshortened or otherwise adulterated perspectives found no favor in his eyes either; they reminded him too strongly of the illusionistic devices used in rococo painting. The strain of adapting his aesthetic to a new medium, from sculpture in the round to murals, led to further imbalances of judgment. Only on later visits to Herculaneum and Pompeii did he gain the more generous view of Campanian painting which is documented in his reports to Bianconi and in the

History; even then, he remained imprisoned in the web of his own prejudices. Committed on the one hand to the twin notions of the excellence of all things Greek and the moral superiority of classical over rococo art, and faced on the other hand by works that were not only mediocre but often appallingly lascivious, he consulted what was to him the last court of appeal: the ancient writers. Pliny having stated that the arts had been in a state of decadence during the early Empire, Winckelmann felt free to assign the bulk of Herculanean and Pompeiian paintings to the period of Nero.

Perplexed by the cold reception he found in Herculaneum and Portici, Winckelmann experienced a sense of disillusionment that informed his whole attitude to the Naples region and its inhabitants. He mildly disliked the latter, judging that they were too loud and altogether too fond of cheating; but if he never rose to the raptures that Naples inspired in such later visitors as Goethe and Lamartine, he did not hate the Neapolitans as much as De Brosses had done when he called them "the most abominable rabble and loathsome vermin that ever infested the earth."[10] There were even some features of their life that he found to his liking: the famous Naples cauliflower, Lacrima Christi and other local wines, and the general aura of nonchalance that seems to permeate the city. It impressed (and continues to impress) many tourists, including a contemporary of Winckelmann's, a Scotsman who described an instance of it with eyebrows visibly raised in Presbyterian wonderment at such abandon: "The [*lazzaroni*] strip themselves before the houses that front the bay, and bathe themselves in the sea without the smallest ceremony. Their athletic figures [may be seen] walking and sporting on the shore perfectly naked, and with no more idea of shame than Adam felt in his state of innocence, while the ladies from their coaches and the servant maids and young girls contemplate this singular spectacle with as little apparent emotion as the ladies in Hyde Park behold a review of the Horse Guards."[11] It is a scene that Winckelmann is the less likely to have missed as he was frequently shown around the city by friends. Already on this first visit, the spectrum of his social contacts was much broader than had been the case when he first arrived in Dresden and Rome. Winckelmann *was* somebody now, a man who might be helped or hindered in his work, but could no longer be ignored. The scholars and academicians had seen to it that his reception at court was no more than polite, no more than was due to a well-recommended visitor from Dresden, where the Queen had lived as a young girl. Count Firmian, however, introduced him to a young compatriot, Johann Jakob Volkmann of Hamburg, and urged the two of them to visit Paestum, rediscovered just then after centuries of oblivion. Winckelmann returned overwhelmed by the beauty of the temples, and convinced that they were the oldest of all surviving Greek buildings: a pardonable error for a man who never saw Greece itself. He also met Giovanni Maria della Torre, curator of the Farnese collection, and the Galianis: the Marchese Bernardo, an amateur philologist who was then as well known as his famous brother, the Abbé Ferdinando, that terribly clever little man who shortly afterward moved to Paris, where he graced many a salon as a wit and *philosophe* who had an iron in every learned fire.

Gratified as Winckelmann was to be accepted by the intelligentsia of Naples, he soon found that these contacts could not make up for the hostility that was shown him by most of the men connected with the excavations as such. They were mediocrities who did not gain on closer acquaintance, such as Mazzocchi, the leading Greek scholar among the Italians of his generation and as such the would-be translator of the papyri, but so dismal a writer that Passionei had refused to buy his works. Mazzocchi's enemy and colleague, Jacopo Martorelli, on

G

173

the other hand, was as brash as the former was timid. The author of a 734-page disquisition on the inkpots used by the ancients, Martorelli had remained unaware that the object on which he had based his whole argument had been no inkstand at all, but a jewelry box that someone had found in the excavations. In the end, Charles III forbade him to publish the work, not because it was spurious but because it contained slashing attacks on Mazzocchi, the royal favorite. Anxious to reinstate himself in the good graces of his sovereign, Martorelli devoted himself henceforth to the glorification of the Neapolitan past; in fact, he became such a fervent patriot that he ended by "proving" that Homer had not only lived in Naples but founded an academy there, so that he, Professor Martorelli, was actually occupying the chair that had once been warmed by Professor Homer. Until recently, there had also been Ottavio Antonio Bayardi, a relative of the hapless Mazzocchi and a prize fool already as a young man, when Prospero Lambertini had first made his acquaintance. "On October 16, 1730," the later Benedict XIV recalled, "in the ground-floor apartment that Cardinal Bentivoglio occupied in Albano, Bayardi, buried in a leather armchair with his left leg dangling over the right knee, explained to me after an interminable coughing fit that he had lying about, ready for the printer, forty volumes of corrections regarding the chronology of Church history." When Winckelmann arrived in Portici twenty-eight years later, Bayardi had just been dismissed for his failure to get on with a similarly expansive and useless project. Instead of cataloguing the finds made at Herculaneum, he had compiled a number of *prodromi*, or introductory essays, dealing not with the excavations but with the exploits of that Hercules after whom the town had supposedly been named. The elaborate retelling of these well-known fables created much discontent among the scholars and collectors, who were less interested in the Augean Stables just then than in what had recently been discovered underground. When these rumblings had become too loud to be disregarded, Charles III dismissed Bayardi and entrusted the work to the Academy of Herculaneum. This body of experts, established in 1755 with Mazzocchi, Martorelli, and Bernardo Galiani among the founding members, was to issue a series of volumes entitled *Antichità d'Ercolano,* the first of which appeared two years later. With their plates of statues, coins, vases, etc., these publications were instrumental in spreading to the far corners of Christendom, from Tsarskoe Selo to the Syon House in Isleworth and, indeed, to Jefferson's Monticello, the Herculanean and Pompeiian motifs that eventually found their way into the architecture, the painting, and above all the interior decoration of neoclassicism.

Although Winckelmann and the French antiquary Anne-Claude-Philippe de Caylus criticized the academy for the dilatoriness of its editorial work, the nine volumes that were eventually issued represent a milestone in the history of archaeology as in that of printing. The academy met every two weeks, under the chairmanship of the Prime Minister himself, in order to pass around and examine three objects that had been excavated since the previous meeting; when each member had handed in a written report on each find, the secretary collated and published these briefs in the form of a definitive description of the relevant item. The academy's work may well be the earliest known example of scholarship-by-committee, and the results were predictably inaccurate: the descriptions contained in the *Antichità d'Ercolano* in no way measure up to the magnificent binding and illustrations. However, the jaundiced eye with which Winckelmann himself regarded these proceedings may also have been due to his chagrin at not having been invited to join them. He was a better judge of antiquities than any of the fifteen academicians, but the statutes forbade the election of foreigners. When he returned to Rome in the spring of 1758, he must have felt that this first encounter with the scholarly establishment of Portici had ended in a draw. If *they* had seemed to be an Immovable Mass, *he* could have been likened to the proverbial Irresistible Force loosed upon it. They had not given an inch; he, enraged rather than disheartened, swore that he would return to the attack.

His second visit, made in 1762 in the company of Heinrich von Brühl, the Saxon prime minister's youngest son, confirmed him in his suspicion that the entire project of excavating the buried Campanian cities and of preserving and cataloguing their contents was being grossly mismanaged. In fact, matters had if anything got worse in the interval. The academy's work had no sooner started than Charles III and Maria Amalia were forced to relinquish Naples and to exchange the Sicilian crown for that of Spain; in return for agreeing to the installation of the Bourbons in Naples, the Austrians had exacted a stipulation that the kingdoms of the Two Sicilies and of Spain were never to be governed, in personal union, by one and the same sovereign. On the death of his half-brother Ferdinand IV of Spain, in 1759, Charles accordingly transferred his court to Madrid and entrusted Naples and Sicily to his son, also named Ferdinand, who was then a boy of eight.

Ferdinand IV of the Two Sicilies, or Ferdinand I as he called himself after the Congress of Vienna, reigned from 1759 until 1825, to the delight of the Neapolitan mob, which fondly called him *Nasone* on account of his bulbous nose and recognized in him one of their own: a *lazzarone* who spoke dialect, sold in the public market and at a stiff price the fish he had caught in the bay, and was as skillful as his humblest subject in warding off the evil eye. Neither Tanucci, who had been appointed regent until the Prince came of age, nor Maria Carolina, the daughter of Maria Theresa, who became his consort, nor his father, who attempted to guide him by means of letters sent from faraway Madrid, were able to ruffle Ferdinand's indolent bonhomie or to puncture his indifference to anything not directly related to his physical well-being. Sir William Hamilton, who became resident English minister in 1764 and thus had many opportunities to observe Ferdinand's development, has described the young Prince as follows:

On the morning after his nuptials, which took place in the beginning of May 1768, when the weather was very warm, he rose at an early hour and went out as usual to the chase, leaving his young wife in bed. Those courtiers who accompanied him, having inquired of His Majesty how he liked her: *"Dorme come un'ammazzata,"* replied he, *"e suda come un porco"* [She sleeps like a corpse, and sweats like a pig]. Such an answer would be esteemed, anywhere except at Naples, most indecorous; but here we are familiarized to far greater violations of propriety and decency . . . When the King has made a heavy meal and feels an inclination to retire, he commonly communicates that intention to the noblemen around him in waiting, and selects the favoured individuals, whom, as a mark of predilection, he chooses shall attend him. *"Sono ben pranzato,"* says he, laying his hand on his belly, *"adesso bisogna una buona panciata"* [I have eaten well; now I need to move my bowels]. The persons thus preferred then accompany His Majesty, stand respectfully around him, and amuse him by their conversation during the performance.[12]

No sustained interest in anything like the excavations could be expected of this man, and that none was forthcoming, beyond the brief thrill of novelty, is attested by the account that Joseph II left of his visit to Herculaneum and Pompeii. It was on this occasion that Maria Carolina made the memorable comment that her husband, the King of the Two Sicilies, was "a right good fool"—*"ein recht guter Narr."*

How foolish Ferdinand was in regard to the excavations is

borne out by his order that the stepping-stones placed athwart the street, which had enabled the ancients to cross dry-footed while yet allowing chariot wheels to pass unhindered, be removed so that the low-slung royal carriage could drive through (they have since been replaced). In Ferdinand's reign, three abuses which had begun in his father's day became general practice: the arbitrary restoration of one damaged object even if it meant pilfering another; the removal of earth and ashes not away from the site altogether, but merely from one building to another that had been excavated, so that the total area cleared increased hardly at all; and the habit of considering the work site as nothing more than a source of supply for the royal museums. In a perversion of physiocratic reasoning, Ferdinand looked upon the archaeological treasure buried in his kingdom's soil as so much potential dynastic wealth. Only the most valuable and best preserved finds were therefore taken to Portici, and later, when Vesuvius threatened to engulf the region once more, to the Museo Borbonico (now Nazionale) in Naples. Everything else was smashed, left lying about, or carried off secretly like the two bronze candelabrae that Goethe admired in Hamilton's house, where they had, as the poet tactfully put it, "found their way" from the Pompeiian tombs. Motivated as it was not by scholarly but by prestige and pecuniary factors, the work turned into a treasure hunt and as such had to be carried out in secret. As late as 1849, Friedrich Hebbel recorded that a Pompeiian cicerone had advised him: "Take a good look around. If anything strikes your fancy, let me know. I shall steal it for you as soon as the moon is full."

When he returned to the excavations in 1762, Winckelmann found that while a total of fifty men had been assigned to the digging, only eight were working on the most promising site, that of Pompeii, which was not identified as such until the following year. The work gangs were made up of Barbary pirates captured in the innumerable skirmishes between the Neapolitan and Turkish fleets, and of convicts so tightly chained together that they could barely move, let alone wield a spade with the requisite care and agility. The scene of the excavations shifted back and forth between Herculaneum, Pompeii, and Stabiae, as chance or the royal whim dictated. Thus, the Villa of Julia Felix in Pompeii, first discovered in 1755, had been left half unearthed while the diggers hurried on elsewhere; on February 8, 1764, and in Winckelmann's presence, some mosaics by Dioscorides of Samos were found in the deserted edifice, which was then covered up again, as holding no further promise of treasure, and not completely cleared until 1953. Some splendid works of art were secured, but much time was also wasted on trivia: a sun dial, examined by Winckelmann but lost since; a small table at which he drank a bottle of Lacrima Christi one evening, in the company of the despised Paderni; and some Priapic statuettes which he described with sophomoric glee in a letter to Bianconi. Taken as a whole, however, the results stood in no relation to the effort that had been expended, or for that matter, to the anticipation of great discoveries which the Neapolitan Court had done nothing to discourage. Having reconnoitered the ground, Winckelmann now launched a frontal attack by publishing his *Sendschreiben von den Herculanischen Entdeckungen*. Ostensibly addressed to young Brühl, who had been his companion on this trip, this "Open Letter on the Discoveries made at Herculaneum" was actually a carefully planned and planted exposé which had been forwarded to Walther in Dresden with instructions about the complimentary copies that were to be sent to art patrons and fellow-scholars in Paris, Vienna, and elsewhere. Naples did not figure on this list of addresses, and for good reason. The author had been given to understand that the publication of this pamphlet would make it difficult for him to be readmitted to the Kingdom of the Two Sicilies.

In the "Open Letter" and the supplementary *Nachrichten von den neuesten Herculanischen Entdeckungen* ("Report on the most recent Discoveries made at Herculaneum," published 1764 and dedicated to his Swiss friend Johann Heinrich Füssli, who had accompanied him on a more or less clandestine trip to Naples that year), Winckelmann gave vent to his accumulated ire. He spared no one—neither Paderni, nor Martorelli and Bayardi, those scholarly mountains that had labored so mightily and given birth to mice, nor yet Roque Joaquín de Alcubierre, a Spanish engineering officer who had been guilty of a truly grotesque blunder: having come upon a set of bronze letters attached to the wall of a house in Herculaneum, he had removed these letters and proudly presented them to the King in a basket, while neglecting to read and record the inscription in which they had been arranged. At the same time, Winckelmann gave his readers an idea of the pall of mistrust and suspicion which hung heavily over the scene. In fact, the engraving of Demosthenes' bust which was reproduced at the end of the "Open Letter" had had to be stealthily sketched by Mengs, who had meanwhile visited Portici on his own.

What made Winckelmann's two publications so effective was the fact that they contained, along with the vituperative passages, others in which he implicitly demonstrated the loss that accrued to the world through the obscurantism of the bureaucrats in Portici and Naples. From what little he had been allowed to see, he was able to determine that many of the surviving inhabitants of Pompeii had returned after the eruption of A.D. 79 in order to salvage what they could of their own, and steal what they could of their neighbors', possessions. Many key passages in Vitruvius Pollio and other architectural writers of antiquity, he found, could be fully understood only now that one was (or ought to be) able to compare, for example, the large orchestra of the Greek with the smaller one of the Roman theater, or to reconstruct on the spot the machines used for changing the scenery within a play. These and similar observations were couched in Winckelmann's very own blend of academic preciseness and sensual imagery. The following passage, inspired by nothing more poetic than some pitchers and vases from Herculaneum, illustrates his gift for proceeding inductively from the examination of details to the formulation of widely applicable statements on aesthetics: "These vessels owe their beauty to their gently curving lines, which as in beautiful young bodies are not fully grown but still maturing, so that the eye neither exhausts itself in beholding perfectly shaped semi-spherical outlines nor comes up against corners or points. The sweet sensation conveyed by such lines may be likened to [the touch of] a soft, tender hand. In the presence of such harmony, our very thoughts become light and limpid."[13] If one visitor, constantly hemmed in by red tape, could so illuminate the characteristics of Greek pottery and the nature of beauty itself, what heights might scholarship not attain if the excavations were thrown open to men from all lands, to measure and copy and meditate as they pleased? Had not Horace Walpole already observed that "there might certainly be collected great light from this reservoir of antiquities, if a man of learning had the inspection of it; if he directed the working, and would make a journal of the discoveries," and added: "But I believe there is no judicious choice made of directors"?[14] Such, no doubt, were the reflections of many who read Winckelmann's accounts of Herculaneum, among them the Count de Caylus, who, having himself feuded with the Neapolitans, now saw a chance of getting even with them by having the "Report" translated into French in order to give it wider publicity. Like its predecessor, the "Open Letter" of 1762, it had attracted little attention at first because it was written in German, a language that was only just beginning to be accepted as a vehicle for learned communi-

G*

cation. But when the Abbé Galiani, at that time secretary to the Sicilian ambassador in Paris, gave Sir William Hamilton a copy of the French text to take along to Naples, Ferdinand IV was incensed at what he considered a grave indiscretion on Winckelmann's part. The latter, in turn, became so apprehensive that he confessed to a friend his fear that "a beating, if not something worse" would surely await him on his next trip south. Stung into making a reply to the charge of incompetence that had been leveled against them, Bernardo Galiani and another Neapolitan scholar hastily got out an anonymously published pamphlet in which they made fun of Winckelmann for believing, and passing on as gospel, "every scrap of misinformation whispered in his ear by some convict or other on the site."

It was unfortunate that the storm should have broken just then. A period of particularly intensive digging was about to begin, during which several major buildings were found in Pompeii and much incidental information brought to light which enabled the experts to flesh out, as it were, the bare shells of these buildings with suggestions of the life that had once pulsated within their walls. In the Temple of Isis, for example, the remains of the eggs and fish were discovered which the priests had been preparing for their meal when they were struck down, and the position in which their bodies were found demonstrated in dramatic detail the story of their thwarted flight. The discovery of the Great Theater in 1764 confirmed much of what had previously been surmised about the construction of such edifices, while that of the adjacent Gladiators' Barracks furnished the raw material for some poignant reminders of the cruelty of fate. Two skeletons were found with their wrists shackled; the men had evidently been in prison and died a horrible death. Elsewhere in the building, the indiscreet visit—if such it was—of a bejeweled woman, whose body was found on these pre-eminently male premises, showed that these men were not only the victims, but to some extent also the heroes of Roman society. This has since been borne out by the Pompeiian graffiti extolling the athletic and amatory talents of such stalwarts as Auctus (who vanquished fifty foes), Severus (fifty-six victories in the arena), and Celadus, the *suspirium puellarum* who evidently broke as many hearts as his colleagues had - cracked skulls. Temporarily banished from the scene of these finds, Winckelmann had to rely on others to keep him abreast of them. One can imagine with what impatience he listened to a description of the Temple of Isis that was given him by young Louis-Alexandre, duc de La Rochefoucauld-Guyon, and how proudly he forwarded to the painter Charles-Louis Clérisseau a sketch that someone had sent him of the Gladiators' Barracks.

It turned out to be an unnecessarily roundabout way of exchanging news. The royal displeasure was of short duration, and on the occasion of Winckelmann's last visit, in 1767, the amenities were observed on all sides. As a token of forgiveness, Tanucci presented him with the fifth volume of the *Antichità d'Ercolano*, and Winckelmann on his part undertook to review the publication, containing magnificent reproductions of 120 bronzes in the Portici museum, in a spirit that for him was downright mellow. To be sure, he never changed his opinion of King Ferdinand, whom he characterized as "a little beast of sixteen" that had only once set foot in the museum and whose greatest pleasure consisted in watching the vivisection of pregnant deer, or of Paderni, "that fourth-rate draftsman who had been on the point of dying of hunger in Rome when he was lucky enough to be commissioned to copy the antique paintings." Yet on the face of it all was well, and Mount Vesuvius even treated the distinguished visitor to a spectacular eruption, which he watched in the company of his favorite disciple, the young Baron Johann Hermann von Riedesel.

．　．　．

Winckelmann's visits to the Campanian cities were a historical event in the truest sense of that overworked term. As a private citizen, he lacked all power to remedy by executive fiat the many abuses that he witnessed. Persuasion had to be his weapon, and he wielded it with such skill in the manipulation of public and learned opinion that he eventually forced those in charge of the excavations to place the whole project on a scientific basis. He accomplished this not by means of naïve appeals to the cupidity, ambition, and vanity of these men, but by helping to raise this type of research to a level where it could no longer be left in incompetent hands. Once Diderot had become interested in it in Paris and the Society of Dilettanti had taken it up in London and Goethe had followed suit in Weimar, its practice could no longer be left to men like Martorelli and Mazzocchi. Once Winckelmann had been invited to Potsdam by Frederick the Great and received by Maria Theresa in Schönbrunn, and his *History* placed in the anteroom of Napoleon's study in the Tuileries, its support was no longer left to sovereigns like Charles III and Ferdinand IV. In thus helping to transform a hobby into a profession, and exemplifying this process in his own person, he shaped the course of all later archaeological work.

In the shade of Vesuvius, practices were initiated that eventually came to be perfected in Peru and Mexico and Egypt and India and wherever else remnants of ancient cultures are dug up, dated and otherwise identified, catalogued, and in the end exhibited for the benefit of later generations. By putting Pompeii and Herculaneum on the map of localities in which the unfolding of Western civilization can best be observed, Winckelmann brought about a major change in our view of that civilization. Whereas we once saw the ancients in the harsh light of heroic and historiographic literature, as giants stepping forth from the pages of Homer and Plutarch, they now appear to us, as often as not, in the gentler radiance of their domestic concerns.

Winckelmann himself did not live to see this change, itself a healthy reaction to the stress that Piranesi and others were placing just then on the monumental aspects of ancient and especially of Roman art. It may have surprised, but it would also have pleased him to know that he, who so celebrated the *Apollo* and the Torso, should prove in retrospect to have taken a hand also in preserving for us the loaves of bread that had been baked in Pompeii a few hours before the city's destruction. The humble baker has not supplanted the gods and heroes. But he has taken his place by their side, steadying a balance that had previously swung between hypertrophy and miniaturization. As a result, our image of classical antiquity has acquired a sense of life and immediacy that can no longer be straitjacketed into such slogans as The Glory That was Greece or The Grandeur That was Rome.

Although modern archaeologists have advanced far beyond the primitive procedures employed in Winckelmann's day, they are still beholden to him for their mental stance. He brought to the discipline certain qualifications that have been demanded of its practitioners ever since. They must be able to reason both deductively and inductively, to analyze a given object by itself and to assign it to its proper place not only within the temporal range in which it is found, but also in such seemingly extraneous categories as the political, climatic, religious, economic, and other conditions of the time. They must be able not only to dig and collect, but to write, and to buttress their writing whenever applicable with literary and pictorial evidence. In so far as he was the first to harness these skills to the exploration and interpretation of Greek and Roman antiquities, Winckelmann may in truth be called the first classical archaeologist.

185

FLORENCE
AND ROME

I

Were he alive today, Philipp von Stosch would be making a fortune playing the role of Prussian *Junker* in the movies: tall and handsome, monocled (a rarity in the eighteenth century), and so eccentric that he kept an owl in his study because watching it flutter about cured him of hypochondriac moods. He did not need a fortune because he was born with one; but a *Junker* he was, a man of such aristocratic bearing that Pier Leone Ghezzi wrote under the portrait he painted of him: "Truly a baron, in fact—*baronissimo!*" Born a doctor's son in the Pomeranian town of Küstrin, Stosch had been a secret agent for the British government, which charged him with keeping an eye on the machinations of the House of Stuart and its Continental sympathizers. As erudite as he was adventurous, he had also found time to collect engraved gems, and to publish a book on intaglios that bore the artists' signature. On reaching forty, in 1731, he decided that his cloak-and-dagger days were over. Devoting himself full-time to his hobby, he settled in Florence, although his broker's shrewdness in gauging the market in antiquities made him travel to the far corners of Italy whenever a museum was opened, a collection auctioned off, or an archaeological discovery announced.

When he unpacked the copy of the "Reflections" that Winckelmann had sent him, Stosch found that it was accompanied by a self-deprecatory little note in the author's hand: "I am taking the liberty of presenting to you . . . a brief brochure on the arts, of which you are the greatest connoisseur and most competent judge . . ."[1] It was an ingratiating gambit, and the *baronissimo*, notwithstanding the aura of vaguely sinister elegance that surrounded him, was a warmhearted and generous man. A lively correspondence ensued between the two, in French, because Stosch was a gentleman of the old school. He invited Winckelmann to be his guest in Florence, and on his own recommended him to his friend Alessandro Albani, whose uncle, Pope Clement XI, had done him some diplomatic and financial favors. Winckelmann accepted the invitation, and made plans to visit Florence in the summer of 1758. But when he returned from Naples that May, he heard that Benedict XIV had just died and that a conclave had been called to elect a successor. Since his patrons Archinto and Passionei were among the leading candidates, he decided to wait out the conclave in Rome rather than continuing on to Florence.

Archinto, who enjoyed the backing of the French and Austrian factions in the Cardinals' College, made a promising start, only to lose out in the end on account of his relative youth. At sixty, he was considered altogether too likely to outlive those who were now his rivals for the papal tiara. Although known to be in poor health, he had evidently failed to convince them that his would be a brief pontificate, at the end of which they would still be eligible as *papabili;* had they been better informed by their medical spies, they would have known that he had only a few months to live. His candidacy, in any case, faded as rapidly as Passionei's, although two months were to pass before Carlo

Rezzonico of Venice was elected (born before Archinto, he nevertheless outlived him by eleven years, reigning until 1769 as Clement XIII). Winckelmann, whose life might have taken a different turn if Archinto or Passionei had become Pope, felt free to leave the capital now. In the meantime, however, Stosch had also died unexpectedly, after requesting Winckelmann in his will to prepare a descriptive catalogue of his gem collection. The Baron, who had never met him in person, had in fact appointed him executor of his scholarly, and, to the extent that the collection increased in value by being catalogued, even of his financial estate.

Winckelmann had no sooner set to work in Florence, in September 1758, than he realized that the job would take years if it were done as meticulously as the former owner had wished. Unlike Lippert, Stosch had disregarded cameos altogether in favor of intaglios. Even though the Persian and Christian items had already been sold by his nephew and heir, Wilhelm Muzel-Stosch, there still remained several thousand intaglios and facsimiles to be identified and described. Many of them were of Renaissance and yet more modern vintage, but had the signatures of ancient gem cutters engraved on them, so that separating the genuine from the forged constituted a major problem in itself. While Muzel-Stosch, an amiable and easygoing young man who needed money in order to be able to travel, wanted a sales catalogue, Winckelmann had been thinking in terms of a *catalogue raisonné*. He was motivated by self-interest as much as by piety toward the deceased, for the collection also included maps, ancient weapons, coins, and other material that would be of value to him in completing the *History*. In attempting to reconcile these differing viewpoints, he hit upon the expedient of listing every item, but restricting his comments to the most valuable ones; for his descriptions of the others, he relied on the notes that had been prepared by the old baron himself. A similar compromise determined his choice of language. Scholarly and commercial considerations indicated that the catalogue should be published in French, in which there already existed a sizeable body of glyptographic literature, by Mariette and others. Winckelmann, however, detested the French at this time as standard-bearers of the rococo, and, perhaps for that reason, felt intimidated by what he calls somewhere "the language ending in -ong." He would have preferred Latin or German, but ended by writing in French after all, even though his command of the language fell short of the level required for publication. At Muzel-Stosch's insistence, the final draft was corrected by Joannan de St. Laurent, a friend of his late uncle and himself the author of a work on the techniques applied by the gem cutters of antiquity. Winckelmann having returned to Rome by then, the job of proofreading quotations in Greek was entrusted to a Florentine professor, who was so incompetent that his emendations had to be checked at every turn by mail. Winckelmann insisted not only on the utmost accuracy in such matters, as befits a scholar, but also on the use of the most legible Greek type. The appearance of books in that language, he thought, had been deteriorating ever since Robert Estienne had stopped printing Greek works in sixteenth-century Paris. After many delays caused by these checks and controls, the *Description des pierres gravées du feu Baron Stosch*, dedicated to Cardinal Albani, was issued in Florence in early 1760.

Winckelmann's first work, the "Reflections," had been a gracefully written essay full of sweeping if well-reasoned conjectures, unburdened by any scholarly apparatus except that which was contained in the appendices: the "Open Letter" and "Commentary" that he had flung so contemptuously at the feet of the pedants. His second major publication, the *Catalogue of the Engraved Gems of the late Baron Stosch*, is heavily footnoted and replete with recondite detail. It reads like the cata-

logue it is, or rather, it does not "read" at all but is meant to
be consulted as a reference work. Hence the worrisome labor
that had been expended on correcting the manuscript. Unlike
the "Reflections," in which Winckelmann had addressed himself
to the public at large, the new work was written primarily for
the benefit of gem collectors, a group of vociferous enthusiasts
who were not known for their forbearance of other people's
mistakes. The author realized that when identifying, say, the
item listed under Class II, Section vi, Par. 307 as "a carnelian
showing Diana of Ephesus between two stags, her hands resting
on an object that Minutius Felix calls 'pillars,' " he would be
called upon to provide evidence of a very different nature from
that given in the earlier work. The *Catalogue* would stand or fall
on the accuracy of its documentation, and Winckelmann accordingly took care to instrument his score with footnotes,
quotations in the original language, variants, and the like. The
publication was reviewed by Mariette himself, favorably enough
as far as the author's scholarship was concerned, but not without
the kind of innuendo that the *baronissimo's* life and personality
tended to evoke among his contemporaries: "Will posterity
really believe," Mariette asked in the Paris *Journal étranger*,
"that Baron Stosch acquired these rich and valuable collections,
these immense treasures, with the revenues of a private gentleman?" Neither he nor the other critics questioned the validity of
Winckelmann's basic premise, namely, that the development
of ancient civilization could as well be traced on the strength of
glyptographic as on any other evidence. This was a commonly
held opinion at the time, when many larger-scale examples of
antique art were as yet undiscovered, or, if located in Greece
itself, inaccessible to Westerners; until the publication of the
first volume of Stuart's and Revett's *Antiquities of Athens*, etc.,
in 1762, even the Parthenon was known only by hearsay. Nor
does anyone seem to have commented on the author's unmistak-

able preference for intaglios showing male over those depicting female divinities or persons.

Even in this, his most pedestrian work next to the *Monuments* (see pages 229–34), Winckelmann's erudition was not of the kind that mirrors itself Narcissus-like in the reflection of its own cleverness. An example will show that his glance, directed at the totality of ancient life, always managed to penetrate the foliage of technical minutiae and to illuminate some previously dark corner. "A warrior mounting his steed," we read in his description of the scene engraved on a gray jade, "placed his right foot in a metal loop affixed at a certain height to the shaft of his spear. We know that the ancients had no stirrups, but no one has yet observed that they possessed a substitute for that device."[2] Until then it had been assumed that they had used for this purpose the raised stones seen by the side of some Roman roads, but not even Ruhnken, as experienced a horseman as he was a philologist, seems to have asked himself how they had managed in open country or on the battlefield. Sustained by a conscientiousness that was never dulled by fatigue or hurry, Winckelmann did not rest until the results of inspiration had been confirmed by those of perspiration. Leafing through the excerpts that he had been making ever since his student days, he came upon a passage in Xenophon which not only supports his interpretation of this scene, but makes no sense unless we assume that the ancients had indeed mounted in this fashion, and from the right rather than the left.

Among the reasons for Winckelmann's trip to Florence had been his desire to examine the Etruscan sarcophagi, urns, and artifacts in the city's museums. He arrived at a good time because the fashion of *etruscheria* had just reached its crest. Dedicated to the study of the Etruscans, who in the eyes of their partisans had been bearers of light and culture when the Greeks and Romans were still barbarians, this fad had recently received a boost by the rediscovery of a book that had first been published almost a century before: *De Etruria regali* by Thomas Dempster, a Roman-Catholic Scot who had taught law at the University of Pisa. Reissued in Florence in 1723-6, it contained engravings of Etruscan antiquities, which now fired a number of Florentine patriots, who had little enough to occupy them in their sleepy little grand duchy, to bethink themselves of their regional heritage. Another fountainhead of *etruscheria* was the Academy of Cortona, which had been founded in that remote mountain village in 1726 for the purpose of establishing a museum and library and subsidizing the publication of scholarly books; it held yearly meetings at which papers were read and a new president, called *lucumone* in revival of an Etruscan term, was elected amidst much antiquarian hocus-pocus. Even though *etruscheria* swept through northern Italy and found a distant echo in England when Josiah Wedgwood launched his "Etruria" line of porcelain, it failed to make much of an impression on the sophisticated Romans. (Far from priding themselves on residing in a city that had supposedly been founded by the Etruscans, they had resented the influx of Florentines who followed their compatriot Clement XII to Rome. One of the most popular acts of his successor, Benedict XIV, had been to send these hangers-on back to the banks of the Arno.) As the *History* was to show, Winckelmann shared this supercilious attitude, being not only repelled by Etruscan art, but believing for some reason that the dour and superstitious mentality of that people had been passed on to their descendants. He thought that such hereditary traits accounted for Savonarola's masochism and for the overpowering force, achieved at the expense of grace and beauty, of

Michelangelo's work. These prejudices did not prevent him from asking St. Laurent to put him up for membership in the Academy of Cortona, which after all counted men like Muratori and Montesquieu among its corresponding members. The Academy duly elected him in 1760, with a citation praising his work on the *Catalogue*. Shortly afterward, he was also initiated into the Roman Academy of St. Luke, and, on the recommendation of Muzel-Stosch, who happened to be in England at the time, into the Society of Antiquaries in London.

Winckelmann's dislike of the Florentines was based on more than his distrust of *etruscheria*. Expressed in repeated references to Florence as "the seat of ignorance," it was nourished by the tone of the city's intellectual life and by the antics of its scholars. While the intellectual life of Rome revolved around the study of antiquities and music, that of Florence was concentrated on the recitation of poetry, much of it in dialect. In the former city, that life had been epitomized by worldly abbés who wished to revive their spirits after a day's work; in the latter, it had become the preserve of catty *littérateurs*. In Rome, writers and artists assembled on an evening in someone's palace; in Florence, critics discussed the gossip of the day in cafés, in the manner later taken up by so many French and Viennese intellectuals. These discussions, Winckelmann found, rarely dealt with matters that would be of interest to people beyond the confines of Tuscany. Apart from the cultivation of *etruscheria*, the only learned work of any importance done locally was the publication of the *Museum Florentinum*, a catalogue of the art treasures collected over the centuries by the Medici family, which had just become extinct with the death of Gian Gastone in 1737. It was indicative of the prevailing lethargy that no Florentine should have tried to preserve for his city, if necessary by outright purchase, the Stosch collection that reposed within its walls; it was eventually bought by Frederick the Great, and fetched a price of

10,000 ducats or about $62,000 because Winckelmann had done such good work in cataloguing it.

Giving the local scholars a wide berth, Winckelmann stayed in Muzel-Stosch's house and had his host introduce him to Sir Horace Mann, the resident English minister who had gathered about him a lively circle of Italians, English exiles, and other foreigners who passed through on their grand tour. Mann received the visitor as hospitably as his colleague Sir William Hamilton later did in Naples, and as a mark of true friendship lent him his copy of John Cleland's *Memoirs of a Woman of Pleasure*, alias *Fanny Hill*, which Winckelmann pronounced "the most wanton book the world has ever seen, but written by a master in the art." Perhaps he had become sensitized to the subject by the liaisons that he was carrying on simultaneously: homosexual ones with Franz Stauder, a pupil of Mengs, and with the young Florentine Niccolò Castellani, as well as an affair with a twelve-year-old ballerina he had seen at the opera. The mock-heroic fashion in which he bewailed to Bianconi the loss of his *verginità* leads one to believe that whatever else may have gone wrong, his heart was not involved. It was as well, perhaps, for even that tolerant century did not look kindly on middle-aged abbés who got involved with pre-pubescent Lolitas.

In surveying the pattern of Winckelmann's relationships with the scholars of Rome, Naples, and now Florence, one ends by wondering whether the man was, perhaps, a snob who did not consider these men worth knowing. It *is* strange that he should have been accepted as readily as the social configuration of the age permitted by Archinto, Passionei, and Muzel-Stosch, yet failed to establish any lasting contact with the large majority of those who were not only his professional colleagues, but had mostly sprung from the same background as himself. The record, however, points to a different rationale for his attitude. Such snobbish instincts as he possessed—and they were less pronounced than Boswell's or Ruhnken's—were balanced by his egalitarian view of mankind, by his sharp ear for the tears that could even then be heard in the fabric of pre-revolutionary society, and by his loyalty to old friends. When he boasted to them of his successes, and intimated that he might visit Germany so that they could admire him in all his glory, he did so not because he considered himself superior to Uden and Berendis and the others, but because he was accustomed to viewing himself with a dispassionateness that bordered on naïveté: "Who would have thought," he seemed to ask, "that I would get so far?" This tendency to regard his life as a spiraling ascent toward the sun of social acceptance was never more marked than in this period, when he disarmingly confessed, in a recommendation written on Volkmann's behalf, that he had been so insignificant until now that this was the first time anyone had asked him for an introduction. It never occurred to him to believe that well-born men like Bünau, Archinto, or Stosch were *ipso facto* better than he, the cobbler's son. Although the contrast between their circumstances and his own made him bitter and led him to reflect, with more than a grain of wistfulness, on the connection between democracy and cultural life that had existed in ancient Greece, he took the world as he found it and wasted little time lamenting its imperfections. He believed in ability and achievement, and was perfectly willing to honor them wherever they might be found, in a scholar like Giacomelli or an artist like Mengs, in aristocrats like Passionei and Albani or in self-made men like Lippert and Oeser. What angered him was not social injustice, which he regretted but could not change, but social and intellectual pretense. It was his misfortune that in Naples and Florence he came up against scholars—as he had against preachers and teachers in Prussia—who had risen through such pretense to positions of a modest prominence. Yet it is not recorded that he ever blamed the system that had allowed them so to rise. Had he done so, he could not have lived as he did.

This being said, we have no reason to spend more time than he himself spent with the learned luminaries of Florence: with the archaeologist Francesco Gori, who had not once set foot in Rome; with the intaglio expert Domenico Antonio Bracci, who did not dare to criticize the *Catalogue* until after its author was safely in his grave; or with Giovanni Lami, editor of the city's leading review, the *Novelle letterarie*. Others have described these men in much the same light in which Winckelmann saw them, including Lami, who, about to be bearded in his den by another German visitor, had been observed rushing out of the house "dressed in slippers and a purple gown, hatless and with his long hair streaming behind him, wearing one red and one black stocking, as they happened to have fallen into his hands when dressing."[3] It is not surprising that Winckelmann kept out of the way of this "bloated toad"—"*aufgeblasene Kröte*"— as he called him on account of his self-important air, and preferred the company of worldlier men. This predilection for the mundane life, in turn, hastened his alienation not from scholarship itself, but from most of his fellow-toilers in the vineyards of art history and glyptography. He did not need them. The harvest of his sojourn in Florence was rich and varied enough without them. He had satisfied his curiosity about Etruscan relics, and had made a friend in Muzel-Stosch, although their relationship had to be patched up, on one occasion when Winckelmann's nose was out of joint, by the gift of 150 lbs. of coffee which the other sent him from Constantinople. Tedious though it had been, Winckelmann's work on the Stosch collection represented, in a way, a fortunate repetition of his experiences with Lippert, Oeser, and Mengs: once again, he had been granted insights into the work of specialists whose field was close to his own, but which he had neither the time nor the talent to master for himself. Deposited in the *Catalogue* and in several brief essays that he took back with him in manuscript form, the gain of the nine months spent on the Arno outweighed the worries with which he faced the prospect of returning to Rome, where much had happened during his absence.

II

Winckelmann had originally set out for Rome with the idea of spending a year or two there, after which he would return in order to take up some minor, never clearly defined position at the Saxon Court. Having found that the city was indeed the spiritual home that he had imagined it to be ever since his schoolmaster days, and that the job of cataloguing its art works was part of the bigger task of analyzing the nature and relevance of ancient art as a whole, he determined to entrench himself in Rome so firmly that nothing could dislodge him. It was a wise precaution. He was never officially recalled to Saxony, or threatened with the forfeiture of his stipend until it formally ran out in 1762. But during the early years in Rome, his perseverance was repeatedly put to the test by developments over which he had no control.

The outbreak of the Seven Years' War in 1756, which forced Augustus III to leave Dresden and take refuge in his Polish domains, caused the stipend to be left unpaid for the better part of a year; as we saw, Winckelmann only just managed to get by. In 1758, he was faced with two further crises: his failure to bring back any real news from Herculaneum, and Archinto's defeat in the conclave. The first endangered his position at the Court of Saxony, which might have decided then and there to replace him with an emissary more acceptable to the Neapolitan scholars; the second meant that the prospects of his chief patron, who could so easily have procured a job for him in the Vatican, had been permanently checked. There followed the death of Stosch, and, a few months later, that of Archinto himself. Just as Winckelmann was about to extend his Italian base by establishing a bridgehead in Florence, its center threatened to collapse in Rome. Archinto was dead, Passionei was becoming senile (he died in 1761), and the new Pope had little in common with his scholarly predecessor. Whereas Benedict XIV had taken an active interest in antiquities, Clement XIII paid no more attention to them than was required to ensure that fig leaves were attached to nude statues. It was one thing for Winckelmann to refer mockingly to "His Fussiness"—"*Sua Scrupulosità*"—on the throne of Saint Peter, but it was another to envisage a life in which he could no longer count on the help of highly placed friends in Rome. That winter, he took up a plan that he had earlier dismissed as impractical: he would hire himself out as a guide to some wealthy tourist who wished to see Greece. At the moment, Lady Orford, Sir Horace Walpole's erratic daughter-in-law, was the most likely prospect. Winckelmann met her in Florence through Sir Horace Mann, and seriously entertained her suggestion that he accompany her to Athens on board the ship that she proposed to charter for the purpose. Having been warned that she harbored scholarly ambitions of her own, he extracted from her an agreement to the effect that he would be free to publish under his own name any writings, a guidebook or whatever, that might result from this enterprise. As it developed, he never went to Greece, with Lady Orford or with anyone else. Without knowing it at the time, he had already reached the southernmost point of his travels at Paestum. For at this juncture, fate intervened in the form of a letter from Cardinal Albani, who invited him to become his secretary and librarian. Assured of an extension of his stay in Rome, Winckelmann accepted immediately. On returning to Rome, he collected the belongings he had left behind in the Cancelleria and moved into a four-room apartment in the attic of the Palazzo Albani, now Palazzo del Drago, in Vià Quattro Fontane on the Quirinal. As was his custom, he celebrated the occasion with a sartorial extravagance, a straw hat that Muzel-Stosch had to send him from Florence. Out of deference to his new standing as member of a cardinal's personal staff, he had it covered with black silk.

Although Winckelmann had been recommended by Giacomelli and Stosch, Albani's job offer represented an extraordinary act of faith, shown to someone who had not even been interviewed for the position. But then, the Cardinal was an extraordinary man.

Alessandro Albani, old and almost blind when Winckelmann became a member of his household, was born in Urbino in 1692 as the third son of Orazio Albani, whose brother Giovanni Francesco became Pope in 1700 as Clement XI. Young Alessandro distinguished himself as a student of history and classical languages, although he was hampered even then by an eye disease which forced him to spend weeks at a time lying in bed in a darkened room. A fine horseman despite this handicap, he joined the army and might have followed a military career if his father had not died in 1712, leaving the three boys to be looked after by their uncle. The latter, however, while still a cardinal had openly condemned the nepotism rampant under Innocent XII; now that he himself was Pope, he dis-

covered that this misplaced zeal had made it all but impossible
to do much for his own relatives. He therefore decided that
Annibale, already a prelate, should remain in the Church while
Carlo, who had married into the Borromeis of Milan, continued
the family; Alessandro, the most volatile of the three, would
move into the Vatican, where he could keep an eye on him.

It proved to be an impossible task. Handsome, rich, and a
born ladies' man, the ex-colonel of Papal Dragoons felt irresist-
ibly drawn to the *dolce vita* of Rome. His clerical garb notwithstanding, he spent his days gambling, flirting, and riding to
hounds—the last-named a pastime through which he gained a
topographical knowledge of the countryside that stood him in
good stead when he went digging for antiquities in later years.
Having become involved in a love affair that was altogether too
spectacular for someone supposedly bound by Vatican decorum,
he was shipped off as Nuncio Extraordinary to Vienna. After
the death of Clement XI, Innocent XIII recalled Alessandro to
Rome and made him a cardinal at the age of twenty-nine, although he still had not taken holy orders. Believing as he did
in the steadying effect of responsibility, the new pope also appointed Albani Protector of the Holy Roman Empire. As such,
he had to preside over the German congregations in Rome,
introduce German visitors at the Papal Court, and digest for
the use of the Holy See the dispatches sent from across the
Alps by diplomatic courier. (A minor benefit of the position,
but one that became very dear to Winckelmann once he could
share in it by virtue of having become part of the Cardinal's
official family, were the free mailing privileges that went with
it.) Albani continued in this charge through the reigns of the
next two pontiffs, and himself figured among the more promising
candidates in the conclaves of 1740 and 1758. By the latter
date, his position had if anything gained in importance: it was
through Albani's office that the actions of Frederick the Great,

whose armies moved so unpredictably all over the map, first
became known to the Vatican and the diplomats accredited to
it.

Albani had been fortunate to find, early in life, a constructive
outlet for the vitality that had made him strain against the bonds
of clerical restraint. Born too late to be the patron of great
artists, in the manner of the Renaissance churchmen whom he
resembled in temperament and talents, he became a collector
instead. He began in his twenties, under the guidance of Stosch,
with whom he excavated in Nettuno and Tivoli. Within a few
years, he had built up a collection of Roman coins that numismatists considered superior to the one that the Medici had been
gathering over so many generations. When he ran out of money
in the 1720's, he sold the bulk of his holdings to Innocent XIII
and Augustus the Strong, and started a new collection with the
aid of a distant relative, the Duke of Modena, who owned the
land on which Hadrian's Villa and the Villa d'Este stood in
Tivoli. On these properties, Albani, accompanied in later years
by Winckelmann, was allowed to dig to his heart's content.
Much of the statuary now in the Villa Albani had originally
come from Tivoli, while some of the smaller items were found
in the catacombs, where Carthusian nuns sieved the ashes and
dirt in order to ensure that no remains of sainted bones were
lost before they could be reverently placed in urns. His Eminence
was not above watching these macabre proceedings in person,
ready to pounce on any coin, engraved gem, or other valuable
that might be brought to light.

Feverish and idiosyncratic as it appears to us, Albani's passion for collecting antiquities was no isolated phenomenon. It
was an avocation that flourished not only in Rome, but in Paris,
Madrid, London, Berlin, Dresden, Vienna, and St. Petersburg.
Collections, museums, and galleries were being established all
over Europe, and learned societies founded from whose mem-

H

bership they drew their intellectual and often enough also their financial sustenance. Much of this activity was merely social, as in the early days of the Society of Dilettanti in London, when eligibility was defined by some unorthodox tokens: "The nominal qualification," Horace Walpole, a confirmed teetotaler, wrote to a friend, "is having been in Italy, and the real one, being drunk; the two chiefs are Lord Middlesex and Sir Francis Dashwood [the later Lord le Despencer, Chancellor of the Exchequer under the Earl of Bute], who were seldom sober the whole time they were in Italy."[4] Yet it was also this society which in soberer moments sent Stuart and Revett to Greece, and subsidized the publication of their work. There is no doubt that the museums and galleries of many lands would be poorer but for the support given them by these learned bodies, which fulfilled a function akin to that performed nowadays by the great foundations. The neoclassicist movement, in particular, and such fashions within it as *etruscheria* and *chinoiserie*, might have remained local fads if the impulses that gave them birth had not been transmitted over this network which covered the continent. The wave of antiquarian scholarship and collecting reached a crest in Rome, where Cardinal Lambertini, who, as Benedict XIV, became the most learned pope since Hadrian VI, revived or founded a whole cluster of academies. His favorite one was that of Papal History, a subject to which he had himself contributed a definitive account of the canonization of saints. Among the others were the Academy of Liturgy, the Academy of Councils, and the Academy of Roman History and Profane Antiquities, in which Albani played a leading role and which had a secretary in Winckelmann's friend Baldani, a place of business near the Capitol, and a constitution and membership roster of its own. Like some modern universities, these academies favored the rise of the type of scholarly executive who teaches little and writes less, but derives his influence from controlling

the sources of information on which his more productive colleagues depend. An example in point was Contucci, who published nothing, seldom did field work (but when he did,
discovered in Tusculum the mosaic with the Head of Pallas
that is now in the Hall of the Greek Cross in the Vatican), and
lives on nonetheless in the writings of his disciple Winckelmann and in the texts to Piranesi's prints.

Although he was criticized for the superficiality of his
scholarship by Baumgarten and others, Lambertini indulged his
antiquarian interests even after he had become Pope. He had
each academy meet once a month, when he would listen to the
reports that were given and compliment the speakers. He took
an equally active part in other aspects of the city's literary and
artistic life, visiting theaters—without actually attending a
performance, although that privilege was still enjoyed by the
lesser clergy—and embellishing many buildings and other land-
marks. It could no longer be said in his reign, as it was in that
of so many of his predecessors, that "what the barbarians left
undone, the Barberini finished"—"*quod non fecerunt barbari,
fecerunt Barberini.*" Like the other Roman families who had
despoiled the ancient monuments in order to decorate their own
palaces with the stolen materials, the Barberini were henceforth
forbidden to touch the ruins that had served as a convenient
quarry during so many centuries. Initiated when Alexander VII
had the Pantheon cleared of the wooden booths that had been
put up inside, this reversal of a long-established practice continued under Clement XII, who ordered the Arch of Constantine
to be repaired, and was formalized when Benedict XIV con-
secrated the Colosseum as a place of public worship on September 19, 1756. It was also the *buon coglione* who had the Fontana
Trevi finished and the Capitol transformed into one of the
world's great museums. Statuary had been placed on that knoll
as long ago as 1471, when Sixtus IV had donated the bronze

she-wolf that can still be seen there. In the course of time, more and more sculptures came to be exhibited in the square that had meanwhile been laid out by Michelangelo, and in the Palazzo dei Conservatori, which faces it. The latter collection, now in the Capitoline Museum, was further augmented by the busts and inscriptions sold by Albani, and by gifts made by Benedict XIV himself, who had the *Capitoline Faun* placed there along with other works taken from Hadrian's Villa. Although the museum soon became the "archaeologist's Bible" (Barthélemy), the evocative aura of the whole locale, where the span of ancient history could be taken in at one glance, must have outweighed the impression made by any individual work. Winckelmann, at any rate, who often visited the spot during his early Roman years, barely mentions the *Faun* or the *Dying Gaul*, and no more deigned to take notice of the *Capitoline Venus* than he had of the *Aphrodite of Cnidus*.

Albani, in short, was only one collector among many, albeit a very learned one whose particular forte lay in the identification and dating of intaglios. He collected them himself, and helped Winckelmann in sorting out those in the Stosch collection. It was in acknowledgment of his services as godfather, which Muzel-Stosch and Winckelmann called him for having "christened" so many hitherto unnamed gems, that they had dedicated the *Catalogue* to him. This collaboration initiated a process that neither the Cardinal nor his secretary could have foreseen when they first met. They became friends, despite the many obstacles that seemingly stood in the way of such a development: an age spread of twenty-five years, the fact that one man was dependent for his livelihood on the other, and a difference in background and social standing that would be all but unsurmountable even today. Before they could enter into this relationship, each of the two had to come to terms with the circumstances of his own life.

Winckelmann, in looking back, realized how tortuous the
road had been that led him from Seehausen to the Palazzo
Albani: "Enjoy the best years of your life," he advised young
Leonhard Usteri, who had come to see him from Zürich, "mine
were wasted in sorrow, want, and labor."[5] Looking ahead, he
knew that the *History* would be followed by other works, for
the writing of which he required a measure of peace and security.
It was at this time that he took to calling himself *spätklug,* one
who acquires wisdom late in life. Borrowed from Theophrastus,
a pupil of Aristotle, the term bespeaks a self-knowledge that
transcends the intellect. In Winckelmann's case, it included the
realization that his precarious affective life would always leave
him exposed to the tribulations that fall to the lot of the proud
and the lonely. He had learned to live with these afflictions, as
he was learning to live with the intrigues and jealousies brought
on by his pederasty. For there is little doubt but that he was an
active homosexual at this time, even if we hesitate to take at
face value Casanova's report of having surprised him, when entering unannounced one day, in a compromising situation with
a young man; adjusting his clothes, Winckelmann is supposed
to have remarked that while such practices were foreign to his
nature, he had taken them up because they had been current in
ancient Greece. When writing to console Francke on the death
of his wife, he rationalized differently: denying that he had
ever been an enemy of the fair sex himself, he added that his
freedom from the responsibilities of husband and father had
enabled him to devote more time to his work than he could
have done as a married man. Be that as it may, his awareness
of his own vulnerability in this as in other respects was reinforced by the darkening fate of Costantino Ruggieri, a close
friend and fellow-abbé. Three years older than himself, Ruggieri lived in circumstances that must have seemed to Winckelmann frighteningly similar to his own. He was an enormously

learned but impecunious librarian who spent his days doing scholarly odd jobs for Passionei, Benedict XIV, and other influential churchmen, without ever finding the permanent position that would have given him security and a modicum of public esteem. Embittered and alienated even from his friends, he ended his life a few years later in the English fashion—*all'inglese*. He shot himself, an unheard-of action for a cleric.

Winckelmann, more fortunate but also made of sterner stuff, now found in Albani an employer who gave him room and board with a small salary, while making only the most minimal demands on his time. This man, furthermore, was a powerful protector, in an environment in which a scholar without private means could not hope to survive unless he had patronage. He was also a wealthy and knowledgeable collector of antiquities, and, although every inch a *grand seigneur*, a jovial and congenial soul. Albani, on his part, found in Winckelmann an experienced librarian and a companion who possessed the special touch required of those who live with the blind—a skill that he had acquired many years ago in the service of Principal Tappert of the Stendal school. Their needs and personalities thus complemented each other to a remarkable degree. At work, the Cardinal, who in addition to his other duties had been appointed Passionei's successor as head of the Vatican Library, drew on Winckelmann's expertise in that field. The latter, in turn, was able to use not only his employer's own collections of sculptures, gems, engravings, and the like, but also those to which he had access *ex officio*, by virtue of being a cardinal's secretary. At home, Albani called on him whenever he needed advice regarding the purchase of a work of art, or wanted to be read to on sleepless nights; Winckelmann meanwhile occupied a comfortable apartment of his own and was made privy to the latest ecclesiastical and archaeological news. In society, the Cardinal enjoyed the services of a presentable aide who was also a shrewd judge of people, while Winckelmann found an entry to many houses that would have remained closed to him if he had been on his own, or in the employ of a less popular host and guest.

Infirm and almost blind, Albani continued to attend concerts, to receive distinguished visitors to Rome, and to play cards with the Countess Cheroffini and other aristocratic dowagers whom he had first charmed when they had been pretty young things, and he, a dashing young officer and diplomat. It was on one of these occasions that Winckelmann met the painter Benjamin West, who created a stir in that jaded society by being himself: not the noble savage in a feather headdress that had been expected, but an unassuming and exceedingly pleasant young Philadelphia Quaker. He was taken about the city on an excursion in which some thirty carriages took part. The tour ended in the Vatican, where the others, anxious to hear the visitor's comments, stood back expectantly as the custodian opened the closet in which the *Apollo Belvedere* was then kept. West lived up to the occasion by exclaiming, "My God, a young Mohawk warrior!" Turning to his astounded hosts, he explained that the statue reminded him of an Indian brave who follows with his eyes the course of the arrow that has just left his bow. Although it differed from his own belief that the work shows Apollo returning from victory rather than going out to gain it, Winckelmann must have been pleased by the American's reaction. Here was proof, if any were needed, that the Greek divinities as fashioned by the great sculptors were indeed archetypal figures of man.

Although there remained a line between them that was never overstepped, Winckelmann felt very much at home in Albani's employ. "I hope that you are well and happy," he wrote Berendis in 1761,

> because I am. I eat and drink and sleep as soundly as I did in my youth . . . I enjoy greater freedom here than I ever did in my

life, and I am, in a manner of speaking, the master of my master and of his country seats [Albani owned properties in Porto d'Anzio by the sea and at Castel Gandolfo in the mountains, where his estate adjoined the Pope's summer residence], which I visit whenever and in whatever company I wish. Twice a week I accompany the Cardinal to receptions and musicales. In this manner, life passes agreeably and without regrets. The Cardinal, seventy years old, is my confidant, whom I frequently entertain with a recital of my loves. [Elsewhere in the same letter, he mentions "a beautiful young eunuch who eats with me tonight, and will join me in drinking to your health."] The nobility here are not proud, and the great lack all pedantry. Here, they know better than in Germany what makes life worth living. They enjoy themselves, and let others do likewise.

III

When his second collection had become so vast that the Palazzo
Albani could no longer accommodate it, the Cardinal commissioned Carlo Marchionni, who had designed the sacristy of St.
Peter's, to build him a villa on the outskirts of town. By the
time Winckelmann moved into the attic of the palazzo in Via
Quattro Fontane, the construction of the Villa Albani (now
Villa Torlonia, in Via Salaria) was well under way. Inaugurated
in Winckelmann's presence in 1763, it was the last Roman villa
to be built in the grand manner. Instead of arranging his statues,
reliefs, sarcophagi, etc. in prosaic rows, Albani incorporated
them into the buildings and grounds in such a fashion that they
give the impression of having been expressly designed for their
present location. The total effect made by the buildings, severely
Palladian in concept with touches of Sansovino in the decorative
detail, and of the architecturally laid-out gardens is therefore
more organic and homogeneous than that conveyed by the
Villa Medici and Villa Borghese, with their distracting mixture
of antique and modern motifs. In accordance with the over-
all design of the whole complex—the villa itself, the gardens,

H*

and the coffee house, or semicircular portico which closes off the propect—Albani had the statuary and paintings in each room or flight of rooms grouped around a pivotal work that sets the historical and aesthetic theme for that part of the property. In so doing, he created one of the earliest examples not only of a "living" museum, but of one organized from a scholarly viewpoint. At the same time, the Villa Albani is also the only eighteenth-century museum that has been preserved practically unchanged. It owes this distinction to a unique concatenation of circumstances, which may well be unraveled here even if it extends beyond Winckelmann's own life span.

On Alessandro Albani's death in 1779, the property passed to his nephew, Carlo's son Giovan Francesco, who became a cardinal himself and as such later advised Pius VI against making any concessions to the leaders of the French Revolution. After Napoleon's invasion of Italy, the possessions of the Albani family, along with those of the Colonna, Borghese, and others that had remained faithful to the Pope when the latter was deposed in 1798, were confiscated and largely removed to the Musée Napoléon in Paris; among the objects taken from the Villa Albani were many of the manuscripts that Winckelmann had left behind when starting out on his last journey. At the Congress of Vienna, it was decided that all the art works sequestered by the French should revert to their rightful owners. The Albani family, however, proved to be unable or unwilling to pay the shipping charges back to Rome. It took the intervention of Antonio Canova, the greatest sculptor of his age, to ensure that at least the relief of Antinoüs, one of the best of all antique works of its kind, was returned to the place to which Albani and Winckelmann had originally assigned it in the villa. (It is ironic, in view of Winckelmann's opinion of Paris as "the seat of foolish notions"—"*Sitz der törichten Lüste*"— that the bulk of his manuscripts should repose to this day in the Bibliothèque Nationale.) When the Cardinal's family died out in 1854, the villa narrowly missed being purchased by the City of Rome and converted into a public museum, whose holdings would inevitably have been adulterated through the sale of old and the acquisition of new items. For a number of years, the villa and grounds belonged to the Counts Castelbarco of Milan, and the collections, to the Chigi family of Rome. This precarious situation came to an end when they were reunited in the possession of a single owner, the Roman tobacco magnate Prince Alessandro Torlonia. In 1870, the property was threatened with destruction when the troops of the newly founded Kingdom of Italy breached the defenses that had hurriedly been thrown up by the papal army at nearby Porta Pia. The Villa Albani not only escaped major damage but became the scene of an historical event: the Sala della Pace on the second floor saw the signing of the armistice which sealed the disappearance of the Papal States from the map, its former territories with the exception of Vatican City being absorbed into modern Italy. During the past hundred years, the Villa Albani with its Raphaels, Peruginos, Van Dycks, and its countless antique statues, mosaics, funerary urns, and the like, has remained the private property of the Torlonia family. One of Prince Alessandro's first acts as owner had been the unveiling, in the memorial year 1868, of a bust of Winckelmann that had been donated by Ludwig I of Bavaria.

The most impressive part of the main building is the so-called *galleria nobile*, a flight of rooms decorated with much statuary and with reliefs set into walls lined with polychrome marble. It also contains, on the ceiling of the great hall, a major work by Mengs: the *Parnassus*, also called *Apollo and the Nine Muses*. A much-admired painting in its own time, this fresco reflects, in the pair of female dancers on the left, the Herculanean motifs that were just beginning to be popular. Mengs, a better portraitist than fresco painter, had employed models that were instantly recognized by their contemporaries. To us, the figures on either side of Apollo (whose face is as saccharinely sweet as that of any calendar Jesus, while his physique approaches Winckelmann's ideal of the hermaphrodite) look like so many other heavy-lidded ladies whose likenesses adorn the walls and ceilings of Italian palazzi. To their friends, they represented Vittoriuccia, the Countess Cheroffini's oldest daughter, shown as Mnemosyne, the Muse of Memory who touches her ear as a token of remembrance, and on the god's other side, Margareta Mengs, who holds in her hand a scroll on which her husband's name and the date are inscribed. The artist had moved into the unfinished building in 1760, and, after finishing the fresco the following spring, departed for Madrid "aboard a man-of-war of seventy guns," as the awed Winckelmann remarked, which Charles IV of Spain had expressly sent to fetch him. Appointed First Painter to the King, Mengs spent the next few years in Madrid and Aranjuez, with a princely salary that included free accommodations and the use of a carriage emblazoned with the royal arms of Spain. Winckelmann was not to see him again.

On a more commercial level, the collaboration between Albani, Winckelmann, and Mengs which had given birth to the *Parnassus* was paralleled by intricate negotiations with contractors, art dealers, and others whose services were required for the completion of the villa. It was the largest building project in Rome, and the orders placed by Albani were big enough to whet the appetite of the dealers and antiquarians who had their stalls around Piazza Navona. Occupied as he was with official duties, the Cardinal let his secretary look after many of the details. Winckelmann had to keep his wits about him to avoid being victimized by these men, some of whom thought nothing of removing such identifying marks as crucifixes and escutcheons from medieval sculptures which could then be sold as antique. Even more blatant were the abuses practiced by the restorers, who had an ally of sorts in Albani himself: possessed by the idea of creating a living museum, he insisted on the restoration of any statue that could possibly be made whole. In a few cases, as in Piranesi's restoration of the relief of a woman with mirror in the Villa Albani, the operation may be said to have succeeded; in other instances, notably in the *Antinoüs* with his clumsily repaired hands, it clearly failed. In all such cases, Albani and Winckelmann had to tread warily lest they be taken in by unscrupulous craftsmen, whose work was facilitated by the fact that relics of antique statuary were still being dug up in the city and its environs. Not all of these dealers and sculptors were able to resist the temptation to "improve" such fragments, and the price for which they could be sold to unsuspecting foreigners, by the addition of whatever parts happened to be missing. Many eighteenth-century houses, in England and elsewhere, still contain statues which their owners would not have recognized if they had seen them in their pristine state of fragmentation, that is, as they had looked when the restorers had purchased them, often for the price of the material only, from a peasant who had found them when plowing his fields. Winckelmann, who as we saw disliked the whole idea of restoring damaged works, came to rely increasingly in all these problems on the judgment of his friend Bartolommeo Cavaceppi. This sculptor, a fair artist in his own right, had drawn up a regular theory of restoration, which he later published with a companion volume showing engravings of statues that had passed through his hands. According to Cavaceppi, no restoration should ever be attempted unless three-quarters of the work in question had been preserved. Even then, it should not be undertaken except by a sculptor who knew his art history— who knew, for example, that in Phidias' time the cornea of the eye was not shown by an indentation in the marble or bronze, or that individual strands of hair were not sculpted until the period of Hadrian. Since Cavaceppi's knowledge was matched by his honesty and good taste (which made him recommend, among other things, that the places where restored parts were joined onto the original be not smoothed over but made to look like a normal break in the material), Winckelmann reluctantly agreed in the end that while the restoration of antique works was never desirable, it could on occasion be defended.

Even aside from his dubious predilection for restored statues, Albani was no innocent lamb thrown helpless among the wolves of the Roman art world. He could haggle with the shrewdest collectors and dealers, and often enough came out on top because he did not hesitate to use the weight of his official position even in these matters. On a visit one evening to an aristocratic Roman house, his eye fell on an unusual object in the hall. A round, phallic shaft with reliefs around the base, it was of white marble and stood some ten feet tall. Like a deaf man who will unfailingly pick up any remark made about himself, the Cardinal could see perfectly well when it came to antique works that interested him. But he had to be sure. Calling his secretary aside, he told him to examine the object inobtrusively, and to say what he thought of it. When Winckelmann came back reporting that it was a valuable obelisk, Albani turned to the host and inquired if he would let him buy it. The owner politely declined, and the Cardinal did not insist. Early the next morning, however, when all was yet quiet in the house in which he had just been a guest, he had his own men pick the lock and remove the obelisk to a shed on his own property. The owner could guess at whose door the theft was to be laid, but Albani was such a powerful man in Rome, and known to have such a temper when crossed, that the other thought it wise to acquiesce in his loss. When the man had died, Albani had the obelisk erected in a corner of the grounds of Villa Albani, where it stands to this day in mute testimony to a churchman's unholy passion for antiquities.

Cemented by such exploits, the relationship between Albani and Winckelmann survived intact the strains placed upon it by the petty frictions of everyday life and the intrigues of envious outsiders. Among these was the Count de Caylus in Paris, who had heard rumors about the art treasures that were being assembled in the villa and now tried, through the Francophile Paciaudi, to smuggle a draftsman onto the property in order to make sketches of the more valuable sculptures. Alerted by a friend, Winckelmann easily foiled the plot. He was determined to be the first to examine these works, and to describe them in the *History*: "[Caylus] is trying by various means to have drawings made of the Cardinal's villa," he gloated, "but I headed him off, as I headed off all others. No one shall have what I can use myself." His position as Albani's confidant, and therewith his standing at the Vatican, was important enough to be defended, in dog-in-the-manger fashion if necessary. But it was a temporary position, subject to being terminated if, as was to be expected, the Cardinal should die before him. In order to make it permanent, Winckelmann needed an official appointment which would formalize his tenuous connection with the Holy See. As luck would have it, his friend Muzel-Stosch was traveling through Germany just then, where he recommended Winckelmann to several princes who were looking for an art expert to help them administer their museums and educate their children. The first invitation to return to Germany reached Winckelmann in 1761, in the form of an offer extended to him by the Landgrave Frederick II of Hesse-Cassel. Winckelmann declined, saying that he was loath to leave Rome before the completion of the *History* and that the Elector of Saxony, who still paid him his stipend, would not want him to return unless it be to his own court. At this stage of the proceedings, Mengs, who was still in Rome, cannily informed their mutual friends in Saxony of the offer received by Winckelmann. He was careful not to identify the prince from whom it had emanated, hinting that Frederick the Great himself might be trying to lure his erstwhile subject back to Prussia. The little ruse had the desired effect. Afraid of losing Winckelmann to their enemy in Berlin, Bianconi and Rauch bestirred themselves sufficiently to procure for him a *pro forma* appointment as antiquary and custodian of the Elector's coin collection, the latter a position that had once been filled by Algarotti. Since the Electorate's treasury was empty as a result of the continuing war with Prussia, the appointment was not to take effect until three years after the cessation of hostilities. For the time being, the new appointee was granted permission to exchange the title of *Pensionnaire du Roi,* which smacked of charity, for the more respectable one of *Antiquaire de Sa Majesté le Roi de Pologne.*

Winckelmann had every reason to be content with this outcome. The war showed no sign of ending, and in the meantime, the promise of employment in Dresden, coupled with a similar offer from Vienna, gave him enough leverage to elicit a matching response from the Vatican. Rising to the bait much as Augustus III had done, Clement XIII appointed Winckelmann to the dignity of *Commissario delle Antichità della Camera Apostolica,* or Papal Antiquary, by a decree issued on April 16, 1763. It was a highly desirable job, combining a modest salary with much prestige and, if one knew how to arrange oneself, a quite tolerable amount of work. On paper, Winckelmann had to keep track of all antique statues, paintings, engraved gems, coins, mosaics, inscriptions, etc., in the Papal States, make sure that no such objects were smuggled out of the country, and dispense permits to undertake excavations anywhere within his jurisdiction. In practice, these routine matters were taken care of by his assistants, minor civil servants who earned their pay by registering newly found art works, making the rounds of museums to see that nothing was missing, and checking the cargos of barges being loaded on the Tiber. The Papal Antiquary, or, as he was sometimes called, the President of Antiquities, himself merely acted as a guide whenever prominent visitors were taken on a tour of the city, and advised the Vatican on the gifts of antique works that were customarily presented to such visitors at the conclusion of their stay. Since the latter usually reciprocated by rewarding the antiquary with a small sum of money or a snuffbox or whatever, the office could be made remunerative as well as prestigious. Winckelmann's immediate predecessor, the Marchese Ridolfino Venuti, who had earned his scholarly spurs in the service of the Academy of Cortona, had become so partial to these gratuities that he turned into a regular cicerone who conducted about Rome not only Frederick the Great's sister, the Margravine of Bayreuth, but many ordinary tourists as well. Winckelmann, poor, but busy with his writing and conscious of his scholarly reputation, quietly restored the office to the dignity it had possessed many years before, when its first incumbent had guided the Emperor Charles V through the Eternal City. He conducted only those who could truly qualify as visitors of state, or who came recommended to him as men of sufficient promise or caliber to benefit from the experience. By concentrating on this aspect of the job he also avoided possible conflicts with old friends, who had been merrily greasing the palms of customs officials in order to export works of art, only to wake up one morning to find that Winckelmann had been given the task of stopping precisely this sort of thing.

Winckelmann had been appointed Papal Antiquary not

only because he wanted the job, but because a way had to be found to keep him in Rome despite the offers he was beginning to receive from elsewhere. The position itself called for a man of high qualifications. The Papal Antiquary occupied the top rung of a professional ladder that extended all the way down to the thousands of nameless guides who offered their services to newly arrived travelers. These had no sooner alighted from the coach, in Piazza del Popolo or Piazza di Spagna, than they were beset by a gesticulating swarm of ciceroni who offered to conduct them to an inn, take them sightseeing, change their money, and perform all the other necessary and unnecessary tasks that are so readily usurped by tourist guides. More highly regarded than these public guides were the private ones who had been retained by the great Roman families, the religious orders, and the foreign embassies. Recruited from the ranks of indigent local scholars, these men did not go to meet the stage but were called upon whenever a German bishop or an English lord or a French diplomat wished to be conducted to this or that monument; for "strangers [were] generally advised," Smollett tells us, "to employ an antiquarian to instruct them in all the curiosities of Rome, and this is a necessary expense when a person wants to become a connoisseur in painting, statuary, and architecture."[6] Above them all towered Winckelmann. He alone did the honors of the city on behalf of its sovereign, the Pope. It was a taxing job, and a sensitive one calling for a knowledge of history and of art, familiarity with court protocol, and fluency in half a dozen languages. The man who held it had to be not only highly educated, but tactful, if necessary firm, and thoroughly inured to the idiosyncrasies of visitors who for all their noble origin and exalted rank were often enough men of dubious character and habits. Some were drunkards who expected the Antiquary, who had called for them at their inn at dawn and spent the day trudging about the ruins in the heat and dust of a Roman summer, to join them in their carousals at night. Others had appetites that were less easily satisfied, in which case Winckelmann put them in touch with Viscioletta, a much sought-after call girl of the time. Still others made such a nuisance of themselves that the police had to be called, as happened with Sir Francis Dashwood of the Medmenham Monks and the Society of Dilettanti, who while in Rome made so many outrageous remarks about the Holy See that he ended by being thrown out of the Papal States.

While he had been selected for this post largely on the recommendation of Cardinal Giuseppe Spinelli, a friend of Passionei's who had continued to keep an eye on him after the latter's death, he owed another appointment to his present patron. On May 2, 1763, he was made *Scriptor Linguae Teutonicae,* charged with the cataloguing of certain German manuscripts in the Vatican library, where he worked directly under Albani. Like that of Papal Antiquary, the new office carried with it a certain amount of discretionary power: the *scriptores,* of which there were several for each of the more important languages represented in the library's holdings, had to pass on all applications submitted by scholars who wished to use the library's resources. Unlike the other office, however, that of *scriptor* required the incumbent to be present in his place of employment several mornings a week. Since the distance from Via Quattro Fontane to the Vatican took a good hour to cover on foot, Winckelmann soon began to chafe under this time-consuming obligation. After a year or two, when his standing as a guide had become such that a conducted tour with the Abbé Winckelmann formed the high point of many a sovereign's visit to Rome, the Pope tacitly dispensed him from having to set foot in the library.

With his twin appointments as Papal Antiquary and *Scriptor,* Winckelmann had reached the pinnacle of his worldly career at forty-six. It had taken him thirty years of unremitting hard work to attain these modest distinctions, which were nevertheless considerable in view of the odds against which he had had to fight. If he had not also been an author, art historian, and educator, he would be remembered like Venuti—in a footnote appended to some histories of eighteenth-century Rome. His real distinction, of course, had lain all along in a different field: in his writings, whose cumulative effect was beginning to be felt all over Europe even before the *History* was published.

IV

Winckelmann's literary production extends far beyond the "Reflections," the *Catalogue*, the pamphlets on the excavations, and the *History*. In 1759 alone he published, along with the "Description of the Belvedere Torso," three major essays in a German quarterly whose editor, Christian Felix Weisse, had asked him for contributions while Winckelmann was still working on the Stosch collection in Florence; another one followed as a separate publication in 1762. Since the arguments contained in these four essays ("Suggestions on the Manner in which Works of Art should be viewed," "On Grace in Works of Art," "Architectural Notes on the ancient Temples at Agrigento," and "Notes on the Architecture of the Ancients") were to be reiterated in the *History*, the reader who does not shrink from a discussion of these topics is referred to the last chapter of this book. Three other late works, however, warrant some examination here because they are enlightening from the biographical point of view. The first two frame the *History*, the one appearing just before and the other shortly after that book.

The third is a major scholarly work that was left unfinished at his death, and had to be completed by other hands.

Despite its formidably Teutonic title, the *Abhandlung von der Fähigkeit der Empfindung des Schönen in der Kunst, und dem Unterrichte in derselben* is no more than a brief essay, "On the Nature and the Cultivation of Sensibility to the Beautiful in Art," in which Winckelmann sketches a typology of the art lover. How does such a person differ, he asks, from the general run of mankind, seeing that the ability to perceive beauty in works of art is, like common sense, a gift that every man claims to possess and that is nevertheless very rare? Winckelmann's description is tailored to fit the young man—or rather, the image that he had formed of the young man—for whose guidance the essay was written and to whom it is dedicated: Friedrich Reinhold von Berg, whom we shall meet presently. Receptivity to beauty being a youthful trait, he says, the art lover should be a young person, but not one so young, or so structured, as to be more susceptible to feminine than to masculine beauty. One is tempted to see in this assertion an instance of the author's own predilections in these matters, if Diderot and others had not also confessed that they were tired of the sight of all those white bosoms and pink bottoms with which the painters of the time were regaling them. It was a cardinal thesis not only of Winckelmann's aesthetic, but of the entire neoclassical reaction to the rococo, that sensual involvement hinders rather than helps the free play of sensibility.

The art lover should also be intelligent and well read, but not learned, because "from Plato's time down to ours, works that deal with general concepts of beauty are . . . devoid of sense, useless, and trivial in content."[7] It is the company of men of good taste, rather than the study and the library, that forms the proper environment for the growth of this faculty. Since "we tend to think in the manner in which we are formed," the typical art lover is also likely to be a good-looking person, and, almost by definition, a man of leisure. For while sensibility to beauty is an inborn trait that cannot be acquired through study, it still needs to be brought out and cultivated, a process that is incompatible with working for a living. The ideal place in which to cultivate it is Rome, which abounds in works of art of a quality and diversity that could not be duplicated if one visited all the museums of Europe. The ideal mentor with whom to cultivate it is none other than the author himself, although he does not say so in so many words: a man who has acquired good taste through being exposed to beauty in all its forms, sharpened his own sensibility through the reading of ancient literature, and reached a condition of leisure even if he was not born into it. It is noteworthy that Winckelmann, who by background and inclination would certainly have been a democrat if democracy had then existed as a practical alternative to absolutism, did not for a moment believe in the adage that art is for the people. Far from it: its study if not its practice is an aristocratic pursuit, and he himself is at his most autocratic in the judgments he passes on modern artists. Mengs is placed high above Tiepolo, Michelangelo cannot hold a candle to Raphael, and Poussin's coloring is held to be so defective that it serves as illustration of the fact that the perception of beauty is as unevenly distributed among painters as it is among laymen. In short, Winckelmann here takes up one of his favorite dialectic positions, that of an engineer who throws a bridge across a river. One end is anchored on the Greek masters, granite pillars that do not budge no matter how strongly the tide of contemporary taste presses against them; the other is precariously held up by the moderns, all but a handful of them dwarfs in stature. Once again, one hesitates to cross this bridge, especially in this case where even Winckelmann's style, the railing that guides one across so reassuringly in the "Reflections" and the *History*, is not always firm. Published just before the *History* in 1763, the essay is less interesting for its content than for its *ad hominem* structure. The bond that tied the author to the man for whom he wrote shows up unmistakably on every page.

The *History of Ancient Art* had barely been launched when Winckelmann completed a project on which he had worked intermittently ever since his arrival in Dresden from Nöthnitz. In that winter of 1754-5, the association with Oeser and his discovery of painting had convinced him that the originality shown by painters in selecting their subject matter had failed to keep pace with the perfection of their technical skills. "During the past few centuries," he had already lamented in the "Reflections," "the lives of the saints, legends, and metamorphoses have constituted practically the only themes treated in painting. Modified and refined in a thousand different ways, they have left the public surfeited and exhausted." Now, ten years later, he published his weakest work, *Versuch einer Allegorie, besonders für die Kunst*. Having failed to define the pivotal concept of "allegory," and to set it off from such kindred but far from synonymous terms as "emblem," "figure," "metaphor," etc., he stuffed his "Repertory of Allegories, primarily for the Plastic Arts" with motley observations thrown together under headings like "Allegories based on Color, and on the Material of Implements and Buildings" or "Allegories of Divinities" (he considered even the Greek myths to be allegories, by which term he understood not the figurative treatment of one subject under the guise of another, but quite simply the use of pictures to convey a meaning). Nor did he draw any distinction between various art forms; coins and statues, paint-

228

ings and bas-reliefs, and even literary genres are mentioned as if they were interchangeable vehicles of artistic expression. Although the essay was intended to be used as a handbook by practicing artists, one cannot imagine a painter standing before his easel, his brush in one hand and in the other Winckelmann's essay, which contained such pearls of antiquarian wisdom as "A poet was designated by a lyre, such as Hesiod's statue on Mount Helicon held on its knees" or "In an ancient epigram, loquaciousness is indicated by the figure of a woodpecker."[8] Once again Winckelmann was publishing, as he had done with the appendices to the "Reflections," the leftovers from a major work instead of discarding them. Dedicated to the Königliche Gesellschaft der Wissenschaften in Göttingen, which had just made him a member, this ill-conceived little essay forms the reverse side, as it were, of the medal that shines forth so brightly in the *History*. The critics, including old friends like Oeser and Francke, lost no time in tearing it to pieces. Having started so late as a writer, Winckelmann had reached his late forties before he had to learn to carry on in the face of an almost unanimously hostile reaction on the part of his readers. After an initial show of petulance, during which he threatened to give one reviewer a good drubbing by "washing his head without soap"—"*una lavatura di capo senza sapone*"— he learned to take censure as calmly as he had long received applause.

Monumenti antichi inediti, spiegati ed illustrati is a pioneering work in the field of archaeological methodology. The first two volumes of these *Unpublished ancient Monuments, explained and illustrated* were issued in 1767, with 208 engravings; the third, completed by Stefano Raffei and containing very little from Winckelmann's own pen, was not published until 1772. The term "unpublished" as used here refers not only to coins, statues, cameos, bas-reliefs, and other "monuments" never before reproduced on plates, but also to many that had hitherto been misinterpreted or left entirely unexplained. In the preface, Winckelmann states that he wrote the work because earlier commentators had limited themselves to the examination of sculptures, etc., that were easily identified and interpreted; Montfaucon, for example, had dealt so indiscriminately with everything that "in wishing to take in all; he appears to have come away holding nothing."[9] The whole project was undertaken under the auspices of Albani, to whom Winckelmann dedicated the first two volumes because the Cardinal had offered so much expert advice, along with his financial support, that the *Monuments* is "your work no less than mine.—Am I, too, not yours," he continued, "since I owe my present condition to the generosity with which you received me?" This dedication, and the numerous references to Albani in the text itself, caused Lessing and Goethe to wonder whether the author had not perhaps been too partial, in his selection of the works to be interpreted, to his patron's holdings; these are represented by 114 items, while the Capitoline Museum furnished 62, and the Villa Borghese a mere 50. The two last-named collections, of course, had long been open to the public, whereas the contents of the Villa Albani had been jealously guarded by Winckelmann, who had reserved for himself the right to describe them. If this was a privilege, it also represented an obligation, which he now paid off handsomely both in the main body and in the introductory chapter, or *Trattato preliminare,* an abridged Italian version of the *History,* which serves as a prologue to the plates and explicatory text of the *Monuments.*

The main thrust of the *Monuments* is twofold. It lies in reclaiming for Greek mythology many of the works that had been thought to depict historical events, and in restricting the scope of the originality with which the ancients had until then been credited. In the course of examining many works that had been misinterpreted, Winckelmann became convinced that his colleagues' ignorance of Greek literature, their chauvinism in so far as most of them were Italians, and the lack of a qualitative differentiation between Greek and Roman art had obscured the central fact that Greek mythology had formed the chief thematic inspiration for the artists of antiquity. By calling a certain relief on a sarcophagus in the Villa Medici "The Rape of the Sabine Women," the local antiquaries had in effect appropriated for their own tradition a work that is actually Greek, and shows the abduction of the ·daughters of King Leucippus of Sicyon by the Dioscuri. Multiplied many times, this sort of thing had led many collectors to overestimate the importance of historical subject matter in ancient art, at the expense of the mythological. Compared with works inspired by Greek mythology (in all its modifications from Homer to the last Alexandrian scribe), those that deal with the legendary foundation of Rome, or with the deeds of the Roman emperors as shown on bas-reliefs in the public buildings erected by them, are insignificant. Furthermore, the ancients only rarely represented scenes that had sprung wholly from their imagination; the only major exceptions to this rule are dances, bacchanalia, and other intrinsically fanciful scenes. This applies even to such realistic themes as the many supposed vignettes from the daily life of the ancients, which can be traced back, more often than not, to scenes that are well established in Greek mythology and literature. Not only sheer phantasy, but the mentality that gave birth to genre painting in the Dutch manner, had been all but unknown to the Greeks.

The *Monuments* has been called an erudite book in contrast to the *History,* which is enthusiastic.[10] The point is well taken. The absence of any aesthetic valuation in this work has been explained as a result of Winckelmann's advancing years—

the more exuberant passages of the *History* date from the late 1750's whereas the *Monuments* was written in the mid-1760's —and of his propinquity to the Papal Court, which might have looked askance at too dithyrambic a praise of pagan beauty. More likely, the controlled tenor of the *Monuments* stems from the fact that it is his most methodical work next to the *Catalogue*. Instead of describing what he sees, and doing so as if he were the first to see it, he corrects in these two works the mistakes made by others. It is not the kind of writing that lends itself to flights of fancy or turns of phrase. The section that he read out to Clement XIII in Castel Gandolfo, in October 1763, may serve as an example. It deals with three bas-reliefs in Rome that had been thought to represent the death of Agamemnon, and are now believed to illustrate Orestes' murder of Aegisthus and Clytemnestra. Beginning with a polemical passage against earlier commentators, Winckelmann compares the accounts given of these events by Homer, Sophocles, Euripides, and other writers; after retelling the story in his own words, he explains the bas-reliefs, austerely enough for a man of his temperament and convictions, on the basis of this literary evidence, and of such historical and folkloristic observations as only he could provide.

The *Monuments* was written in Italian because Albani, who knew no German, wished it so, because Winckelmann himself was afraid that he might be losing his hold over his native German after so many years spent abroad, and because most of the experts with whom he took issue had been Italians. No doubt there was also pride involved in this (after all, he had already demonstrated that he could write in German and French) and a sense of "When in Rome . . ." He also had to think of the preparation of the engravings, which had to be done on the spot since the plates were heavy, and were likely to be damaged in transit if shipped across the Alps to

Walther or another German publisher. In the days before photography and mass tourism, when only a few readers could be expected to have actually seen a Greek or Roman work, engravings were of course an integral part of any such work. Those in the *Monuments* were done by Giovanni Battista Casanova, a brother of the celebrated Giacomo, and according to Winckelmann "the greatest draftsman in Rome." Casanova, unfortunately, turned out to have prepared reproductions not only of genuine but of some faked antique works, which he submitted to the unsuspecting author along with the others. Someone else might have shrugged off the deception as a poor joke, one that was perpetrated often enough in those days. Winckelmann, however, was hurt in his most sensitive spot, his reputation as an expert in all matters relating to ancient art, including that of discriminating between the genuine and the false. To make matters worse, Casanova, who had himself invested in the *Monuments* by taking over a share of the production costs, suddenly made himself scarce without informing Winckelmann. The latter was now forced not only to shoulder the whole financial burden by himself, but to engage other engravers, less skillful than his partner had been, for the remaining illustrations. He sued Casanova in court and had him convicted of fraud, *in absentia* since the engraver had meanwhile moved to Dresden. But the damage had been done: the publication of the *Monuments* had to be postponed several times, and the plates were of very inferior quality.

A staggering amount of work and worry lies hidden beneath the innocuous-looking words "Published at the Author's Expense" on the title page of the *Monuments*. It entailed asking friends to sell subscriptions to the work, and when they had done so, arguing with bankers about the rate of exchange to be applied to the drafts that Wiedewelt sent from Copenhagen, Muzel-Stosch and Nicolai from Berlin, Mengs from

Madrid, Barthélemy and the Duc de La Rochefoucauld from Paris, Sir William Hamilton from Naples, Berg from Riga, and others from Dresden, Vienna, and even Constantinople. It entailed hiring engravers and supervising them at work, and packing the cases with his own hands before shipping them off to all these destinations. Winckelmann did all this in addition to his duties as a scholar, guide, and librarian. He did it, furthermore, at a time when there existed no effective copyright legislation and when business practices in general were of a complexity and unpredictability to frighten all but the hardiest speculators: in the century that had begun with Law's Mississippi Company and was to end with the bankruptcy of the French State. While he was not a successful businessman, in the sense that his dream of achieving financial independence with the publication of this book did not materialize, he did it well enough to break even.

V

So many visitors to Rome insisted on being conducted about the city by Winckelmann that an entertaining "Who Was Who in the 1760's" could be compiled from his notes alone. Among the English, there was Frederick Calvert, Lord Baltimore, "proprietor of all Maryland and Virginia, with an annual income of £30,000 which he is unable to enjoy: one of those beastly, malcontent Englishmen who are surfeited with everything under the sun." Baltimore later turned up in Vienna, with a harem of eight women, on whom he experimented by feeding sour foods to the fat and a meat-and-dairy diet to the lean ones. Asked by the chief of police which of the eight was his wife, his lordship replied that it was his habit to answer such questions with a challenge to a boxing match, and if the challenge was turned down, to depart forthwith with all his ladies. Depart he did from Vienna as he had from Rome, where Winckelmann had found him so unbearable that he would have no more to do with him. John Ker, Duke of Roxburgh and a leading member of the Society of Dilettanti, was a man of the same kind; so was the Duke of York, brother of George

III, and in Winckelmann's eyes "the greatest ass I know, no credit to his rank or country."[11] The most flamboyant of them all was Edward Wortley Montagu, an inveterate traveler and one of the first men to be successfully inoculated against small-pox, in a medical feat that was celebrated by Voltaire. Winckelmann was impressed by his uncommon skill in speaking German, which Wortley Montagu had learned in Leipzig, and thought at one time of accompanying him to Egypt. He did not go along because the trip would have entailed a long absence from Rome, but he eagerly followed his friend's escapades from afar: his abduction of the wife of the Danish consul in Alexandria—Wortley Montagu not only cuckolded the husband, but sent him on a trumped-up errand all the way to Holland—and his conversion to Roman Catholicism, which had been dramati-cally timed to coincide with a visit to the Holy Sepulcher. When he announced his discovery of an Egyptian bust to the Royal Society in London, Wortley Montagu in turn was gracious enough to preface his report with an acknowledgment that was duly read by the president: "As to the Figure I need say nothing as I here send the Opinion of Abbé Winkleman [*sic*], than whom no one has greater skill in antique statues."

Not all of Winckelmann's English friends resided on the outer fringes of sanity. Many were eminently rational men, such as Robert Adams, Sir Horace Mann, Sir William Hamilton, and James Boswell, who after making Winckelmann's acquain-tance praised his "fine and classical taste." Gibbon, strangely enough, does not seem to have met him in Rome; but another English visitor added a characteristic touch in remarking that "[the] Abbé Winckelmann had not the gaiety or gallantry of a lively French abbé, but he had ease and good breeding with a sufficient knowledge of the world."[12] This estimate is particularly striking in view of its source: the author and demagogue John

XXII. *Etruscan funerary urn, with battle scene. Florence, Museo Etrusco.*

XXIII. THE CANON OF BEAUTY:

The Apollo Belvedere—*"The so-called Greek profile...consists of an almost straight or a slightly depressed line formed by forehead and nose..."*

XXIV. THE CANON OF BEAUTY:
The Albani Pallas—*"In ideal
heads, the eyes are invariably
set deeper than in nature . . .
The chin is not bisected by
a dimple . . ."*

XXV. THE CANON OF BEAUTY:
*Roman copy of the spear-
bearer* (Doryphorus) *of Polyclitus—"According to several
ancient writers, a beautiful
forehead is supposed to be
low . . ."*

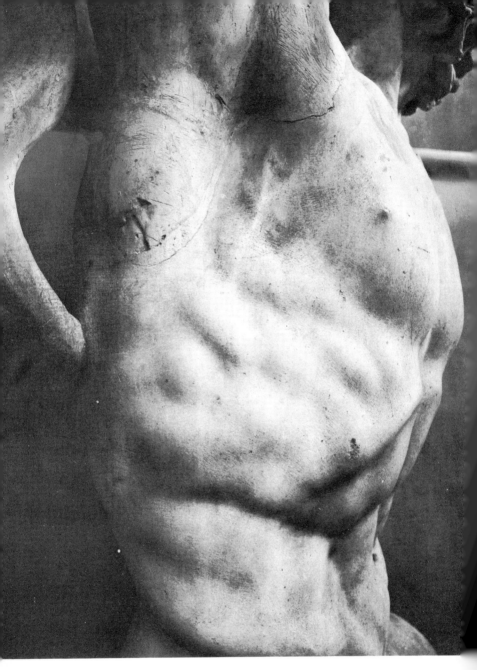

XXVI. THE CANON OF BEAUTY:
Laocoön, *detail—"A wide and deeply arched chest was regarded as a universal mark of beauty..."*

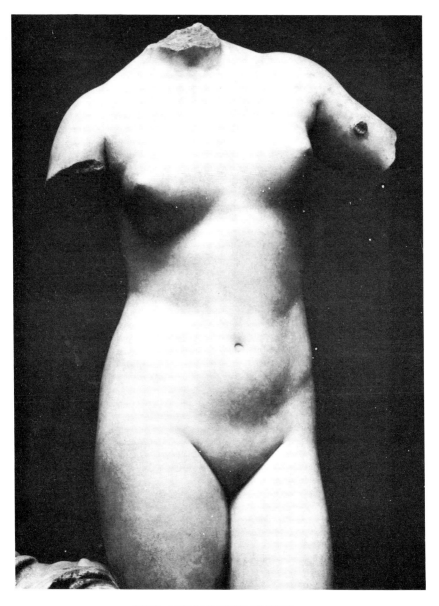

XXVII. THE CANON OF BEAUTY:
The Aphrodite of Cyrene—"*The bosom of female figures is never overly full...The navel is markedly indented, especially in female figures, where it is drawn in an arch and occasionally in the shape of a small semi-circle pointing downward ...*"

XXVIII. THE CANON OF BEAUTY:
*Greek athlete—"... The abdomen is
... without belly... Of the
testicles, the left is always larger ...
In youthful figures, the knees are
... smooth and simply arched, without tensing of muscles..."*

XXIX. ASPECTS OF THE NON-BEAUTIFUL:
1) *Caricature: Drunken Hercules.*

XXX. ASPECTS OF THE NON-BEAUTIFUL:
2) *Realistic portraiture: Bust of Caracalla.*

XXXI. ASPECTS OF THE NON-BEAUTIFUL:
3) *Carnality:* The Rape of Proserpina, *by Bernini.*

Wilkes, like Wortley Montagu a one-time Member of Parliament, Lord Mayor of London in 1774, and of course the coiner of some of the most devastating *bons mots* of that malicious century; it was he who on being warned by the Earl of Sandwich that he would end on the gallows or of disease, replied: "That depends, my lord, on whether I embrace your principles or your mistress." Wilkes's point of reference is well taken, for the blending of scholarly with social competence was indeed more common in France than elsewhere. It was, at any rate, almost unknown in the Germany of that time: the step that Winckelmann took so nimbly from the study into the salon was one that other and greater Germans—Lessing, Schiller, Beethoven—took either not at all or with dubious grace.

His esteem for individual Englishmen notwithstanding, Winckelmann held a low opinion of the aesthetic sensibilities of the race as a whole. With Montesquieu and Voltaire, he believed that the lethargic temperament of the English, coupled with the unfortunate climate in which they had to live, was bound to inhibit any development of the arts among them. He must have expressed these views with some vehemence, because an English painter with whom he had argued in Rome found it necessary to refute them in a vigorously worded defense of his countrymen's artistic patrimony.[13]

Winckelmann's attitude to the French was more complex. Like Lessing and Goethe, he felt that he could not strike out on his own until he had fought free of the French influence that lay so heavily on all facets of Germany's cultural life. Like them also, he looked upon France with a mixture of admiration, dislike, and envy, aiming the shafts of his ridicule not so much at the French themselves as at the numerous Germans (among them almost all the reigning houses) who aped that nation down to the last mannerism. In Winckelmann's

I

development as in that of the two poets, a residual ambivalence may be observed in this regard to the very end. On the one hand, he castigated the habit of many French travelers of considering themselves missionaries to the unenlightened tribes of Germany and Italy; on the other, he was quick to acknowledge that such men as Clérisseau and the Duc de La Rochefoucauld were among the century's finest artists and collectors. While he attacked Claude-Henri de Watelet for having wrongly identified certain antique statues in his *L'art de peindre* (1760), he became so fond of him on personal acquaintance that he regretted having criticized his scholarship. Although he frequently made fun of the French language, he wrote the *Catalogue* in it, and remained far more sensitive to the reception his works found in Paris than to what the critics thought of him in Dresden or Rome. In the end, it remained for two Frenchmen to define the common denominator of these contrasts: Diderot praised him as a "charming enthusiast," while Caylus took him to task for the "misplaced enthusiasm" of his writings, which supposedly makes these so hard to translate.[14] Winckelmann's messianic manner of argumentation was indeed totally at variance with the pretended objectivity of the Académie Royale des Beaux-Arts.

Varied and fruitful as all these contacts were, it is well to remember that they formed an exception. Most of Winckelmann's personal and professional relationships were not with Englishmen, Frenchmen, or even Italians, but with the Germans and Swiss who came to visit him in Rome. With them, he was free to speak and correspond in his own tongue, and they, in turn, were affected most immediately by his work and personality. The Swiss occupied a special place in his affections ever since the portraitist and art historian Hans Caspar Füssli had taken up a collection on his behalf in 1758. Among them were several members of the Usteri and Füssli families, who had long played a role in the intellectual life of Zürich. It is a pity that the most talented of them, Caspar's son Johann Heinrich (a cousin and namesake of the Füssli who had accompanied him to Herculaneum), did not make his way to Italy until 1770, when Winckelmann was no longer alive. As Henry Fuseli, he eventually settled in England, where he translated the "Reflections" and gained renown for his paintings of scenes from Shakespeare and *Paradise Lost;* he was elected to the Royal Society, and lies buried in St. Paul's Cathedral next to his protector Sir Joshua Reynolds. Winckelmann's ties with the Swiss, even with those he had never met, such as Wille, Sulzer, Bodmer, and Gessner, were particularly close because he thought that he could detect in these men a love of freedom that contrasted favorably with the obsequiousness of so many of his own compatriots. Unlike Rousseau, Gibbon, and others who had actually spent some time in that country, he was spared the discovery that civic and religious pusillanimity had a way of making life fully as unpleasant in republican Switzerland as it was in the more openly repressive French and Prussian monarchies; J. H. Füssli himself had been constrained to leave Zürich, where he had incurred the enmity of an elected city official, with the same dispatch that Wolff had shown when escaping from the King of Prussia. Winckelmann's Swiss friends, on their part, labored under a similar illusion when they regarded him solely as a pendant to Rousseau, as a reformer and purifier of the arts in times of decadence: it was in keeping with this illusion that Füssli followed up his translation of the "Reflections" with a book on the philosopher. Admiring and misunderstanding each other in this fashion, Winckelmann and the Swiss got on so well that he could hardly wait to visit Zürich: "Keep a little room free for a pilgrim from Rome," he advised Leonhard Usteri as early as 1766.

. . .

239

On the face of it, this last period of Winckelmann's life should have been a period of calm, a plateau on which he could rest and catch his breath after the laborious ascent of so many years. The position of Papal Antiquary had been secured, the construction of the Villa Albani completed with its inauguration in 1763, and the *History* had been published at the very end of that year. To a superficial observer, it must have seemed that Winckelmann had done his work and could now sit back to enjoy its fruits. There he was, the great scholar, sought out by distinguished men and promising youngsters who came from all over Europe in order to be guided and instructed by him. In the winter months, he occupied his comfortable apartment high up in the Palazzo Albani, in the center of Rome; after Easter, he accompanied the Cardinal to the country house near the beach at Nettuno; July and August were spent in Castel Gandolfo, where so many guests assembled for dinner or to play cards and dance far into the night that their neighbor, the Pope, complained on more than one occasion that he could not sleep on account of all this revelry. There he was, the Papal Antiquary, reading aloud to the Holy Father from the manuscript of the *Monuments,* drawing for the preparation of that work on all the scholarly resources of the city, and called upon whenever a famous tourist wished to see the Colosseum, the Appian Way, or the Capitol. When he had had enough of all this and wanted to relax, he was free to go to the opera or to attend parties and receptions, at which he not only heard the latest gossip but renewed acquaintance with the men and women who had given rise to it . . . with Giacomo Casanova, for example, or with Vittoriuccia Cheroffini, who had married a rich man and now wanted a divorce, claiming that the marriage had not been consummated and that, anyway, she was in love with another man—a eunuch, as it happened. It was one of the spicier scandals in the capital of Christendom, spicy enough, in fact, to be mentioned many years later by Goethe and Stendhal. At the time, Winckelmann was concerned lest Albani, who had been the lover of Vittoriuccia's mother, become involved in it and as a consequence lose his standing in the Vatican. There he was, the famous author whose works were reviewed in many lands and tongues, having his portrait done by Anton von Maron and Angelika Kauffmann, and ordering, through Walther in Dresden, his very own set of Meissen porcelain: blue plates, a teapot, six gold-rimmed cups with handles, and six without. Another status symbol, one that money could not buy, came to him in the form of a first biography, even if it was little more than a newspaper article. Entitled *Kurzgefasste Lebensgeschichte und Character des Herrn Präsidenten und Abt Winkelmanns [sic] in Rom,* it was written by Paalzow, who had once been his *Rektor* in the school at Seehausen and had recently asked him for details about his youth. When no information was forthcoming—we have already noted Winckelmann's compulsive reticence in this regard —and he had exhausted his own reminiscences of the subject, Paalzow published this "Brief biographical and personal Account of the Abbé Winckelmann, President [of Antiquities] in Rome" in 1764. Winckelmann, who had just dismissed as premature a similar request for information made by a Göttingen professor, was furious because the article contained a number of inaccuracies, including the misspelling of his name. This was the more galling as he had already instructed Walther never again to leave out the "c," as had happened in the first edition of his "Notes on the Architecture of the Ancients": "Thus [i.e., "Winckelmann"] my father wrote *his* name, and I, the last of my line, do not wish to change the spelling." At the same time, he was touched to see that for all of Paalzow's clumsiness, the good man held him in such awe that he felt it necessary to explain at some length that the celebrated Johann Joachim

Winckelmann was indeed identical with the young teacher who had been, only a few years before, his subordinate in a small country school in remotest Prussia.

Despite such accolades, Winckelmann found little leisure in which to rest on his laurels. His energies were in fact strained to the utmost by his duties as a guide, his continuing obligations toward Albani, the need to finish the *Monuments* even as he prepared the second printing of the *History,* and the demands made on him by his correspondence. On a fairly typical day, April 18, 1767, he wrote in his own hand three long letters totaling some 1,250 words, the equivalent of four double-spaced typed pages. It was all he could do to keep in touch with old friends: "Please convey my apologies to Mr. Francke," we read in a business letter to his publisher; "I owe him a reply, but God knows that I scarcely find time to eat. The Prince of Mecklenburg, the Reigning Prince of Anhalt-Dessau, and the Duc de La Rochefoucauld are in town, each of them desiring me to spend the whole day with him alone. My patron also wants his share, every foreigner in Rome comes bearing a letter of introduction, and there is much other correspondence waiting to be answered. I have very little time left for my own work, to which I should be devoting every minute." This kind of explanation, however, only served to fan the flames of envy and resentment at home, where it was widely believed that Winckelmann was becoming altogether too fond of the company of his betters. He knew that this impression had got about, but the imputation of arrogance is one that must be countered by deeds, not words, and there was little he could do to correct it from Rome. In any event, not many of his compatriots viewed this development as charitably as Goethe did when he commented on Winckelmann's "unremitting drive to be esteemed and highly regarded." Most Germans would rather have agreed with Moses Mendelssohn, who was repelled by his "childish boasting" about his friendships with important people and the "snide contempt" with which he looked down on German professors (Goethe and Mendelssohn admired Winckelmann's work, but never met him and wrote after his death).[15]

Which of the two was right? The truth lies somewhere in the middle, and is worth getting at because it throws light on a problem that is as topical now as it was then: How can a creative person preserve his integrity on being accepted by the establishment of his time? It is a moral problem and one of manners. In German history, it is nicely posed in the famous anecdote about Goethe's meeting with Beethoven in Teplitz. The two had made each other's acquaintance in that fashionable spa in 1812, and are said to have been taking a walk through the park when they saw, coming toward them on a narrow path, the Empress of Austria with her retinue. Goethe had no sooner recognized her than he respectfully stood aside, doffed his hat, and bowed. But Beethoven took no notice of her at all: head held high, he walked right through the group of courtiers . . . and afterward berated Goethe for what he considered his servile behavior. After parting, the two proceeded to express their opinion of one another to third parties. Goethe thought that the composer might well have been right in believing that he was the equal of any crowned head, but that he was only making things difficult for himself and others by refusing to observe the civilities. Beethoven, on the other hand, suspected that Goethe was fonder of keeping company with people of rank and position than befitted a great poet. As in most such archetypal confrontations, the contrast is exaggerated for the sake of dramatic effect; Goethe was not nearly the sycophant, or Beethoven the boor, that the story would seem to indicate. But the problem is a real one for all that, a hurdle that has to be faced by any successful artist or intellectual who intends to remain committed to his craft or cause. It is instructive to see

how Winckelmann took that hurdle, because it loomed larger
for him than it did for the others. He came from a background
that was much humbler than Beethoven's, let alone Goethe's;
in the eyes of many, he had already jeopardized his integrity by
his conversion; and he lived in pre-revolutionary times, when
the power to grant acceptance to outsiders was vested in individuals who could revoke their blessing as arbitrarily as they
had bestowed it. In Winckelmann's day, a minor French aristo-
crat could give Voltaire a beating and have him thrown into
the Bastille. In Goethe's and Beethoven's day, public opinion
had become so powerful that Napoleon himself was not able
to silence Madame de Staël. It is against this background that
we must gauge the validity of Mendelssohn's criticism.

Clearly, a man who could refer to the King of England's
brother as an "ass" was no mere namedropper. Equally clearly,
a man who could write that "fifty years hence, there may be no
Pope and no priest left, [and] some crazy Englishman will get
a notion in his head to have Trajan's column transported to
London," was no believer in the permanence of social institutions. On the contrary: Winckelmann's prophetic talents
were of such a high order that they allowed him to foresee the
advent of the French Revolution, the deposition of Pius VI,
and the removal to foreign lands of much Italian art (it was
this eventuality that made him speed up the revision of the
History, while the works described in it were still in their
accustomed place). If he reveled nonetheless in his familiarity
with men of rank, it was because he liked some of them as individuals and found them useful as vehicles for the dissemina-
tion of his ideas. After all, who were the men for whose sake
he had neglected his correspondence with Francke? George
Augustus of Mecklenburg-Strelitz, the youngest brother of
Queen Charlotte Sophia and brother-in-law of George III, was
a boy in his teens who had been tutored by Genzmer and gave

every indication of possessing a genuine interest in antiquities. Leopold III Frederick Francis of Anhalt-Dessau, then in his early twenties, had been accompanied on a portion of his Italian journey by Laurence Sterne, and later became one of the most enlightened princes of Germany; while still under Winckelmann's spell, he built the neoclassical palace at Wörlitz. We have already met the Duc de La Rochefoucauld among the connoisseurs and art collectors of the time. These visitors, in short, were not only titled personages, but men who promised to amount to something in their own right both as human beings and as forces in the cultural development of their respective countries. (It was in part his desire to renew his connection with several German princes of this caliber that launched Winckelmann on his fateful journey of 1768.) On the other hand, he did not hesitate to turn away, as forcefully as circumstances would allow, some very influential callers who did not meet his standards of intelligence and character, such as the Duke of York and Lord Baltimore. If such men happened to be Germans, he sometimes used his unique position in order to make suggestions about political reforms of a nature that his compatriots at home, even if they happened to be men of courage like Mendelssohn or Lessing, could not possibly have advocated in print. Winckelmann may have exaggerated a little when he claimed to have told a visiting German potentate some truths that the latter would never have heard at home, "where everybody who does not happen to be a foreigner, trembles before him" (and well they might: the prince in question was Charles William Ferdinand of Brunswick, Jerusalem's pupil, and so odious a creature that he gave orders to leave the wounded behind when he recalled his troops from America after the War of Independence). Yet Winckelmann's treatment of the greatest of these princes, his own former sovereign, shows that while he had learned to be a diplomat and had no

I*

doubt become a bit of a snob, he had by no means turned into a toady.

When the position of director of the Royal Collection of Antiquities and Medals fell vacant in Berlin in 1765, Winckelmann's name was placed on the list of candidates by Karl Gottlieb Guichard, who had studied with him in Halle and meanwhile become a colonel in the Prussian army. It was true that Winckelmann was not a Frenchman, which would militate against him in the King's eyes; but there were others in Berlin who supported his candidacy. Among these were the philosopher Johann Georg Sulzer, the author Friedrich Nicolai, and the musicologist Friedrich Wilhelm Marpurg, a childhood friend of Winckelmann from Seehausen who had recently been appointed Director of the Prussian State Lottery. Frederick the Great himself, who had of course read the *Catalogue* before buying the Stosch collection, had a high opinion of Winckelmann's scholarly and literary skills; if the applicant had the misfortune of having been born a German, the King may have reflected, he at least wrote good French. It had even been informally arranged that if Frederick ever found time to visit Rome, Winckelmann would do the honors of the city. Nothing came of this project, or of a similar visit that the Emperor Joseph II, who had also stipulated that he wished to be guided by him, planned to undertake at about the same time. But if the sovereign had been unable to come to Rome, he could at least avail himself of his ex-subject's services in Berlin.

When the offer reached him in August 1765, Winckelmann was at first tempted to accept. There was much to be said in favor of returning to the country of his birth. Although he had once written that he "shuddered from head to toe to think of Prussian despotism and of the royal slave driver, who will yet make that land, cursed by Nature and covered by Lybian sands, into an object of universal detestation," such Old Testament

imagery made no allowance for the undoubted fact that the
royal slave driver was also the greatest sovereign of the age.
If Winckelmann were to return, he would see Berendis, Genzmer, Guichard, Uden, Marpurg, and other old friends again,
who were living in or within reach of Berlin; and he would meet
Lessing, Sulzer, Nicolai, and Mendelssohn, who had read his
works and were themselves engaged in similar investigations
into aesthetics and art history. His beloved Lamprecht resided
in Prussia, as did his enemy Schnakenburg, who would have
to grovel before him if he now returned on the invitation of
the King himself. Winckelmann was almost forty-eight, and
no doubt felt that if he was ever going to move, now was the
time to do so. And if it came to moving, what destination
could be more desirable than the court of the sovereign who
had been celebrated by Voltaire, even before the glorious deeds
of the Seven Years' War had been accomplished, in the
quatrain

> *Il est grand roi tout le matin,*
> *Après le dîner grand écrivain,*
> *Tout le jour philosophe humain*
> *Et le soir convive divin ?*

These tantalizing prospects did not prevent Winckelmann
from making certain stipulations in his correspondence with
Marpurg. If he accepted at all, he wrote, the King would have to
wait until the following spring before asking him to undertake so long and uncomfortable a journey; his salary would
have to be 2,000 *Taler* a year, with moving expenses paid in
advance; he required a guarantee that the *Monuments* would
be printed in Berlin even though the work was written in
Italian; and he must have a written contract, if only to show
to the Pope (who, he cleverly intimated, would be most reluctant to lose the services of a man possessing so intimate a

knowledge of Vatican politics). The negotiations were at this stage when the Francophile King, incensed at Winckelmann's demand of a salary of 2,000 *Taler* for a position hitherto budgeted at a mere five hundred, terminated them with the remark that "one thousand *Taler* are quite sufficient for a German." By then, Winckelmann himself had reconsidered. Clement XIII had given him to understand that he did not need to take his duties in the Vatican Library too seriously; Albani was heartbroken at the very thought of losing his trusted companion; and another cardinal with antiquarian interests, Giovanni Francesco Stoppani, promised to pay him a small pension if he would only remain in Rome. In the end, his pride and his ancient loathing for Prussia broke through the diplomatic veneer: "Does the King not realize," he wrote to Berlin, "that he would have to pay at least as much to a man who is to exchange Rome for Berlin, and who has no need to offer his services to anyone, as he pays to a person who is recalled from Saint Petersburg on the Arctic Sea? [The mathematician Leonhard Euler had just returned to Berlin from Russia.] Surely he knows that I can be of more use than a mathematician, and that the experience of ten Roman years far outweighs in importance a decade spent on the calculation of parabolic lines, which can just as well be carried out in Smyrna as in Tobolsk."[16]

Except for an ironic final touch that was still to come, Winckelmann's contest of wills with Frederick the Great thus ended in a stand-off, with both men indignantly drawn up to their full height. It was a characteristic posture for these contrasting and yet germane figures who had issued, respectively, from the very top and the very bottom of eighteenth-century Prussia. Their differences of opinion notwithstanding, they had much in common: ambition and high intelligence, self-discipline and executive ability, and a masculine outlook on life coupled with markedly homosexual tendencies. Although the

roles they played were so disparate, they even shared a sense
of alienation which made them view themselves as actors.
Winckelmann's exhortation to J. H. Füssli that "we should
play as well as we can the part that is assigned to us, be it
good or bad," finds an exact complement in the report that
Frederick sent to Voltaire after his defeat at Zorndorf: "I am
much obliged to the hermit of Les Délices for his interest in
the adventures of the Don Quijote of the North. This Don
Quijote leads the life of a traveling comedian, playing now in
one theater, now in another, sometimes hissed, sometimes applauded. His last piece was the *Thébaïde* [Racine's tragedy
in which all the protagonists die]; there was scarcely anyone
left to snuff the candles . . ."[17]

It was inevitable that the acquaintances which Winckelmann
made in his capacity as Papal Antiquary should have been of
short duration and low intensity. The more illustrious among
the visitors spent only a few weeks in Rome, and the tour with
Winckelmann was merely one of many entertainments that were
laid on for them. On only a few such occasions was he really able
to give free rein to his pedagogical impulses. He had resigned
from the Prussian school system, years ago, not because he disliked teaching but because the circumstances under which he
taught had been all but unbearable. Since then, these impulses
had been absorbed by his writing, which had become the more
effective for it. But as he grew older, he found that he could
renew his own energies only through steady contact, in person
or if necessary by letter, with receptive young minds on which
he might imprint his aesthetic beliefs. This need, which could
not be appeased in any methodical fashion in Rome where all
formal instruction was the preserve of the clergy, had been
among the factors that made him toy with the idea of returning

to Germany, where he would have been free to teach as well as write. Nothing having come of these plans, he had to make do with the material at hand—with the young Germans and Swiss who looked him up or wrote to him from afar. They were not men of such stature as to have a call on his official services as Papal Antiquary. He guided them not because it was his duty, but out of affection or for the sake of those who had recommended them to his care; and they became his real disciples, who continued in his footsteps long after the princes and potentates had gone home. Once the Revolution had broken out, these had little time to spare for the arts. The Duc de La Rochefoucauld, for example, joined the revolutionary movement by becoming a deputy to the Estates-General of 1789 (only to be later stoned to death before the eyes of his mother and his wife), while the Duke of Brunswick combatted it until he died of the wounds he had suffered in the Battle of Jena. For them, the days they had spent with Winckelmann in Rome were soon turned into memories, recollections of a world that had become as remote to them as that before 1914 is to our fathers.

The work of spreading Winckelmann's gospel had to be carried forward by others, by disciples less conspicuously involved in these momentous events. Some of them deserve to be remembered: Johann Friedrich Reiffenstein, who, having come to Rome as tutor to a nobleman on the grand tour, decided to follow Winckelmann's example by becoming an art historian and a guide himself; Friedrich Wilhelm von Erdmannsdorff, the favorite of Leopold of Anhalt-Dessau and the architect who designed the palace at Wörlitz; and especially Johann Hermann von Riedesel, who had been planning to visit Sicily with Winckelmann when his mentor decided to go to Germany instead. Riedesel's account of the journey he then undertook by himself, *Reise durch Sizilien und Grossgriechenland* (1771), shows how deeply he was committed to his teacher, after whose

example he checked his own observations against those made by
the writers of antiquity. It is not too much to say that it was
Riedesel who discovered Sicily for the modern tourist; among
other things, he was the first to measure the dimensions of the
Temple at Segesta and to draw attention to the valuable pottery
preserved on the island. His *Journey through Sicily and "Magna
Graecia"* was translated into French and English, and was consulted by Goethe on *his* Italian travels.

The least scholarly of these men, but the closest to Winckelmann as a person, was Friedrich Reinhold von Berg, the Baltic
baron to whom he had dedicated "On the Nature and the Cultivation of Sensibility to the Beautiful in Art." Berg had
visited Rome for a few weeks in 1762, and after a stopover in
Paris returned to his native Riga. Once again, Winckelmann
had been swept up by a torrent of emotions that left him
drained and embittered in the end. Once again, he had considered himself bound to another man in a heroic friendship
patterned after those between Theseus and Pirithous or Achilles and Patroclus, a friendship cast in the pagan mold glorified
by Montaigne and Shaftesbury. Once again, he had urged the
other man to read Homer, Plutarch, Pope, above all Plato's
Phaedrus: the authors and books that had given meaning to
his own youth. Once again, he had found solace in poetry,
addressing Berg in Cowley's lines (from the ode "Platonick
Love"):

> *I Thee, both as Man and Woman, prize;*
> *For a perfect Love implies*
> *Love in all Capacities*

and in telling others about his happiness: "I might as well admit
it," he wrote to Leonhard Usteri, "that I have fallen in love,
and how! with a young Livonian . . ."[18] And once again he
had consoled himself with the reflection that his friend would

beget children who perpetuated his beauty: "[To return to Rome] was the promise you made," he sighed at the end of the essay, "when I carved your initials in the bark of a magnificent, leafy sycamore, that day in Frascati, when I recalled my own stunted youth, and we sacrificed to our guardian angel. Remember that angel, and remember your friend. Enjoy the prime of your life in a noble leisure, far from the vanity of the courts; live according to your own lights, as you are able to do, and raise up children and grandchildren in your own image."

It was Lamprecht all over again, pederasty tempered by pedagogy, called forth in both cases by a good-looking young man who was quite unable to respond on any of the levels on which he was being importuned. Lamprecht ended his days in the Prussian civil service; Berg, equally undistinguished, lived out his life on his estates near Riga. The former did not repay the money that Winckelmann had lent him; the latter forgot to thank him for the dedication of the essay (a disappointment that was sharpened by Füssli's silence on receiving the "Report on the most recent Discoveries" and by the failure of the Saxon Court to acknowledge the homage paid to the Elector Frederick Christian in the *History of Ancient Art*). As Lamprecht had betrayed Winckelmann's spirit for the sake of a career under Frederick the Great, so Berg now violated a similar trust in forsaking Rome for Paris. The only difference between Winckelmann's first love and his last lay in the fact that whereas he and Lamprecht had been almost of the same age, he had now reached forty-five while Berg was a mere twenty-six. Hence the bitterness of his lament about the "stunted" years of his youth. He could not retrieve them, any more than he could change his emotional, erotic, and aesthetic fixation on his own sex. No one believed him when he made the startling announcement, two years later, that he had "finally"—"*endlich*"

—managed to fall in love with a woman. He did not believe it himself. It was a piece of bravado, a last bit of play-acting before the curtain fell on the tragicomedy of his sexual involvements.

Margareta Mengs, who had followed her husband to the fleshpots of Madrid, returned to Rome in 1764, alone and for reasons of health. It was early summer when Winckelmann, who had been squiring her about the city, took her to Albani's villa in Castel Gandolfo. "As attractive as she looks," he reported from there to Muzel-Stosch, "I had hitherto always regarded her rather indifferently. But now, her constant companionship . . . engendered a familiarity which, except for one ultimate delight, could not have been any greater. On more than one afternoon, we took our siesta lying on the same bed. In the end, she lost her mind from want of the best [*"aus Mangel des besten"*]. Her husband [who had remained behind in Madrid] only knew that she had not been feeling well. Although he no doubt guessed that her wanton nature would reassert itself once she had recovered her health, he now sought to give her the highest proof of his love: he ceded all his rights to me, urging her to put health before chastity." Mengs had, in fact, given his wife *carte blanche* with one hand, and taken it away again with the other by stipulating that she was to see no one but Winckelmann. If it sounds like a risky thing to do, on the part of a husband who was a thousand miles away while his wife and his best friend were consoling one another in a secluded villa, it must be admitted that Mengs knew his man: "In this predicament," Winckelmann's report continues, "virtue came to my aid. After some time, the woman regained her senses, and was able to set out on the journey home." It is greatly to Margareta's credit as a person that once she had rejoined her husband in Madrid, she added her regards whenever the latter wrote to Rome.

Thus ended Winckelmann's "affair" with one of the most attractive women of his time, the only one with whom he had felt sufficiently at ease to include her among his correspondents; years before, she had teased him about the women he met in Florence, and he had replied, with a homosexual's mocking gallantry, that they were not nearly as enchanting as the ladies of Rome. He must have presented a challenge to many a spirited woman, this handsome and brilliant man who was so patently impervious to their charms, and endowed besides with the aphrodisiac of fame. But not even Margareta—enticing, lonely, and *"jolie, honnête, et très exacte dans les devoirs de femme"* in the opinion of as seasoned an observer as Giacomo Casanova —could make him stray from the path of what he chose to call his "virtue." She might never have bothered to try if she had known the question that Winckelmann asked in all serious-ness of Paul Usteri: "After all, what does a woman have that is supposed to be so beautiful? . . . A magnificent bosom does not last, and besides, Nature has made this part of the body not for beauty's sake, but for the nourishment of the young . . ."[19]

VI

Winckelmann's decision to visit Germany in 1768 remains the most enigmatic action of his life. He never explained it himself, and the reasons adduced by his biographers, while plausible enough, are not sufficiently cogent to account for a step that ran so counter to the whole previous course of his life. It is true that he had been thinking of returning to Germany, off and on, for a number of years. But there was no specific reason for him to go at this particular time, if ever: the return to Germany, like the never-realized plan to visit Greece, might well have remained in the realm of the potential. He wanted, of course, to see his new friends in Switzerland and to be seen in all his glory by such old ones as Uden and Berendis and Francke in Germany. It was natural that he should have wished to indulge this vanity, and indulge it he did to the full—in his correspondence. They all knew that he had become a famous and important man, and there was no need to prove it to them in person. Furthermore, he did not travel via Zürich, and turned back long before reaching Dresden, let alone Berlin. He also wanted to further a pet project of his last years, the excavation of the stadium at Elis in Greece, which he proposed to finance by selling shares, with each buyer receiving a number of art works proportionate to his investment; with the exception of Leopold of Anhalt-Dessau, however, none of the would-be shareholders, among whom were Cardinal Stoppani and the Duc de La Rochefoucauld, resided in Germany. Finally, he had become so wary of pirating publishers that he wished to oversee in person the printing of a revised translation of the *History*, of which truncated French versions had been issued in Paris and Amsterdam; like a gunner removing the breech block, he had sent the manuscript to Berlin while withholding the quotations and footnotes, in order to make sure that this scholarly barrage would not be fired until he was ready to give the order. But he never went to Berlin, and this whole project, too, could as easily have been carried out in Rome, or better still, in Paris. After the endless annoyances arising from the preparation of the plates for the *Monuments*, he was overworked and badly in need of rest; but a journey over the Alps was bound to be an added burden on his strength and his nerves. His father and mother had been dead for many years, and Stendal, in the heart of the Prussia he so detested, did not lie on his itinerary in any case. He thus had no discernible reason of a professional or sentimental nature for going to Germany at this time. But he went there, nevertheless, instead of accepting Riedesel's invitation to join him on a trip to Greece.

The decision makes no sense within the context of as rational a life as Winckelmann had not only endured, but actively carved out for himself, up to this moment. His biographers have therefore tried, with varying degrees of credibility, to interpret this ill-considered journey as the result of a spell cast over Winckelmann by some evil power. What else, they argue, could have made him announce his impending journey to Francke in terms as hauntingly prophetic as these: "Finally, peace will come over us in the very place where we hope to meet again and rejoice in each other's company . . . There, I shall depart from this world even as I arrived in it: a wanderer, but lightly burdened . . ."? However, every remark in which the cloud of fate thus darkens the horizon, can be balanced by one in which his inner landscape is lit up with the kind of joyful anticipation that usually precedes a voyage of this kind: "I never wrote you with more happiness than I feel now," he informed the same correspondent a few weeks later,

when I have the pleasure of telling you of my planned arrival in Nöthnitz. It is scheduled for the middle of May, unless some illness should overtake me on this voyage. I intend to leave here before the middle of April, and have already received the Pope's and my master's permission to do so. But since I intend to travel as quickly as possible to my first destination, the palace of the most excellent Prince of Dessau, and will therefore pass through Dresden in a hurry because I need to see only you and Mr. Walther there, I would ask you to keep this entirely to yourself . . . When the time comes, you might let [Walther] know whenever you are in Dresden, so that I will know where to find you. In Dessau I expect my friend Muzel-Stosch, whom the good Prince will invite at my request. From there we are going to take a trip together to the Hereditary Prince of Brunswick, and thence to Berlin. I will be accompanied on the whole trip by Cavaceppi, the well-known Roman sculptor, who is coming along for my sake and for the good of his health.[20]

Whatever the motivations that impelled Winckelmann to undertake this journey and the expectations with which he set out, a sense of being about to meet his doom did not figure greatly among them. If the journey had not ended as it did, no one would have gone looking for such phantoms. Beginning with Goethe, however, Winckelmann's admirers have found it difficult to face up not only to his conversion and his homosexuality, but to the fact that he suffered a severe nervous break-down on returning to Germany in 1768. It is true that the spectacle of this incisive and tautly strung mind snapping before our eyes is as unsettling to behold as that of the "believer" who bartered away his "faith," or that of the connoisseur of Greek beauty who adored his Adonises in the flesh as much as in marble. Yet Cavaceppi's account of the voyage, and Winckelmann's own actions, leave us in no doubt about what happened. Nor is there any cause for surprise: it would have been odd if this man, who had so long carried the dismal burdens of poverty, loneliness, and sexual abnormality, had *not* faltered under the additional strain of having to re-enter a sphere that he had hated with every fiber of his being. One rather marvels that he had not broken down before. This much seems certain: Winckelmann came to grief not in Trieste, but when he broke off his journey in Ratisbon. His mission was fulfilled at that point, and the pilgrim had literally begun to double back on his tracks. It is not inconceivable that Arcangeli's knife spared him the long agony suffered by Hölderlin and Nietzsche, two other wanderers who came home demented.

After leaving Rome on April 10, Winckelmann and Cavaceppi stopped briefly in Loreto, Bologna, Venice, and Verona. While they were making their way up the Brenner Pass, the former began to complain so inordinately about the height of the mountains and the ugliness of the houses that Cavaceppi thought at first that he must be joking. On seeing that his companion was serious and exhibited *"una aversione incredibile"* toward his surroundings, he tried to reason with him by saying that if anyone had a right to be shocked by such unaccustomed sights, it was he, the Italian who had never seen them before, rather than Winckelmann, who had come down this very road some thirteen years earlier. In the end he had to explain, as one would to a child, that Alpine houses have sloping roofs because they would otherwise be crushed under the weight of the snow that fell on them in winter—this to Winckelmann, who had never been in Greece and yet laid bare so masterfully the connection between that country's climate and its art and architecture. When they approached Munich, Cavaceppi began to suspect that his companion, who whenever spoken to monotonously replied, "let us return to Rome"—*"torniamo a Roma!"*—had indeed lost his mind.

Although received "with the honors due to his merits" by the antiquarians and art patrons of Munich, Winckelmann remained so listless and melancholy that Cavaceppi had to "drag" him—*"strascinarlo"*—on to Ratisbon. They had no sooner put up at an inn there than the sick man asked for stationery and wrote to Albani, declaring that he had resolved to return to Rome and asking that his apartment be got ready to receive him. Cavaceppi, who had been arguing with him all the way to the posthouse, was unable to dissuade him from sending this letter. It was all he could do to make sure that Winckelmann would at least return via Vienna, in order to deliver the dispatches that the Cardinal had entrusted to him. They were addressed to Maria Theresa and her chief minister, the Chancellor Prince Kaunitz, whom Cavaceppi had managed to forewarn about his friend's condition. If the Italian is to be believed, Kaunitz himself now took a hand in the matter by appealing to Winckelmann's sense of obligation toward his companion. "How can you be so heartless," he is supposed to have asked, "as to leave your friend here, who is more concerned about you than he is about himself? Can't you see that he will have to traverse by himself vast lands of which he knows neither the customs nor the language?" But Winckelmann could not be moved to reconsider his decision, and the sculptor, who had business of his own to look after in Germany, had no choice but to leave him behind, "pale and trembling, with eyes as empty as a dead man's."[21] Cavaceppi continued his journey to Dessau, and reached Berlin at the end of June. On hearing of his arrival, Frederick the Great summoned him to the palace and gave him the news of Winckelmann's murder. Cavaceppi was so upset that he refused at first to believe it, whereupon the King tartly observed that his ministers were not in the habit of telling him fairy tales.

Winckelmann, after spending a few days alone in a Vienna hospital, had left the capital on May 28, bound for Trieste.

THE HISTORY
OF ANCIENT ART

I

It is not always easy for us to read the *History of Ancient Art* "straight": as naïvely, that is, as if it were still the gospel that the author proclaimed it to be in the 1760's. (The lack of a readable English version does not lighten the task; the last of several poor translations was published over a hundred years ago.[1]) We nevertheless owe it to Winckelmann, and to the truly incalculable influence that this work has had on later generations including our own, to summarize it briefly before evaluating it from the vantage point of the two centuries that have elapsed since. During these centuries, art history has advanced as far beyond Winckelmann as, say, penology has beyond Beccaria, whose *Essay on Crimes and Punishments* was published within a few months of the *History*. What matters is not that Winckelmann overstressed one aspect of Greek art at the expense of all others or that he misread this or that text, but that he established the ground rules of a new discipline. What has taken place in that discipline since then has been, by and large, a mere filling in of the spaces that he perforce had to leave blank.

In the preface, he defines his project as tracing, "wherever feasible on the strength of the surviving ancient works themselves, the origin, growth, changes, and decadence of art, as well as the styles of the various nations, periods, and artists."[2] The need for a book of this kind, he adds, springs from his colleagues' refusal to acquaint themselves as thoroughly as they should have with antique sculptures and paintings. Instead of examining these with their own eyes, critics and historians had been content to copy the accounts left by the Greeks and Romans, and to use the actual frescos, statues, etc., as mere shelves on which to display their scholarly baubles. Even the best of them, Jonathan Richardson, Jr., had seen some works only once and others not at all, so that he too became guilty of describing the palaces and villas of Rome, and the statuary that these contain, "like a person to whom they had only appeared in a dream." The common denominator of these books, according to Winckelmann, was in fact their descriptive rather than analytical tenor. They therefore contain numerous mis-identifications, wrong ascriptions of authorship, and, worst of all, failures to distinguish between originals and restorations or later additions. Had they possessed a critical knowledge of the works themselves, and that over-all familiarity with all other aspects of classical civilization that Winckelmann here claims for himself, earlier historians would (to give but one example) not have considered as genuine an equestrian relief in the Palazzo Mattei, on which a horse is shown as shod although horseshoes had been unknown in antiquity.

We are entitled to expect much of a writer who dismisses so cavalierly the efforts of his predecessors. That much will be given is implied in the author's listing of his own qualifications for the job: a true vocation ("The love of art has been my strongest impulse since youth," he states with some exaggeration, "and although my upbringing and the circumstances of my life have led me along a wholly different path, this call never failed to assert itself"), a first-hand knowledge of the subject matter ("I have myself repeatedly seen and examined everything that I adduce by way of evidence, paintings and statues no less than coins and engraved gems"), and a willingness to engage in what might be called controlled speculation. Since our incomplete knowledge of the ancient world would otherwise compel us to take "big jumps over many blank spaces," some speculative procedures, Winckelmann believes, are as indispensable to a work of this nature as the postulation of working hypotheses is in scientific research. At the same time, he insists that conjectures must be based on defensible premises and never be applied for their own sake. They are the scaffolding, not the building.

II

The work is divided into two partially overlapping sections: a philosophical INVESTIGATION INTO THE NATURE OF ART and the briefer, and more properly speaking historical, treatise on GREEK ART AS SEEN FROM THE CHRONOLOGICAL VIEWPOINT. The first, or theoretical, section, a statement of first principles, consists of five chapters which now call for our attention.

A) INVESTIGATION INTO THE NATURE OF ART.

1) The Origins of Art, and the Causes of its Diversity among the various Nations.

"Like all other inventions," Winckelmann declares in the lapidary style of his best Roman period, "the pictorial arts were born of necessity. Afterward, men looked for beauty, and in the end, there followed excess. Such are the three main stages of art." The cradle of art (which began with sculpture, painting being added later as decoration) must not be sought in any one country; art arose spontaneously, in response primarily to religious impulses, in many countries but not necessarily at the same time. Thus, the graven images of which the Bible tells us are older than any Greek works, which are also antedated by the Egyptian obelisks; "yet those who speak of the origin of a skill or custom," we are cautioned, "in terms of its transference from one nation to another, are mistaken all and sundry because they draw general conclusions from the resemblance of individual features." Greek art, then, developed later than (but independently of) that of the Near Eastern nations. It grew out of the need to represent divinities, originally in the form of square pillars and hewn blocks of wood on which heads were later placed as on the *hermae*. Legs and an indication of sex then came to be shown in the lower part of the block or pillar, with the rest of the figure emerging subsequently. These straight-faced primitive Etruscan and Greek sculptures, often embellished with writing, eventually lost the rigidity that they had shared with those of the Egyptians, and began to express movement first in the extremities and then in the whole stance of the figure. Because the ancient languages do not seem to have made a distinction between the potter's trade and that of the sculptor, clay may be assumed to have been the earliest material used. Glazed and painted, it continued in use even after others had been introduced. Wood was especially popular in Egypt, where it was often painted and gilded; of ivory, already mentioned by Homer, little has come down to us because "it calcified in the ground, as do the teeth of other animals excepting only those of the wolf" (!);[3] tufa was first used in Greece, travertine mainly in Rome, marble in both; many surviving statues, not to mention passages in ancient authors, attest to the use of such metals as bronze, brass, and silver. (In other words, Winckelmann saw the various archaic styles as conditioned by the material used, whereas we like to think that any given style will select its own material.)

The diversities that may be observed in the art of different

nations are, primarily but not solely, the result of climatic variations. In an elaboration of arguments first propounded in the
"Reflections," we are given to understand that physical perfection is more often found in temperate zones than elsewhere
("The degree to which a pleasant climate enhances beauty can
be gauged from the particular attractiveness of the women of
Malta: for that island knows no winter"); even the language,
in fact a nation's entire cultural life, are strongly influenced by
climatic factors. However, the artistic primacy which Athens
enjoyed in classical, and Florence in more modern, times is not
so exclusive that Northerners are inevitably prevented from
sharing it, provided that they are willing to leave their fog-
bound shores behind them at least in spirit: "Holbein and
Dürer, the fathers of German art, have shown astonishing gifts,
and if they could only have learned from the ancients as Raphael, Correggio, and Titian did, they would have become as
great as these, and perhaps greater." These men form the exceptions which confirm the rule that great art is the prerogative
of those who dwell in a temperate climate and benefit from the
customs, institutions, and values that tend to develop in such a
setting. At the same time, a favorable climate is not the only
determinant of a nation's greatness. Winckelmann has this to
say of the contrast between the Athenians, and the Ionians who
settled on the coast of what is now Turkey: "Among the Greeks
of Asia Minor, whose language became softer after their migration from Greece, and richer in vowels and more musical because they dwelt under a sky that was even more smiling than
that which looked down on their compatriots elsewhere, this
very sky awakened and inspired the first poets. Greek philosophy
developed on that soil, and their first historians sprang from it;
indeed, the painter of grace, Apelles, was begotten under that
sensuous sky." But because these Greeks had not been able to
defend their liberties against the Persians, it had been in Athens

rather than Asia Minor that "the sciences settled along with the arts."

2) Art among the Egyptians, Phoenicians, and Persians.

No such development can be discerned in the art of Egyptians, which Winckelmann describes as having "failed to progress appreciably beyond the style of their earliest works." The reasons for this ossification are to be found in the dour temperament of this race (according to a passage that he misread in Strabo, they knew neither music nor poetry and were altogether "not made to enjoy life"), in their static social order, which inhibited the rise of a separate class of artists so that these were considered as "little more than workingmen," and in the lack of anatomical knowledge resulting from their excessive veneration of the dead. Forbidden by their religion to perform autopsies, they "considered making a single incision [in a corpse] as tantamount to murder." The depiction of animals, or divinities with animal heads, was the only escape from the rectilinear style to which their artists were otherwise restricted. Even so, a distinction may be drawn between an early period lasting until the country's conquest by Cambyses, a later phase during which Persian and Hellenistic influences came to the fore, and a kind of epilogue marked by the imitations of Egyptian works in Hadrian's reign.

The handful of coins which is all that we have left of Phoenician art is again taken to reflect an equable climate: for if the portraits on these coins are any indication, "that race, which according to Herodotus was the healthiest of all, must have been very well-proportioned." The Persians have left only a few engraved gems, none of which shows nude figures since their notions of propriety did not allow them to portray these. For political as well as social and religious reasons, much the same applied to the ancient Hebrews and Parthians. Although

K

less rigorously so than in the case of the Persians and Egyptians, their form of government was still too hieratic to have encouraged any artistic growth beyond the more or less stylized rendition of sacred motifs. These ancient Near Eastern monarchies knew neither the religious tolerance nor the social give-and-take, for example between ruler and subject or between different classes, which are second only to the climate as prerequisites for a flowering of the arts.

3) The Art of the Etruscans and of their Neighbors.

Some measure of freedom, Winckelmann thought, must however have prevailed among the Etruscans. If their art, in which three stages of development may be discerned, falls short nevertheless of that of the Greeks, it is because they, like the Egyptians, seem to have been of a melancholy cast of mind, given to soothsaying and other superstitions. It is no coincidence that it was the Etruscans who introduced the gladiatorial games that were eventually copied by the Romans; Etruscan funerary urns, in particular, bear witness to a penchant for the gloomy and violent that would have been quite out of place in Winckelmann's Greece. According to him, this trait may still be observed in their distant progeny (". . . even in more recent times, self-flagellation was first practiced in Tuscany"), not excluding such latter-day Etruscans as Daniele da Volterra and even Michelangelo (". . . it has been said with good reason," Winckelmann observes in regard to the latter, "that he who has seen one of his [sketched] figures, has seen them all"[4]). In the final instance, however, all these differences between the two nations, even that between the Greek predilection for showing the musculature and the Etruscan emphasis on bone structure, cannot obscure the "fact" of their common derivation from the Pelasgians. What we might at first sight be tempted to call typically

Etruscan, such as statues of divinities carrying a thunderbolt, inevitably turns out on closer examination to have been present in Greece as well. All such motifs are proof not of the originality of Etruscan, but of the universality of Greek art.

Winckelmann must have suspected that he was skating on thin ice when making these statements. His customary incisiveness, in any event, is strangely muted in this chapter, which, as the *Anmerkungen* or "Comments" to the *History* show, was to have been recast in the second edition. As it stands, it abounds in passages like "I cannot help lamenting the insufficiency of our knowledge, which does not always allow us to tell the Etruscan apart from the archaic Greek"; or "We do possess a number of Etruscan figurines, but not enough statues in the round to gain a really systematic view of their art; after a ship-wreck, one cannot very well construct a seaworthy vessel out of a few planks." He has even less to say of the Etruscans' neighbors among the Italic tribes, although he differentiates between the Oscans and Samnites who inhabited Campania, and the Sardes to the North.

4) Art among the Greeks.

In this, the longest and by all tokens the pivotal chapter of the entire work, Winckelmann examines five different aspects of Greek art:

i) The Causes of its Superiority over
the Art of other Nations.

The exemplariness of Greek sculpture and painting stems from three considerations: it is so superior in quality that it represents an absolute standard; it is so superior in quantity that we cannot possibly expect to know it all; and it is so superior in substance that, whereas the study of Egyptian and Etruscan works merely "sharpens our perception and corrects our judgment," that of Greek art provides the raw material for the edifice of critical evaluation and normative creativity that Winckelmann considered as the *raison d'être* of his work. "The *History of Ancient Art* that I intend to write," he had already announced in the preface, "is no mere description of the sequence of its development and of the changes it underwent; rather, I take 'history' in the broader meaning it possessed in Greek [information, tidings], and therefore propose to design a systematic doctrine." The climate, which actuated and continued to nourish the Greek cult of beauty and fitness; a form of government that among other things gave birth to philosophy and rhetoric, disciplines which do not thrive under tyrants; the esteem in which the Greeks held their artists, who were credited with being wise as well as skillful, and were so honored that many of their names defied the passing of time; and the uses to which art was put by them (to reward outstanding athletes and other citizens as well as to venerate the gods) are cited among the causes of the superiority of Greek sculpture, painting, and architecture over those of other nations. Of the three art forms, the two first-named, which began with the imitation of nature, reached perfection earlier than the more cerebral craft of architecture. Buttressed with quotations from ancient authors and analyses of specific works, these statements are intended also to castigate modern practices. "The works of a given artist," we read in one such aside, "were not conceived after the wretched taste and half-baked notions of a judge appointed by flatterers and time-servers, but evaluated and rewarded by the wisest men in the land . . . it was before such a jury that Aëtion presented himself with his *Marriage of Alexander and Roxanne*. The foreman who handed down the verdict was a man by the name of Proxenides, and he gave the artist his own daughter for a wife."

ii) The Essentials of Greek Art.

In tackling this central portion of his argument, Winckelmann likens himself to a competitor in the ancient Olympic Games held at Elis. His task of defining the essence of art reminds him of that of an athlete about to perform before the assembled public; like one of these champions of old, he, too, sees before himself "not one but innumerable expert judges." Yet the work must be done because too many others have shirked it, preferring instead to lead their readers through "a labyrinth of metaphysical sophistries and subterfuges, for the purpose of compiling gigantic tomes that exhaust the mind through sheer surfeit." Since the creation or reproduction of beauty—read: of the sculpted and preferably the nude human form as an expression of *Gestalt* in a neoplatonic sense, i.e., as a phenomenon that occurs in nature and in art and serves to remind us of the divine—is "the ultimate aim of art and its very core," we must first remove the various obstacles that prevent us from creating beauty as artists or recognizing it as beholders. Among these is the passion it awakens, which causes us all too often to perceive beauty through the senses rather than the mind, as happens with young men who think that some women are goddesses merely because their faces show "a languishing or lubricious expression." Then there is the failure of some artists to let their perception of the beautiful ripen to maturity, as was the case with Michelangelo and Bernini. The former, admittedly "magnificent in the rendition of strong bodies," did poorly in his youthful and female figures, while the latter "sought to ennoble, by exaggeration, forms that he had borrowed from nature at her coarsest, [figures] . . . whose expression is often at variance with their actions, like Hannibal, who [was said by Livy to have] laughed in extreme distress." Still other such hindrances are the belief that color is as important as line, and the even more widespread one that beauty constitutes a regional or ethnic rather than a universal standard. Once again, Winckelmann goes to some length to demonstrate to his own satisfaction that the protruding lips of Moors (explained by reference to the African climate) and the slanting eyes of Orientals (which disturb him because they distort the "T" formed by the horizontal of the eyebrows and the vertical extending from the top of the nose to the point of the chin) cannot represent a universally acceptable measure of beauty, which nevertheless exists and, we are told, is acknowledged as such "by a majority of civilized nations, in Asia and Africa as well as in Europe."

Like its stillborn predecessor in the "Reflections," the definition of beauty which Winckelmann attempts at this point proceeds by abstraction as well as eclecticism. Any artist's concept of beauty, he insists, derives partly from measurements and proportions, and partly from his understanding of form. This form can be individual, such as it may in rare cases be found in nature, or ideal in the Platonic sense. "Like a skillful gardener who grafts shoots of various noble plants onto one stem," the Greek sculptor, and among the moderns such men as Raphael and Guido Reni, selected from their models this or that specific feature and infused the resultant work—which is now composite and no longer individual—with the ideal beauty that makes it come alive even as Galatea did in the hands of her creator. Singled out for emphasis among various instances of composite beauty are the Greek hermaphrodites, and the eunuchs of Winckelmann's own time, when castrati were still in vogue at the Papal Court and elsewhere. Their fleshy hips and smooth backsides seem to have corresponded more closely than either the male or the female to that nebulous "line of beauty" that Winckelmann, along with generations of philosophers (not to mention contemporary artists as disparate as Hogarth and Mengs) sought so eagerly.

Although Winckelmann tells us that a beautiful figure need not be perfect in every detail, it is primarily with physical features that he concerns himself here. Before doing so, however, he designs his famous "scale of beauty." In ascending order, it comprises realistic portraiture, idealized portraiture, representations of heroes and demigods, and pictures of divinities, which constitute the sublimest embodiment of the human form and possess in addition the ennobling trait of ethical perfection. Next to form and such general prerequisites of beauty as unity and simplicity, Winckelmann mentions *Unbezeichnung*: the stress on the generic rather than the individually conditioned traits of a given subject. The better we are able to take in a work at one glance, the more likely is that work to be beautiful ("It is for this reason that a large palace laden with ornamentation appears to be small, and a house large if it is simply built"); the farther removed the work is from portraiture, the closer it is again to being beautiful, like water, which is the better for having been purified of all foreign substances. *Unbezeichnung*, however, is a more elusive quality than simplicity or even verisimilitude. It becomes operative only in relation to its quasi-opposite, *Ausdruck*, or expression, which is defined as "the rendition of the active and passive state of our soul and body, of our passions as well as our deeds." Since a state of complete *Unbezeichnung* is impossible to achieve (and, Winckelmann neglects to point out, undesirable because we could not take much interest in a subject thus presented), a work of art must have *Ausdruck* as well as a form incorporating the quality of *Unbezeichnung*. Beauty of form, to be sure, takes precedence and must be preserved at all costs: no expression must ever be so violent as to affect "the facial features and the body's posture, and thus the very forms on which beauty depends." Violent emotions can, however, be represented, provided that the moment chosen is the psychological and physiological one of "freezing." For example, the daughters of Niobe are shown frozen in fear of death, yet with their beauty unimpaired. Another example is *Laocoön*, a "much more learned"—we should perhaps say "sophisticated"—work than the *Apollo Belvedere*.

Defeated once again, as he had been in the "Reflections," in his endeavor to furnish an incontrovertible and all-inclusive definition of beauty, and perilously close to the entrance to that "labyrinth of metaphysical sophistries and subterfuges" of which he had promised to step clear, Winckelmann abruptly switches at this point from deduction to induction by compiling a list of individually beautiful features. This list, it must be remembered, was distilled from only a tiny fraction of the classical sculptures that are now exhibited in museums all over the world.

In facial structure, the so-called Greek *profile* is the foremost characteristic of high beauty. This profile consists of an almost straight or a slightly depressed line formed by forehead and nose, in youthful and particularly in female heads . . . That such a profile represents a source of beauty, may be seen from the opposite: for the more the nose is depressed, the more the face deviates from the beautiful . . . In ideal heads, the *eyes* are invariably set deeper than in nature, a fact that accentuates the upper edge of the socket. Deepset eyes are not in themselves an indication of beauty and do not make for an open countenance; but in this, art could not always conform to nature . . . for in large statues which are viewed from farther away than small ones, the eyes and eyebrows would barely show at a distance because . . . the apple of the eye was left unmarked, generally smooth and blank . . . In this fashion, this part of the face was given a sharper contrast of light and shadow, so that the eye, which would otherwise have been unremarkable and almost lifeless, was rendered more powerful and animated . . . According to several ancient writers, a beautiful *forehead* is supposed to be low; yet a wide and high brow is not ugly, but rather the opposite. This apparent contradiction is easily resolved: the brow should be low in young men, as it is in the springtime of one's years, before the short hair on the forehead falls out and leaves the latter bare. It would thus be against the essence of youth to give it a wide and high brow—which is, however, a distinguishing mark of grown manhood . . . The *chin*, whose beauty lies in the rounded fullness of its arched form, is not bisected by a dimple . . . which, occurring as it does in nature only individually and by accident, was not deemed by Greek artists . . . to be a prerequisite of pure and universal beauty. No dimples are therefore found on *Niobe and Her Daughters* or on the *Albani Pallas* . . . or on the *Apollo Belvedere* or the *Bacchus* in the Villa Medici . . . The *Florentine Venus* has one, [but] as a token of personal charm rather than as an integral part of beauty of form . . . The *hands* of the *Venus de' Medici* have been completely restored, which points up the ignorance of those who criticized them in the belief that they were original . . . The beauty of a youthful hand lies in a very moderate fullness, with barely visible depressions, mere shadowy nuances, over the knuckles, where plump hands would show dimples. The *fingers* taper like finely wrought columns, with the joints not articulated in sculpture; the tip does not bend upward as it does in the work of newer artists . . . A wide and deeply arched *chest* was regarded as a universal mark of beauty in male figures, and it was with such a chest that the father of poetry [Homer] endowed Neptune, and after that model, Agamemnon . . . the *bosom* of female figures is never overly full . . . in fact, a stone from the island of Naxos was used, which, carefully contoured, was placed over the breasts in order to inhibit their burgeoning growth. The poets likened a virginal breast to a cluster of ripening grapes, and in some less-than-lifesize statues of Venus, the breasts are compact and resemble little hills running to a point, which shape seems to have been considered the most beautiful . . . on virginal breasts and those of goddesses, the nipples are not erect, at least in marble . . . Even in male figures, the *abdomen* is like that

K*

of a person who enjoys a good rest and sound digestion, that is, without belly . . . The *navel* is markedly indented, especially in female figures, where it is drawn in an arch and occasionally in the shape of a small semicircle pointing downward or up; on some statues, this feature is shown more pleasingly than it is on the *Venus de' Medici*, whose navel is uncommonly deep and large . . . The *sex organs*, too, have a beauty of their own. Of the testicles, the left is always larger, as is the case in nature, just as they say that the left eye sees better than the right . . . In youthful figures, the *knees* are shaped according to their natural perfection, that is, they are not visibly divided by cartilage, but smooth and simply arched, without tensing of muscles . . .

One is taken aback to find, at the end of this timeless canon of beauty, a tribute to an artist who has meanwhile all but disappeared from memory: "The epitome of all the perfections described as being present in the ancient sculptures is found in the immortal works of Anton Raphael Mengs, First Court Painter to the Kings of Spain and of Poland, the greatest artist of his own and perhaps of future years. Phoenix-like he arose from the ashes of the first Raphael, in order to teach beauty in the realm of art, and to attain in that the pinnacle of human endeavor." Winckelmann, of course, was neither the first nor the last great critic to let his acumen be blunted by personal friendship and contemporary fashion, or to misjudge signally his own posthumous fame in comparison with that of an artist who was highly regarded in his own time. "I am often bold enough to wish," he had written on first meeting Mengs, "that my name may in future be mentioned in the same breath as his: a faraway prospect for me!"[5]

As if to make amends for this idiosyncrasy, Winckelmann now offers a set of "Conclusions drawn for the Layman's and the Critic's Use" which are as valid now as when they were first promulgated. Directed at youthful beginners and tourists—

"junge Anfänger und Reisende"—these admonitions could be reprinted without change in any guidebook, or posted over the entrance to any museum of representational art:

Do not attempt to find faults and imperfections in a work until you have learned to recognize and identify its beauties. This advice is the fruit of long experience, namely, that most men miss the beautiful altogether because they criticize before they have even begun to learn. They are like so many schoolboys who are smart enough only to probe for the teacher's weaknesses. We are too vain to content ourselves with mere contemplation, and our self-esteem wants to be flattered; hence our desire to pass judgment. However, just as a negative statement is more easily made than a positive one, so is the defective easier to find than the perfect, and it is surely less troublesome to judge others than to teach ourselves. Coming up to a fine statue, a man will praise its beauty in general terms because that costs him little; once his flighty glance has wandered about uncertainly and failed to see the good parts and the reasons for which they are good, it will remain glued to the bad . . . [But if men are taught to expect] much that is beautiful, they will look for it, and a part of it will open out to them. Return many times, until you have found it. For it is there.

Contrary to popular belief in Winckelmann's time as in ours, draped Greek statues vastly outnumber nudes. After a brief discourse on the excellence of antique representations of animals, the author concludes this portion of his argument with a description of women's clothing in classical times, such as it can be reconstructed from literary and pictorial evidence.

iii) The Growth and Decline of Greek Art, and the four Periods and Styles by which its Development may be reckoned.

These are, successively:

a) The Archaic Style (*"Der ältere Stil"*), which has survived in so few statues and reliefs that we have to rely for its characterization mainly on coins and engraved gems. In line, it is harsh, forceful, angular. Since many of the motifs treated in this, the earliest and by far the longest period of Greek art, were of a violent nature, there is more *Ausdruck* in these works than is compatible with beauty. Just as a kinship with Egyptian and Etruscan techniques marks the beginning of this period, a softening of its starkly massive effect may be observed as it reached its culmination just before the age of Phidias and Polyclitus. By that time it had become

b) The Sublime Style (*"Der hohe Stil"*), in which the protruding and "jagged" parts of statues tended to become smoother, movements more fluid, and violent attitudes muted. A certain monumentality nevertheless remains typical of this period, which lasted to the days of Pericles and of whose values the *Albani Pallas* is a prime example. If the early works of Michelangelo remind us of the Archaic and those of the mature Raphael of the Sublime Style, those of Correggio may be said to correspond to

c) The Beautiful Style (*"Der schöne Stil"*), which flourished just before the time of Alexander the Great and is distinguished by its grace and wavelike line. It is indicative of the skill of its protagonists, among whom were Lysippus and the painter Apelles, that this style has given us not only the *Sauroctonus* (and the *Aphrodite of Cnidus* and the *Apoxyomenus* and, as Winckelmann fondly believed to the end, the *Laocoön*) but also many first-rate statues of children, thus laying to rest "a widely-held misconception . . . to the effect that the ancients had remained far behind modern artists in the representation of the young." With the inevitability of an organic process— for such, indeed, it was—there now followed

d) The Imitative Style (*"Der Stil der Nachahmer"*). "Since the proportions and forms of beauty," Winckelmann contends by way of determining the high point of Greek art and the beginnings of its decline, "had been exhaustively studied by the artists of antiquity, and the shapes and contours of figures so finely determined that they could be changed only to their detriment, the concept of beauty could be raised no higher. Thus art, in which as in all emanations of nature no stationary point can be imagined, perforce had to recede since it could not advance any further. Images of gods and heroes having been formed in all conceivable shapes and attitudes, it had become increasingly difficult to think of new ones. Imitation was thus given free rein. But because imitation restricts the mind, and because it appeared impossible to surpass a Praxiteles or an Apelles, it also became difficult to equal them. The imitator has ever been inferior to the creator." Grace as well as monumentality were lost sight of as the sculptors' attention turned to ornamental and other secondary features such as folds in drapery, locks of hair, jewelry, and the like. In an attempt to check this dissipation of creative energies, so many artists returned to the pristine fashions of Egypt and Etruria that, if Juvenal is to be believed, the painters of early Imperial Rome lived by turning out pictures of the goddess Isis. This increased production of "heads and busts, or what is commonly called portraits" (Winckelmann's very wording sounds pained and censorious), was altogether the token of an advanced stage of deterioration. "Lysippus," he acidly observes, "may not have been able to make a better head of Caracalla, but the sculptor of that bust could not have made a statue like Lysippus, and therein lies the difference." In this late period, it became difficult to distinguish the genuinely archaic from the merely archaistic, especially in the many statues made of Spes, the goddess of Hope, and in the purported busts of Plato and other sages. An analogous phenomenon in more recent times is represented by the work of Bernini, who by engaging in theatrical effects and doing highly naturalistic portraits, "singlehandedly . . . introduced corruption into art." A fatuous statement, but not an unexpected one from the pen of a critic who had assigned to realistic portraiture the lowest rung on his scale of beauty.

iv) Mechanical Aspects of Greek Sculpture.

After listing the respective virtues of Parian, Pentelic, and other marble and of bronze, porphyry, basalt, etc., Winckelmann discusses some specific technical problems, ranging from the casts and molds that the ancient sculptors made of their works to the soldering by which the hair was joined onto the heads of statues. As we have come to expect of him by now, he provides supporting evidence in almost every case, from literary sources ("Plato even advocated a law that in his republic, statues were to be made of one piece"—which is not quite what the philosopher had had in mind) or from personal examination, according to which the heads of the *Albani Pallas* and of *Niobe* (the latter a copy which he mistook for the original) had been sculptured separately from the torsos to which they were later fitted. While his statements are not always correct, their inclusion here shows, more tellingly than his frequent asseverations on this point, that Winckelmann was no bookworm even if he spent much of his time in libraries. He describes the manufacturing side of sculpture not only without a trace of the intellectual's condescension toward the artisan, but with such relish and expertise that these passages may well have been actuated by experiences of his own, of the boy who had watched his father cure and sew leather, or of the student who had examined the contraptions by means of which Hamberger had endeavored to discover what makes the human body "tick." In any event he had preserved, even while struggling with the imponderables of beauty and style, an informed interest in questions of workmanship which was quite uncommon among his contemporaries.

"There are two methods of gilding in fire," he states in a characteristic passage,

of which one is called *amalgama*, and the other, in Rome at least, *allo spadaro*, or armorer-fashion. The latter is done through the use of gold leaves while the former requires a gold dissolved in aqua fortis. Mercury is added to this gold-saturated water, which is then placed on a moderate flame in order to let the nitric acid evaporate, whereupon the gold combines with the mercury to form a salve. Carefully cleansed, the heated metal is coated with this salve, which makes it look all black; on being reheated, however, the gold acquires its luster. This gilding, which is so to speak incorporated into the metal, was unknown to the ancients. They used only gold leaf, after the metal had been covered or rubbed with mercury. The durability of this gilding lies in the thickness of the leaves, whose layers can still be seen on Marcus Aurelius' horse.

v) On ancient Greek Painting.

When the *History* was being written, very few antique paintings had come to light; as Winckelmann puts it in one of his favorite metaphors (which tend to be maritime in origin), "we must consider ourselves lucky if we can gather up individual planks, as after a shipwreck."[8] He could therefore do little more than give a brief inventory of what had been found in Rome and Herculaneum, with much antiquarian detail about the precise circumstances of the discovery. Given this paucity of material and Winckelmann's, indeed the eighteenth century's, propensity for considering the visual evidence gathered on classical sites largely as corroboration of what the ancients had written, it is understandable that Pliny, Vitruvius, Pausanias, and other writers loom even larger here than elsewhere in the book. Unable to provide such corroboration in regard to painting, the author is visibly tempted to take one of those "big jumps over blank spaces" that he had threatened to take in the preface. The ancients had intimated that their painting had been as good as their sculpture: therefore it must have been so even though he, Winckelmann, had been unable to discover any real evidence to that effect.

"With the sole exception of four sketches on marble," he writes, "all these paintings were done on walls, and even though Pliny asserts that no famous painter had done frescos, this unsupported statement of his serves to demonstrate the excellence of the best ancient works. For some of those that *have* come down to us—and they must surely have been negligible compared with such masterpieces—do contain great beauties of line and color." Yet there is little he can offer by way of proof other than the *Aldobrandini Marriage*, the *Bacchantes* and *Centaurs* from Herculaneum, and some other odds and ends, none of them Greek. Even within the limited portion of Italy that Winckelmann knew well, the best was still waiting to be discovered, including the bulk of Pompeiian and Etruscan frescos. But his instinct was sound enough. Having jumped across this particular blank space, he landed on both feet in prophesying that "in this region, inhabited by the ancient Etruscans who were called Tarquinians, lie thousands of mounds, each one a tomb made of tufa; their entrances are choked up with rubble, [but] there is no doubt that if someone were to pay to have them opened, he would find not only Etruscan inscriptions, but paintings as well." All this, of course, has since been done. As bad luck would have it, Winckelmann himself described two such paintings, which were among those that the nimble-fingered Casanova had faked, possibly with the aid of Mengs. His failure to recognize these bogus antiques as such was the more embarrassing as he had himself helped to unmask, a few years earlier, the Venetian forger Giuseppe Guerra, "*le plus fameux faussaire de nos jours"* according to Paciaudi, who had sold as originals some sixteenth-century works that he had merely restored; emboldened by this success, Guerra had then taken to fabricating entire panels of "Herculanean" frescos. Yet Winckelmann lived long enough to witness the beginnings of Etruscan exploration, and to report on it in the "Comments" to the *History.* Of Greek painting, however, he had seen next to nothing, and the value of his comments accordingly lies in incidental observations (for example, on the Greeks' preference for blond over dark hair) rather than in any cogent interpretation of the topic at hand.

5) Art among the Romans.

A similar imbalance prevails in this final chapter of the first section, in which the consideration of Roman art is overshadowed by two peripheral concerns: an examination of men's clothing in antiquity to complement that given earlier of women's dress, and polemical shafts directed at Michelangelo and the French antiquary Isaac Casaubonus. The sculptor is faulted for having anachronistically represented his famous *Moses* with stockings tied below the knee under his robe, and the scholar, for claiming that gloves had not been worn in Greece and Rome although they were known already to Homer, who shows Laertes, Odysseus' father, working in his orchard with

> *gaiters fastened and patched together, to prevent scratching, and gloves on his hands because of the bushes . . .*[7]

Winckelmann looks on Roman art, at least of the Republican period, as entirely derivative, an offshoot first of Etruscan and later of Greek art. Despite a disclaimer to the contrary ("Everything that seems to be inferior is called Roman work, without further elaboration"), he does in fact consider it so inferior as to postpone any examination of its later stages—of the six centuries or so that separate the Roman conquest of Greece from the fall of the Empire—to the second section, where it is treated, superficially enough, as a variant of Hellenistic art. The salient point of this chapter lies not in what is said but in what is implied: that contrary to the views held by almost all his contemporaries except Caylus, Winckelmann placed the art of Rome so far beneath that of Greece that it does not warrant being discussed in detail.

B) Greek Art as Seen from the Chronological Viewpoint.

Having in the first section staked out signposts in what was then largely unknown territory, the aesthetics of Greek sculpture, the author records in this second or "applied" section the unfolding of ancient art from its pre-Phidian beginnings to its disappearance in the late Roman Empire. Inevitably, much of what he writes is repetitive; also inevitably, much of his information is hopelessly antiquated by now. It is not a matter of names, although some are given wrongly and others not at all. Nor is it a matter of dates, although his habit of reckoning events as the Greeks and Romans did, in terms of Olympiads and *ab urbe condita,* is annoying to the modern reader, who may well have forgotten that the Greeks celebrated Olympiads every four years beginning with 776 and that Rome was supposedly founded in 753 B.C. Rather, the boredom that occasionally overcomes one on reading these pages is due to the fact that so many blank spaces have meanwhile been filled in.

Had he been able to examine a work like the *Wounded Lioness,* Winckelmann would have realized that excellence in the representation of animals was a characteristic as much of Babylonian and Assyrian as of Egyptian sculpture. In the field of Egyptology itself, advances undreamt of in his day were made from the discovery of the Rosetta Stone in 1799 to the present, and a glance at the *Village Chief* and other naturalistic Old Kingdom and Memphite statuary would have shown Winckelmann the social and artistic dynamism behind the rigid façade of that art. Although some aspects of Etruscan culture, including much of the language (as well as the time and manner of the Etruscan migration to Italy) are still to be investigated, his postulate of a close ethnic relationship between that people and the Greeks has been discarded long ago. His belief in the seniority of Egyptian over Greek art likewise had to be re-examined in the light of Schliemann's and Evans's work; even if the Aegeans did not come of Greek stock, the art they created on Greek soil may well have been synchronous with that of Egypt.

Among major works of the archaic period alone, the following were brought to light after his death: the *Acropolis Maidens* in 1886–90, the Aegina marbles in 1811, the metopes from Selinus in 1822, the *Victory of Delos* in 1877. Had he lived a century or two later, Winckelmann would have had more to say about the use of polychromy, about the genetic connection between relief sculpture and work in the round, about the relative importance of early Roman versus Etruscan pottery, and about some other matters that he touches on but lightly. Since the Temple of Zeus at Olympia was not cleared until the 1880's, he had had to rely on Pausanias for his discussion of so central a sculptural motif as the *Battle of the Centaurs and Lapiths*. The list could be continued at will, down to his refusal to credit the late Roman sculptors with the perfection of illusionist relief work and a truly extraordinary skill in realistic portraiture (which is not as lowly an art form after all, as he would have us believe). None of this, however, detracts from his achievement in having for the first time integrated the ancients' comments on art with the larger panorama of Greek and Roman civilization. What remains of interest in the second section is not the chronological skeleton, but the masterful analyses with which he fleshed it out, among them the paean to the *Apollo Belvedere* and further interpretations of *Laocoön, Niobe and Her Daughters*, the Torso, and the so-called *Antinoüs*. By the strange logic that rules the entire second section, these statues are discussed here for no better reason than that they had been brought to Rome, or copied there, under this or that emperor.

III

We have spoken of Winckelmann's achievement. The time has come to ask: in what, precisely, does that achievement lie as far as the *History of Ancient Art* as a whole is concerned? It lies in the work's novelty, scope, and organization. Its author, to be sure, was indebted to many predecessors, men who had gone with him part of the road and whom he later left behind. Pliny the Elder in his *Natural History* and Pausanias in his *Description of Greece* had collected details about the lives and works of ancient artists, in a tradition revived during the Renaissance by Vasari and continued in Winckelmann's time by Richardson, Barthélemy, and Caylus. Hippocrates, Polybius, Cicero, and other Greek and Roman writers had stressed the importance of climatic factors in cultural life, and Hume and some others had gone a step farther in crediting the Mediterranean races with being "more ingenious" (Bacon) than Northern Europeans. Montesquieu and Vico had popularized an organic concept of history and endowed it with a sense of causality and periodicity. Many artists, among them Michelangelo and Rubens, had commented on the works of the ancients as well as on those of their own contemporaries. But it fell to Winckelmann to weave these and many less visible strands into the tapestry of art history as we know it. By drawing on religious practices, political events, economic conditions, technical inventions, social customs, and much else for his analysis not only of the works themselves but of the background against which they must be viewed and of the laws that had governed their creation, he became in effect the founder of *two* new disciplines: of art history as well as archaeology. Without necessarily being aware of it, he established them in the manner in which all new disciplines are established: by setting them off against those already in existence, assigning them a goal and devising methods by which that goal might be reached, and infusing them with a mystique of their own. It was one thing to dissociate himself as vigorously as he did from the philologists who compiled encyclopedias of classical knowledge, the literary men who left descriptions of ancient monuments, the philosophers weighing new concepts of aesthetics, and the biographers of various artists. It was quite another to replace this haphazardly gathered, fragmentarily recorded, and subjectively presented information with a body of evidence that stands up to close scrutiny: metaphorically speaking, to substitute astronomical for astrological procedures.

Although he arranged his evidence according to the reliability of its sources, the scale is arbitrarily drawn because he assigned priority to the statements of ancient writers, and after them, to his own visionary concept of classical Greece. It was only when these "sources" had been exhausted that he relied, in descending order, on information supplied by librarians, on the opinions of other scholars, and on reports from dilettante travelers. It is not a scale that a modern scholar would care to use, but it represents a method where there had been none before. An example in point, one that fairly makes him speak with forked tongue in his endeavor to reconcile conflicting types of evidence, is his comment on the underclothing of Greek women: "Two undergarments may be seen on the above-mentioned female statues—a petticoat and a gown. But this does not contradict Herodotus, who says that women wore only one undergarment. This must no doubt be taken to mean the petticoat *or* the gown." A question of sartorial semantics, one is inclined to think, compounded by a bachelor's ignorance of the subject, and hence unimportant—if the author's own view of Greece did not likewise take precedence even over nature herself.

Remarking, as so many other tourists had done in that period when malaria was endemic in Italy, on the yellowish pallor with which the inhabitants of marshy regions were afflicted, he writes that "it is just this color that one sees on the faces of people living along the Mediterranean littoral, in the Papal States, in Terracina, Nettuno, Ostia, etc." *Greek* swamps, on the other hand, do not seem to have had any deleterious effect on those who dwelt near them, for he continues without a break: "Swamps, which rendered the air so unhealthy and deadly in Italy, cannot have given forth any harmful exhalations in Greece. Ambracia, for example . . . was situated in the midst of them and could be entered from only one direction."[8] It never occurred to him that Ambracia might have flourished *despite* its foul air, a notion that would have conflicted with his belief that Greece was an earthly paradise settled by paragons of health as well as of all other virtues and qualities. Yet the same man looked and argued so closely that he could also write: "The feet [of Egyptian statues] differ from those of Greek figures in being flatter and more spread, with the toes, which lie completely flat, showing less variation in length and, like fingers, lacking any articulation of joints . . . Also, the little toe is neither curved nor pressed inward, as it is on Greek feet . . . Egyptian children ran about barefoot, and their toes were not forced against one another; nevertheless, the above shape of foot is not the result of walking barefoot, but must be considered to have been imitated from their earliest statues . . . The toenails, without any roundness or curvature, are only suggested by means of angular indentations."

Despite his bias, then, Winckelmann observed carefully, and supplemented his observations with evidence gathered in the most disparate fields: climatology and mathematics, sociology and chemistry, numismatics and philosophy. Pursuing his declared goal of tracing "the origin, growth, changes, and decadence of art, as well as the styles of the various nations, periods, and artists," he analyzed with the aid of these and other disciplines entire series of phenomena that had hitherto been discussed without much reference to their morphological, typological, and comparative dimensions.

Like all outstanding books, the *History of Ancient Art* is in part rooted in its time and in part towers above it. Its eighteenth-century ethos reaches the sublime in the author's praise of liberty as the motive force behind the genesis of so many noble works of art, and touches on the ridiculous in his insistence that the Egyptian and Etruscan sculptors, like so many friends of Dr. Johnson suffering from "melancholick vapours," had for that reason been unable to create great art. The work's encyclopedic character, its tendency to systematize at all costs, and the spirit of religious tolerance that permeates it are as emblematic of that period as is the frequent discrepancy, familiar enough to readers of Voltaire and Boswell, between what it preaches and what the author practiced. Winckelmann's eloquence on behalf of liberty, for example, is a many-faceted jewel that does not glitter with equal brilliance on all sides. In discussing the emergence of the Sublime Style, he says: "[Now] that the era of complete freedom and enlightenment dawned in Greece, the arts also became freer and nobler." The corollary is provided in a passage on the decadence of Athenian sculptors under the Macedonians: "Art, on which liberty had bestowed the gift of life, inevitably sank and fell with the loss of that liberty in the very place where it had blossomed most." So far, so good. Even if Heyne and other contemporary critics were to disagree, the message is clear, and stated in so many words: "This entire history illustrates the fact that the arts had owed their development to liberty." But aside from the dubiousness of the argument itself, which makes little allowance for periods in which artistic creativity and a lack of political freedom had existed side by side as they had in Augustan Rome, Medicean Florence, and the Spain of the Golden Age, there is an element of irony in the message being delivered by an author who had been granted, by such crotchety autocrats as Augustus III of Poland and Cardinals Archinto and Albani, a quite unusual degree of personal freedom. Not only was Winckelmann ever willing to lend an ear to the blandishments of Italian clerics and German petty tyrants; he was, among other things, also too much of a loner to have taken his place at the council table. For all his animosity toward Frederick the Great, it would be hard to imagine Winckelmann as a Swiss burgher or the citizen of a German Free City.

The umbilical cord by which the *History* remains attached to the century that gave it birth may also be seen in the work's curious division into two such dissimilar parts. This division, decided upon in principle as early as 1757, was sharpened by the circumstances of the book's composition. Conceived within a few months of the author's arrival in Italy, it had grown so quickly that his plan of writing on the restoration of antique statues and of listing the monuments of Rome in a sort of inventory had gradually been absorbed by the larger project. Once the question of language had been settled in favor of German (Winckelmann had at various times considered French, Latin, or Italian), the work proceeded at such a pace that a draft of the first section was submitted to Walther in 1757. Having been kept waiting for a reply for several months, Winckelmann then half promised it to Wille in Paris, who wanted to do the illustrations, and to Füssli who hoped to publish it in Zürich; hence the acknowledgment to the two men in the preface. The Saxon Court, however, was not pleased with the prospect that this book, written by a beneficiary of Saxon largesse, might be published abroad while the country was fighting for its survival in the Seven Years' War. Yet Winckelmann had no sooner terminated his negotiations with Wille and Füssli than temptation came his way again, in the form of an offer from the Leipzig publisher Dyck, who promised to pay higher royalties than Walther. Winckelmann now decided to recast the whole work, and withdrew the manuscript which had already been forwarded to Leipzig. While the revision was in progress, 1759–61, he flirted with the idea of having Volkmann submit the book to a publisher in Hamburg, where business had not suffered by the war. Weary of the whole affair and impatient to see the work of so many years in print, he finally sent the revised manuscript to Walther after all. Only then did he hurriedly set to work on the second section.

Although it bears the imprint of the year 1764, the *History* was actually published just before Christmas of 1763, with a dedication to the Elector Frederick Christian. But the farce was not yet played out. The Elector took it into his head to die on December 17, of all times, just as Winckelmann, acting on the advice of Count Firmian, was frantically signaling from Rome to substitute for the dedication to the Elector one addressed to a far mightier patron: Firmian's own sovereign, the Emperor Francis I, Maria Theresa's consort. It was too late. By the time his letter reached Dresden, the two quarto volumes (Winckelmann's favorite format, used for all his books save the *Monuments*, which are in folio) had already been solemnly presented to the Dowager Electress Maria Antonia. Although Winckelmann emerges from the whole transaction in the dubious light of a promoter who outsmarted himself, his actions had been well within the compass of eighteenth-century literary practices.

Winckelmann knew that the *History* was destined to remain an open-ended work. It can never be quite finished in its theoretical portions because definitions of beauty, style, and form are subject to reassessment by every successive generation, or in the chronological and applied portions because every new discovery affects both the total quantity and the respective qualitative standing of all surviving antique sculptures and paintings. In his commemorative essay of 1778, Herder was to ask outright: "Who in the world, unless he be a prophet, a god, or a devil, could write a *complete* History of Art?"[9] Even so, the publication in 1765 of two defective French translations brought home to Winckelmann the urgency of preparing a second and improved German edition, a task that clearly could not wait until the completion of the *Monuments*; but he died before that edition could be made ready for the printer. What we do have from his hand is a set of emendations and additions published in 1766 in Dresden, the *Anmerkungen über die Geschichte der Kunst des Altertums*. Except for their factual rather than promotional nature, these "Comments on the *History of Ancient Art*" resemble the various postscripts with which he had speeded the "Reflections" on their way. Consoling himself with the thought that "it is no disgrace, when hunting in a forest full of game, to miss a few shots," he admitted in the foreword to these "Comments" that the *History* had indeed contained a number of errors. There is little doubt that the manuscript on which he worked during those fateful days in the Locanda Grande in Trieste was the corrected version of the *History*, and that the second or chronological section would have been altered more radically than the first part of the book. As it turned out, the revised edition was completed by others, and published in Vienna in 1776. Among those who commented on the incongruity of the division into two parts was Herder, who thought that despite the title, the author had been more concerned with presenting a historical metaphysics of beauty, abstracted from the Greeks, than with writing an actual history. The observation is true enough. What had made Winckelmann select this approach, and suppress his ingrained distrust of metaphysical procedures, was his didactic intent in establishing a canon, i.e., a normative rather than descriptive view of art, and the need to counter the long tradition of considering art history not as a field in itself, but as an appendage to an artist's biography.

Herder wrote long after the event, and the literary reception of the *History* lies in any case beyond the scope of this book. It is, however, worth recording that another great German critic happened to be finishing a major work of his own while Winckelmann's was being published. In Chapter XXVI of his *Laokoon,* Lessing announced, quite seriously despite the ironic tone, that "Mr. Winckelmann's *History of Ancient Art* has just come off the press. I dare not take another step until I have read it." Lessing had never let his objections to Winckelmann's reading of specific passages in ancient authors, or their divergence of opinion about the *Laocoön* group itself, stand in the way of his admiration for his older and then much more famous compatriot, whose death was to make him exclaim: "I see by the papers that the report of Winckelmann's end has been confirmed. He is the second recently deceased writer [Laurence Sterne having died earlier that year] to whom I would gladly have given a few years of my own life."[10] Lessing commented often and favorably on the *History* and on Winckelmann's other writings. If he failed to see that the seminal aspect of these works lay not in the author's knowledge (the depth and extent of which Lessing continued to admire even as he criticized details), but in the sensibility with which Winckelmann interpreted rather than described classical art and literature, it must be remembered that Lessing's own exposure to ancient sculpture had been restricted, even in the case of the *Laocoön* group itself, to the examination of a few copperplate prints. From what little he had heard of him, Winckelmann on his part was at first inclined to dismiss the younger man as yet another German pedant who wrote on art without having seen any. But he changed his mind on reading some excerpts from *Laokoon* that a friend sent him, and ended by lamenting the fate that had forced him, while still in Germany, to forego the pleasure of reading Lessing's earlier work because he had had to fill his head with "old Frankish chronicles and the lives of the saints." A closer reading of *Laokoon*, however, and his own awareness of the shortcomings of the *History* soon disillusioned him. Lessing's habitual mental stance, that of a fencer who lunges and parries and feints in a display of dialectic one-upmanship, was far removed from Winckelmann's own emotional density, and the latter's old disdain of transalpine book learning broke through in the taunt: "Let him come to Rome, so that we can discuss this on the spot."[11] Matched as it is by a similar outburst from Lessing—"Do you know what makes me angry? That everyone to whom I speak about my trip to Rome immediately brings up Winckelmann. What does he, and the project he worked on in Italy, have to do with my trip?"[12]— it makes one wonder whether these two writers (whose dis-

similar talents, Goethe thought, would have complemented
each other to perfection) could in fact have got along if the
one had still been alive when the other finally arrived in Rome.

Since the publication of the *History*, men have no longer
claimed, as had been the fashion in Winckelmann's youth, that
Roman art is the equal of that of Greece. They have no longer
mistaken the biography of artists for the history of art, or
denied the pivotal importance that he assigned to the best Greek
works. Artists can pay homage to his ideal by imitating it, as
Canova and Thorwaldsen did in Europe ´ and Powers and
Greenough in America, or by consciously rejecting it as our
contemporaries do on both continents. But they have to come
to terms with it if they want to be taken at all seriously. In
England, Winckelmann's credo helped to replace the Palladian
fashion with an architecture and interior decoration that were
inspired directly by classical antiquity. In France, it helped to
bring about that identification of neoclassicism with republicanism which characterized the Revolutionary and Napoleonic
periods. In Italy it helped to revive the sense of pride in the
nation's past that inspired the *risorgimento*. In Germany, it
helped to impart to writers and thinkers an admiration for
ancient Greece that was to transcend national and temporal
boundaries in the works of Goethe, Schiller, Hölderlin, and
Hegel; modified by Bachofen, Nietzsche, and Freud, this
current reached deep into our century with Hofmannsthal,
George, and Benn.

As we stand back for a final glance at the *History* such as
it appears to us so many years after its publication, we can distinguish easily enough the live from the dead tissue. A weather-
beaten ruin, the *History* rather resembles Hadrian's Villa at
Tivoli, which is so often mentioned in it. Like that villa, the

work still impresses us by the majesty of its design and the value of all that has been quarried in it by later generations. The author's emphasis on the first-hand examination of all the available evidence; his habit of looking at cultural history through a wide-angle lens that shows not only the loftiest ideals of antiquity, but also the shoes worn by those who had held these ideals; and his ability to regard works of art as interrelated phenomena, which can be fully understood only if we compare the morphological characteristics of one period with those elsewhere (a line of investigation that was to be perfected by Spengler and Toynbee)—these techniques and modes of thought have lost none of their appeal in the intervening two centuries, which have witnessed our descent from a belief in the perfectibility of man to the fear that we might find ourselves at the end of a major historical period, and perhaps at the end of history. "I have already traced the course of [ancient] art beyond its end," Winckelmann writes in the concluding paragraph of the *History*. "I could not forbear following the fate of these works as far as my eye reached, although the ruin of ancient art made me feel like someone who, in writing the history of his country, has to describe its destruction as if he had experienced it himself. Just so will a loving woman stand by the shore, and look tearfully at her departing sweetheart whom she cannot hope to see again, and imagine that she can recognize his features even on the distant sail. Like this woman, we are left with only an outline of the object of our desires. But our yearning for what is lost is all the greater for this, and who knows? perhaps we regard the copies more attentively than we would ever have examined the originals if we had been in full possession of them."

While this lachrymose way of looking at the past is immeasurably far removed from us, the *History* contains other passages that are particularly rewarding for the modern reader.

Not only is it a pleasure to warm one's hands, chilled by the touch of contemporary art, over the fire of Winckelmann's enthusiasm; there are also many observations in his book that are of greater relevance to the harassed city dweller of the twentieth century than they ever were to his ancestor in the eighteenth. As we make our way from office to bank or from home to school, surrounded on all sides by monumental buildings and by the evidence of a growing contamination of our aesthetic as well as biological environment, we are reminded of Winckelmann's caution that "when I speak of the decadence of ancient art, it must be remembered that I refer primarily to sculpture and painting; for architecture flourished even as these decayed." Surprisingly little has changed in the world since "buildings of a size and magnificence were put up in Rome that the Greeks had not known in their best period, and Caracalla built those astonishing baths whose ruins still stir the imagination, at a time when there were only a few artists left who could draw a tolerable figure." There is solace in this, and the assurance that we are not alone because the symptoms of disease—and, one keeps hoping, of eventual recovery— have ever been the same. "Numismatists have remarked," Winckelmann tells us, "that coins ceased to be minted in Greece after Gallienus. Yet the poorer the coins of that time were in metal content and imprint, the more often the goddess *MONETA* was depicted on them, just as 'honor' is a frequent word on the lips of a man whose honor we have reason to doubt."

NOTES AND SELECTIVE BIBLIOGRAPHY

Notes

EPILOGUE AND PROLOGUE: TRIESTE

1. (*Mordakte Winckelmann*), ed. C. Pagnini, tr. H. Stoll (Berlin, 1965), pp. 116–18.

PRUSSIA

1. Edith Simon: *The Making of Frederick the Great* (Boston and Toronto, 1963), pp. 102–3.
2. *Johann Joachim Winckelmann, Briefe*, ed. H. Diepolder and W. Rehm (Berlin, 1953–7), IV, 244.
3. Thomas Nugent: *The Grand Tour; or, A Journey through the Netherlands, Germany, Italy and France* (2nd edn., London, 1756), II, 230–1.
4. *Briefe*, I, 62, 55, and 69.
5. *Briefe*, IV, 169.
6. *Boswell on the Grand Tour* (New York, Toronto, and London, 1953), I, 14.
7. *Odyssey*, XIII, 200. *Iliad*, I, 287 *ff*.; II, 24. Lattimore's translations.
8. Carl Justi: *Winckelmann und seine Zeitgenossen* (2nd edn., Leipzig, 1898), I, 117.

SAXONY

1. *Johann Joachim Winckelmann, Briefe,* ed. H. Diepolder and W. Rehm (Berlin, 1953–7), I, 90–1.
2. "Denkmal Johann Winckelmanns," in *Gesammelte Werke,* ed. Suphan (reprint of 1892 edn., Hildesheim, 1967), VIII, 445.
3. *"Da lieg ich hässlichs Höllenaas*
   In meinem Sündenkote,
   Daran ich mir den Narren frass
   Als wie am Zuckerbrote;
   Da lieg ich rasend toller Hund,
   An Seel und Leibe krank und wund,
   Und kann nichts mehr als heulen."
   Cited in Cornelius Gurlitt: *August der Starke* (Dresden, 1924), II, 114.
4. *Briefe,* I, 128–9.
5. *Briefe,* IV, 249.
6. "Précis du Siècle de Louis XV," *Oeuvres complètes de Voltaire* (Paris, 1877–85), XV, 335.
7. *Boswell on the Grand Tour* (New York, Toronto, and London, 1953), I, 135.
8. E. M. Butler: *The Tyranny of Greece over Germany* (Cambridge, Eng., 1935).
9. F. Basan: *Dictionnaire des Graveurs anciens et modernes* (Paris, 1767), I, 277.
10. *Johann Winckelmanns sämtliche Werke,* ed. J. Eiselein (Donauöschingen, 1825–9), I, 8.
11. *Aeneid,* II, 222–4. Copley's translation.
12. Mme de Staël: *Corinne, or, Italy,* tr. Baldwin-Driver (London, 1888), p. 140. George Gordon, Lord Byron: *Childe Harold's Pilgrimage* (Philadelphia, 1851), p. 209. Nathaniel Hawthorne: *French and Italian Note-Books* (Boston and New York, 1871), p. 121.
13. "Ardinghello," in *Sämtliche Werke,* ed. Schüddekopf (Leipzig, 1902–25), IV, 250–1.
14. *Boswell on the Grand Tour,* II, 66–7.

15. "Über Laokoon," in *Goethes Werke* (Hamburg, 1948–60), XII, 59–60.
16. Friedrich Nicolai, in *Bibliothek der schönen Wissenschaften*, I (1759), 346.

ROME AND HERCULANEUM

1. Thomas Nugent: *The Grand Tour; or, A Journey through the Netherlands, Germany, Italy and France* (2nd edn., London, 1756), III, 37–8.
2. Charles de Brosses: *Lettres familières écrites d'Italie en 1739 et 1740* (Paris, n.d.), II, 5–6.
3. Casanova: *History of my Life*, tr. Trask (New York, 1966), I, 257–8.
4. *Johann Joachim Winckelmann, Briefe*, ed. H. Diepolder and W. Rehm (Berlin, 1953–7), I, 266.
5. *Briefe*, I, 297-9. *Johann Winckelmanns sämtliche Werke*, ed. J. Eiselein (Donauöschingen, 1825–9), VI, 223.
6. *Briefe*, I, 266–7.
7. *Werke*, I, 227.
8. Tobias Smollett: *Travels through France and Italy* (London, 1776), II, 151.
9. "Salon de 1765," in *Oeuvres complètes de Denis Diderot* (Paris, 1875–7), X, 417.
10. De Brosses: *Lettres* . . . , I, 338.
11. "A View of Society and Manners in Italy," in *The Works of John Moore, M.D.* (Edinburgh, 1820), II, 362.
12. Sir Nathaniel W. Wraxall: *Historical Memoirs of my own Time* (Philadelphia, 1845), p. 95.
13. *Werke*, II, 189–90.
14. To West, June 14, 1740, in *Horace Walpole's Correspondence with Thomas Gray, Richard West and Thomas Ashton* (Yale edn. of Walpole's correspondence), XIII, 224.

L*

FLORENCE AND ROME

1. *Johann Joachim Winckelmann, Briefe*, ed. H. Diepolder and W. Rehm (Berlin, 1953–7), I, 227.
2. *Johann Winckelmanns sämtliche Werke*, ed. J. Eiselein (Donauöschingen, 1825–9), IX, 435.
3. Carl Justi: *Winckelmann und seine Zeitgenossen* (2nd edn., Leipzig, 1898), II, 232.
4. L. Cust and S. Colvin: *History of the Society of Dilettanti* (London, 1898), p. 36.
5. *Briefe*, II, 189.
6. Tobias Smollett: *Travels through France and Italy* (London, 1776), II, 89.
7. *Werke*, I, 240.
8. *Werke*, IX, 110 and 121.
9. *Werke*, VII, 17.
10. H. Rüdiger: *Winckelmann und Italien* (Krefeld, 1956), *passim*.
11. *Briefe*, III, 39–40.
12. Cited in *Briefe*, IV, 243.
13. James Barry: *An Inquiry into the real and imaginary Obstructions to the Acquisition of the Arts in England* (London, 1774).
14. "Salon de 1765," in *Oeuvres complètes de Denis Diderot* (Paris, 1875–7), X, 417. *Briefe*, III, 449.
15. "Winckelmann und sein Jahrhundert," in *Goethes Werke* (Hamburg, 1948–60), XII, 126. *Briefe*, III, 447.
16. *Briefe*, III, 127–8.
17. G. P. Gooch: *Frederick the Great* (New York, 1947), p. 199.
18. *Briefe*, II, 333.
19. *Briefe*, III, 277.
20. *Briefe*, III, 379.
21. *Briefe*, IV, 269.

THE HISTORY OF ANCIENT ART

1. *History of Ancient Art*, "translated from the German of John Winckelmann, by G. Henry Lodge, M.D., with the Life of

Winckelmann, by the editor" (Boston, 1856, with several later edns.).

2. *Johann Winckelmanns sämtliche Werke*, ed. J. Eiselein (Donauöschingen, 1825–9), III, 9–10. Quotations, as always, are from the Eiselein edition of *Sämtliche Werke*; the arrangement of chapters is that used by Wilhelm Senff in his edition of *Geschichte der Kunst des Altertums* (Weimar, 1964).

3. *Werke*, III, 101–2.

4. Lodovico Dolce: *Dialogo della Pittura* (Venice, 1557), p. 48; as cited in *Werke*, III, 363.

5. *Johann Joachim Winckelmann, Briefe*, ed. H. Diepolder and W. Rehm (Berlin, 1953–7), I, 244.

6. *Werke*, V, 102.

7. *Odyssey*, XXIV, 229–30. Lattimore's translation.

8. *Werke*, III, 131.

9. "Denkmal Johann Winckelmanns," in *Gesammelte Werke*, ed. Suphan (reprint of 1892 edn., Hildesheim, 1967), VII, 468.

10. *Lessings Sämtliche Schriften*, ed. Lachmann (Leipzig, 1853–7), XII, 236.

11. *Briefe*, III, 204.

12. *Lessings Sämtliche Schriften*, XII, 245.

Selective Bibliography

Works by Winckelmann:

Johann Winckelmanns sämtliche Werke, ed. J. Eiselein. 12 vols. Donauöschingen: Im Verlage deutscher Klassiker; 1825–9 (reprinted Osnabrück, 1965).

Johann Joachim Winckelmann, Briefe, ed. H. Diepolder and W. Rehm. 4 vols. Berlin: De Gruyter & Co.; 1953–7.

Johann Joachim Winckelmann, Kleine Schriften, Vorreden, Entwürfe, ed. W. Rehm. Introduction by H. Sichtermann. Berlin: De Gruyter & Co.; 1968.

Johann Joachim Winckelmann, Geschichte der Kunst des Altertums, ed. W. Senff. Weimar: H. Böhlaus Nachfolger; 1964.

Monumenti antichi inediti, spiegati ed illustrati da Giovanni Winckelmann, ed. P. P. Montagnani-Mirabili. 3 vols. 2nd edn. Rome: da Torchii di Carlo Mordacchini; 1821.

General:

Althaus, Horst: *Laokoon (Stoff und Form)*. Bern: A. Francke; 1968.

Begenau, Siegfried Heinz: *Zur Theorie des Schönen in der klassischen deutschen Aesthetik (Versuch über die zentrale Kategorie in der deutschen Aesthetik von Winckelmann bis Herders 'Kalligone')*. Dresden: Verlag der Kunst; 1956.

Bendinelli, Goffredo: *Dottrina dell'archeologia et della storia dell'arte* (Storia, Metodo, Bibliografia). Milan: S. A. Editrice Dante Alighieri; 1938.

Biedrzynski, Richard: "The Eagerness to See and Observe," in *Winckelmann, 1768/1968*. Bad Godesberg: Inter Nationes; 1968.

Boroviczény, Aladár von: *Graf von Brühl*. Zürich-Leipzig-Vienna: Amalthea-Verlag; 1930.

Bosshard, Walter: *Winckelmann (Aesthetik der Mitte)*. Zürich: Artemis-Verlag; 1961.

Curtius, Ludwig: *Winckelmann und seine Nachfolge*. Vienna: A. Schroll & Co.; 1941.

Cust, Lionel, and Sidney Colvin: *History of the Society of Dilettanti*. London: Macmillan; 1898.

De Beer, Gavin: *Gibbon and His World*. New York: Viking Press; 1968.

Finsler, Georg: *Homer in der Neuzeit (Von Dante bis Goethe)*. Leipzig and Berlin: B. G. Teubner; 1912.

Furtwängler, Adolf: *Die antiken Gemmen (Geschichte der Steinschneidekunst im klassichen Altertum)*. 3 vols. Leipzig and Berlin: Giesecke & Devrient; 1900.

Gooch, George P.: *Frederick the Great (The Ruler, The Writer, The Man)*. New York: Alfred A. Knopf; 1947.

Graevenitz, Georg von: *Deutsche in Rom (Studien und Skizzen aus elf Jahrhunderten)*. Leipzig: E. A. Seemann; 1902.

Gurlitt, Cornelius: *August der Starke (Ein Fürstenleben aus der Zeit des deutschen Barock)*. 2 vols. Dresden: Sibyllen-Verlag; 1924.

Haake, Paul: *August der Starke im Urteil seiner Zeit und der Welt*. Dresden: W. & B. v. Baensch-Stiftung; 1922.

Hatfield, Henry: *Winckelmann and His German Critics, 1755–81*. New York: Columbia University Press; 1943.

————: *Aesthetic Paganism in German Literature (From Winckelmann to the Death of Goethe)*. Cambridge: Harvard University Press; 1964.

Hautecoeur, Louis: *Rome et la renaissance de l'antiquité à la fin du XVIIIᵉ siècle (Essai sur les origines du style Empire)*. Paris: Fontemoing Co.; 1912.

Hazard, Paul: *La Pensée européenne au XVIIIᵉ siècle, de Montesquieu à Lessing*. Paris: Boivin; 1946.

SELECTIVE BIBLIOGRAPHY

Hinrichs, Carl: *Friedrich Wilhelm I, König in Preussen* (*Jugend und Aufstieg*). Darmstadt: Wissenschaftliche Buchgesellschaft; 1968. Reprint of 1943 edn.

Holtze, Friedrich: *Geschichte der Mark Brandenburg*. Tübingen: H. Laupp; 1912.

Honour, Hugh: *Neo-Classicism*. Harmondsworth: Penguin Books; 1968.

Justi, Carl: *Winckelmann und seine Zeitgenossen*. 3 vols. 2nd. edn. Leipzig: F. C. W. Vogel; 1898. Same, ed. W. Rehm. 3 vols. 3rd edn. Cologne: Phaidon-Verlag; 1956.

Koch, Hanna: *Johann Joachim Winckelmann* (*Sprache und Kunstwerk*). Berlin: Akademie-Verlag; 1967.

Kreuzer, Inge: *Studien zu Winckelmanns Aesthetik* (*Normativität und historisches Bewusstsein*). Berlin: Akademie-Verlag; 1959.

Ladendorf, Heinz: *Antikenstudium und Antikenkopie* (*Vorarbeiten zu einer Darstellung ihrer Bedeutung in der mittelalterlichen und neueren Zeit*). 2nd edn. Berlin: Akademie-Verlag; 1958.

Lavagnino, Emilio: *L'Arte moderna dai neoclassici ai contemporanei*. 2 vols. Rev. edn. Turin: Unione tipografico-editrice torinese; 1961.

Mordakte Winckelmann, ed. C. Pagnini, tr. H. A. Stoll. Berlin: Akademie-Verlag; 1965.

Noack, Friedrich: *Das Deutschtum in Rom seit dem Ausgang des Mittelalters*. 2 vols. Stuttgart: Deutsche Verlaganstalt; 1927.

Pater, Walter: "Winckelmann," in *Studies in the History of the the Renaissance*. London: Macmillan; 1873.

Rehm, Walter: *Winckelmann und Lessing*, and *Johann Hermann von Riedesel* (*Freund Winckelmanns, Mentor Goethes, Diplomat Friedrichs des Grossen*), both in *Götterstille und Göttertrauer* (*"Aufsätze zur deutsch-antiken Begegnung"*). Bern: A. Francke; 1951.

Rosenblum, Robert: *Transformations in Late Eighteenth Century Art*. Princeton; Princeton University Press; 1967.

Rüdiger, Horst: *Winckelmann und Italien*. Krefeld: Scherpe-Verlag; 1956.

———: *"Winckelmanns Persönlichkeit,"* in *Der Deutschunterricht*, 8/2; 1956.

———: *Winckelmanns Tod (Die Originalberichte)*. Wiesbaden: Insel-Verlag; 1959.

311

————: *"Winckelmanns Geschichtsauffassung,"* in *Euphorion,* 62/6; 1968.

St. Clair, William: *Lord Elgin and the Marbles.* London: Oxford University Press; 1967.

Schadewaldt, Wolfgang: *Winckelmann und Homer.* Leipzig: J. A. Barth; 1941.

Schultze, Werner: *"Winckelmann und die Religion,"* in *Archiv für Kulturgeschichte,* 34; 1952.

Schulz, Arthur: *Die Bildnisse Johann Joachim Winckelmanns.* Berlin: Akademie-Verlag; 1953.

————: *Winckelmann und seine Welt.* Berlin: Akademie-Verlag; 1962.

————: *Die Kasseler Lobschriften auf Winckelmann (Einführung und Erläuterungen).* Berlin: Akademie-Verlag; 1963.

Sewall, John Ives: *A History of Western Art.* New York: Henry Holt & Co.; 1953.

Sichtermann, Hellmut: *Laokoon.* Stuttgart: Philipp Reclam Jun.; 1964.

Simon, Edith: *The Making of Frederick the Great.* Boston and Toronto: Little, Brown & Co.; 1963.

Stoll, Heinrich Alexander: *Winckelmann. Seine Verleger und seine Drucker.* Berlin: Akademie-Verlag; 1960.

Sydow, Eckart von: *Die Kultur des deutschen Klassizismus (Leben, Kunst, Weltanschauung).* Berlin: G. Grote; 1926.

Vallentin, Berthold: *Winckelmann.* Berlin: G. Bondi; 1931.

Valsecchi, Franco: *L'Italia del settecento (dal 1714 al 1788).* Milan: Mondadori; 1959.

Zeller, Hans: *Winckelmanns Beschreibung des Apollo im Belvedere.* Zürich: Atlantis-Verlag; 1955.

Index